Advance Praise

"A wonderfully written cookbook with accurate basic nutritional information and colorful anecdotes that makes a nice addition to anyone's library. Even the most inexperienced cook can find easy-to-follow delicious recipes in this book that readily fit into a healthy eating plan."

Eve M. Dansereau, M.S., R.D., L.D.N.

"…a must for the healthy gourmet."

Kathleen M. Zelman, M.P.H., R.D.

"Marcia Williams has developed some excellent recipes that are low in fat and salt. These creative dishes can be used as part of a heart-healthy diet to lower cholesterol and improve cardiovascular health. Marcia Sabaté Williams has shown us that healthy eating does not have to be bland or boring, it can be delicious and exciting."

Pat H. Farris, L.D.N., R.D.

"[Marcia's] inventiveness will help many confused and frustrated heart-healthy dieters to realize that no fat, no salt, no sugar can be so delicious. This book is a complete, information-packed reference on everything from how to stock your kitchen to where to buy hard to find ingredients. It is a step-by-step action plan for anyone who is serious about adopting a heart-healthy eating style."

Rosanne P. Farris, L.D.N., M.S., Hyg.
Assistant Professor of Pediatrics

"As a surgeon seeing hundreds of patients a year with heart and peripheral vascular arteriosclerotic disease, I know how difficult it is for them to suddenly have to restrict their salt, sugar and fat intake.…I am convinced that if more people adopted the dietary practices of Marcia Sabaté Williams's kitchen and taught them to their children, we would become a nation with a reduced denseness of disease related to arteriosclerosis."

George E. Barnes, M.D.

"An excellent variety and collection of recipes for low cholesterol, low fat, low sodium cookery. The text is informative, accurate, and entertaining."

Vickie Meckel, L.D.N., R.D.

"I really enjoy *More Healthy Cooking With No Apologies*. The style is very easy to read and I can identify with everything. Just like *No Salt, No Sugar, No Fat No Apologies*, the ingredients are easy to find in grocery stores."

Paula Brown, R.D., M.S., L.D.N.

"The style is relaxed, friendly, and best of all, HUMAN. Marcia admits to problem times when trying to stay consistent with diet recommendations, and offers possible solutions to dealing with those times . . . She brings out the brightness, friendliness, and intelligence of Louisianians! Thanks."

Janice Taulli, R.N., M.N.

More Healthy Cooking
with no apologies

More Healthy Cooking
with no apologies

Marcia Sabaté Williams

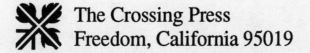
The Crossing Press
Freedom, California 95019

This book is dedicated to my wonderful husband Ray, to my three fine, big boys, R.B., Guillaume, and Alex, and to the memory of my dear mother, Miriam Hubert Sabaté, who passed all her knowledge of good New Orleans Cooking down to me.

Copyright 1991 by Marcia Sabaté Willliams

Cover design by Nina Bookbinder
Interior art by AnneMarie Arnold
Cover photography by William Darby © 1990
Photographed in the studio of 6WDSU-TV, New Orleans
Pritikin is a registered trademark of Pritikin Systems, Inc.

Printed in the U.S.A.

Library of Congress Cataloging-in-Publication Data

Williams, Marcia Sabaté.
    More Healthy Cooking with no apologies / by Marcia Sabaté Williams.
    p. m.
    Includes index.
    ISBN 0-89594-453-7 (cloth)   -- ISBN 0-89594-452-9 (paper)
    1. Sugar-free diet -- Recipes.   2. Salt-free diet -- Recipes.
    3. Low-fat diet -- Recipes.   I. Title.
RM237.8W548 1991
641.5'63 -- dc20   91-2025
                                        CIP

Contents

Foreword

During the past thirty years near miraculous advances have been made in medicine. New drugs, surgical techniques, and x-ray procedures have been successfully employed for the treatment of cancer, high blood pressure, heart disease and strokes. Yet despite all of these advances heart disease continues to be the number one killer in the industrialized world.

It has only been during the past two decades that the medical profession has awakened to the important role of a healthy diet for the well-being of patients. As late as 1975, cardiologists and cardiovascular surgeons were not convinced that cholesterol control was important in the arterosclerotic (hardening of the arteries) disease process. We now realize that control of dietary cholesterol intake is very important. If a person can lower his serum cholesterol below 200 mg. there may be a regression of plaque material in his affected arteries.

As a practicing cardiologist for nearly twenty years, I have become a firm advocate for a healthy diet for all of my heart patients. I have a number of heart patients who have had significant cardiovascular symptoms despite having undergone heart surgery and placement on proper medications. Their symptoms improved only after I was able to convince them to follow a strict Pritikin type diet.

I applaud Marcia Sabaté Williams for writing *More Healthy Cooking with No Apologies*. This cookbook allows cardiovascular patients to eat flavorful, appetizing foods that still meet the American Heart Association guidelines. Louisiana is known for its excellent cuisine which is often high in cholesterol, fat and salt. To get my cardiovascular patients to follow a strict diet has been difficult because they are accustomed to eating foods high in fat and salt. Marcia's cookbook offers many simple and excellent recipes which have been accepted by my patients. I strongly recommend this cookbook, *More Healthy Cooking with No Apologies,* for any person concerned about maintaining a healthy diet and lifestyle.

Michael Charles Finn, M.D.
Fellow American College of Cardiology
and American Board of Internal Medicine

Preface

My first book, *The No Salt, No Sugar, No Fat, No Apologies Cookbook*, was published too quickly. Even while it was being printed, I was making up new recipes, and it's been like that ever since. I just keep thinking up new ways to make old favorite recipes. For instance, my son, R. B., said, "Mom, why don't you ever make meat loaf any more?" Good question. I didn't have a meat loaf recipe in my first cookbook. Well, there's one in this book.

That's the way many of the recipes in this book came about—by request. Some ideas came from people who bought my first book and called to say, "You know what I just did? . . . I thought you might like to try it." And there are many brand new concoctions I thought up.

It's amazing to me how many good things have happened to me since my first cookbook came out. The Louisiana State University School of Medicine is using my first cookbook as a teaching tool for student dietitians. Because of that, Rosanne Farris, a registered dietitian at the medical school, asked me to speak to dietitians, psychiatrists, and pediatricians from all over the United States at a convention in New Orleans. That was very exciting. I've been asked twice to judge the Culinary Heart's Cook Off in New Orleans, which is put on by the New Orleans Dietetic Association and the American Heart Association. Famous local chefs compete by cooking low-salt, low-fat, sugar-free food. I've been on television several times, and on the radio. Once, in Wisconsin, my book and some of my recipes were on television, and I didn't even know it. People all over the United States are being helped by my cooking techniques, and I understand that even in New Zealand, Australia, England, and Canada people are cooking my recipes.

It's been wonderful, too, to meet people from many cities around the United States who have called to ask me questions. I've made friends I never dreamed of by cooking healthy.

For those of you who haven't read my first cookbook, I got into this no-salt, no-sugar, no-fat cooking because my husband was going to pot (mostly you know where). He looked terrible and felt terrible. He had just about everything you can think of wrong with him. That man was on his way out. If the diabetes wasn't going to get him, the high blood pressure was. He had to go in the hospital to get straightened out.

The doctors put my husband on what they said was a no-salt, no-refined-sugar, no-fat regime called the Pritikin Diet. He wasn't allowed to eat egg yolks, cheese, butter, margarine, oil, alcohol, avocado, coconut, coffee, tea, (except herb teas), soft drinks (with or without sugar), caffeine, organ meat, barbecue, nuts (except water chestnuts and Italian chestnuts), potato skins, black or white pepper, and no artificial sweeteners. I thought, "Dang! That's ridiculous!" when I heard all that.

Well, you see, when Ray and I first got married, I cooked like Paul Prudhomme. Have you ever watched him on television? He uses butter like water. If something needs liquid, he uses melted butter. Not that his food doesn't taste good. It does. But using butter like water isn't good for anyone. Anyway, when we first got married, Ray got awfully fat eating that way. I gained a few pounds, too. But then, I'm not a big eater, so I didn't gain as much as Ray did.

At one point I took Ray off starches and gave him big steaks and vegetables, thinking he would lose weight. You know what happened? He developed gout—too much uric acid in meat. By the time he was 35, he started falling apart. The doctor reduced the meat to 3-1/2 ounces per day. And he had to add starches to his diet.

Unfortunately, Ray really needed an even more restrictive diet and a change in lifestyle. By the time he was 45, he was a borderline diabetic. He had high blood pressure, high cholesterol, high blood sugar, and high triglycerides. He suffered from gout occasionally. He was also very overweight. He checked into the hospital to get on a sensible diet; otherwise he knew he wasn't going to last long. On the new eating plan, his cholesterol and triglycerides, blood pressure, and weight came down. Fast.

At first, I didn't think I was going to be able to cook within the restrictions of the new diet. I had to struggle to adjust to it, but after a while, it got easier, and here I am after many years, still cooking that way. It really isn't that hard, and it's good food, regular food, not weird food. I think that's why I'm still able to cook this way. I'm still preparing the same dishes, except I just cook them a little differently, using chicken stock, vegetables, water, or wine to moisten the food, instead of butter. The results are just fine, sometimes better than the original recipes.

Other people are able to do this, too. A lady who had lost 21 pounds cooking and eating out of my first book told me, "This is the first time I've ever been on a diet that doesn't make me feel I'm going crazy. This is the first diet book that doesn't make me feel like a wart." She had a history of cardiac problems aggravated by being overweight. It made me feel good to think I was helping her.

After this lady called me, I thought, I really need to help more people like her who get thrown a directive by their doctors to get off salt, sugar, and fat without being given any instructions on how to cook such food. If I can help people find tasty methods of cooking healthy food, that's got to be a good deed.

No one writes a book like this all alone because there are so many things that have to be researched. It's good to know experts who are willing to help.

Many thanks go to Ilene Pritikin, widow of the late Nathan Pritikin, who has been an inspiration to me for the past nine years, and to her son Robert Pritikin who has taken so much of his time helping me; to James J. Kenney, Ph.D., R.D., Nutrition Research Specialist, Pritikin Longevity Center, author of *The L.A. Diet*, who didn't seem to mind all my questions; to Denise Vilven, R.D. Director of Pritikin Systems, Inc., for her help; to my friends the dietitians in the New Orleans area hospitals: Clare Miller, R.D., former president of the Louisiana Dietetic Association, Vickie Meckel, L.D.N., R.D., Pat H. Farris, M.S., R.D., L.D.N., Eve Dansereau, M.S., R.D., L.D.N., Paula G. Brown, M.S., R.D., L.D.N., Kathleen M. Zelman, M.P.H., R.D., L.D.N., and Rosanne Farris, P., M.S., H.Y.S. for much help; to Dr. Neil Vancelow, Chancellor of Tulane Medical School and his wife Mary for their help; to Pharmacist, Al Capace, R., P.H. and to Bill Friedrich of the Federal Drug Administration, Washington, D.C., for their expertise; to Cheryl Geiger, St. Bernard Parish home economist for her help; to Joyce Dakin, Nutritional Food Store, and Ruby Bouchard, of Ruby's Health Food store, for looking up many things for me; to William de Marigny Hyland, attorney, historian, and linguist for his help in both historical and linguistic research; to the librarians at Slidell Library; Rebecca Taylor, Marilyn Bennkers, Josie Athey, Diane Barringer, Judy Crawford, Kathleen Ezell, Bee Galadas, Jeanne Hays, Eda Parker, and Fran Thomas, who saved me many trips by looking up things for me on the phone; to Licatas Seafood and Boga River Nurseries for expert information; to Jeannette Sapdone, K & B Drugstore, for looking up information for me; to Ron Yager, Channel 6, WDSU-TV, for his help with the cover of this book; to my cousin Muriel Hubert for her advice and inspiration; to my friends, Shirley Templet, Palma Leitz, and Ken and Janine Hembel for their encouragement; to my editor, Andrea Chesman, for all her help and advice; to my publishers at The Crossing Press, Elaine and John Gill, for making me feel like part of the family; to Jane Somers at The Crossing Press for her concern and help; and last but not least to my sons, R. B., Guillaume, and Alex, and my husband, Ray, who not only ate my cooking but who were my expert testers. They complimented me when something was good and were truthful enough to say "blah!" and make faces when they didn't like something. Thanks to them, the "blah" recipes didn't get into this book.

1

**Cooking
and Eating
the Heathy Way**

"No sugar, no salt, no fat, no fun," a lady I met at a party said when someone mentioned my first cookbook. Then she said, "I'm just kidding." But she wasn't kidding at all. And I'm sure if you have never tried to cook without those ingredients, you might say the same thing.

So can you have fun when you diet and don't drink? Sure. You can still go to parties. And you know what? No one will even notice that you don't drink, especially at big parties. People are so interested in what *they* are doing, they never notice that you are drinking Perrier with a twist or orange juice. How can they know what's in your glass?

I do find people insistent about alcohol at small dinner parties where the host or hostess may try to get you to have wine or another type of alcoholic drink. But if you stick to your guns, he or she will admire you for trying to take care of yourself. We always bring something we can drink because most people offer only colas as an alternative to alcohol. Sometimes we bring nonalcoholic wine and beer. The new ones are wonderful. You can't tell from the taste that they don't contain alcohol.

However, if it's going to make you absolutely miserable when you can't have an alcoholic drink, and you may chuck the whole diet if you can't have a beer or some wine, it's better to go ahead and have your one drink. That is, of course, if you can keep it down to one drink.

Food at a dinner party is a much larger problem. You can't simply refuse to eat. We just try to eat as wisely as we can at such functions, not going overboard. If you can't resist the desserts, just take a very small piece of the one that looks the best. If you can't eat lightly, it's best to close your eyes when the desserts are served or refuse to go near the dessert table.

Restaurants are another problem, but it is possible to ask for things cooked without salt. It's difficult to get dishes cooked without fats. Salads are simpler—you can bring small bottles of your own salad dressing. You have to do the best you can in restaurants.

Will you feel deprived? Honestly, yes, but not as much as you would think. Other things make you feel deprived, too, like going to someone's brand new, gorgeous house. (You might feel deprived when you see someone 19 years old in a bikini and you haven't seen 19 in years.) Deprivation is relative. You're alive, aren't you? I want to keep you that way so you can continue to have fun. And feeling slightly deprived does not keep you from having fun.

I can hear you telling me, "Yeah, but years ago people didn't even know anything about the effects of fats, sugar, and sodium. My grandma used to cook everything in bacon grease and she did okay."

A few years ago I started looking through death records in New Orleans from 1850 to see if I could find out where my great-great grandfather Numa Hubert was buried. I was astounded to go through one hundred names before I found a person who lived to the age of 60. And while searching for about an hour, I never found one person who lived longer than 60 years. Mortality of infants and children was high, and many, many people died in their 20s. Most people back then didn't live long enough to develop the medical problems people over 40 face today (high blood pressure, heart disease, and diabetes). The ones who survived past 40 probably had wonderful genes.

(Did I find my great-great grandfather Numa? Yes, I did. While I was looking him up in New Orleans, it turned out he was in San Francisco fighting a pistol duel with some man because the man put his foot on the back of Numa's chair at the opera. Numa won, but died shortly after—at the age of 35—and was buried in the now nonexistent Greenwood Cemetery in San Francisco. What was a New Orleans attorney who lived on St. Charles Avenue doing fighting pistol duels in San Francisco? The gold rush maybe?)

"No Salt, No Sugar, No Fat, No Food"

I get that irritating bit of sarcasm all the time. You will, too. I'm always so amazed at the ignorance of the remark that I fail to retort, "Is that all you eat—salt, sugar, and fat?"

You're eating all the same foods everybody else eats when you omit the salt, sugar, and fat—it's just your cooking methods that are different. You'll still get custard when you want custard, vegetable soup when you want vegetable soup, and pot roast when you want pot roast.

The alternatives for sugar are fruits and concentrated fruit juices. For whipped toppings, you can use gelatin mixed with baked bananas and evaporated skim milk instead of heavy cream and sugar. For salt you use juice concentrates, wine, and sometimes a bit of vinegar. Pepper helps, too. Instead of using oil, you use nonstick pots and pans, stocks and water or juice concentrates, or other liquids—sometimes vegetables that contain a lot of water. I think you get the idea.

What Makes You Keep to the Diet?

Fear of dying, for one thing, and for another, fear of pain. A person in good health will not have the same motivation to stay on this type of diet as a person who has just had open-heart surgery.

Even so, I know people who have had two open-heart surgeries who followed their diets carefully and exercised hard for about a year. Then I saw them backsliding with junk food and cheese. When they went to cardiac re-hab gyms, instead of exercising, they chitchatted with everyone . . . until they had another heart attack. If that one didn't kill them, they tightened up for a good while again. When people feel better, they tend to forget they are in danger.

Pain is probably the best motivator. Sometime back I felt my heart bumpity-bumping, as if I was in love, and this went on for four days. The only person who was around me was my husband, Ray, and we had been married for 23 years. I called the doctor.

The doctor told me to come right in and, sure enough, he found I had an extra heartbeat. He said it was probably caused by stress and by caffeine. Previously, one of my sons was in a car wreck and had to be operated on. Nervous with nothing to do in the hospital but chew my fingernails, I drank several cups a day of the coffee the hospital set out for visitors, even though I knew it wasn't good for me. After my visit to the doctor, I cut out all coffee and tea and I got better. But later I allowed myself one cup of black tea a day, and sometimes I sneaked two. I also drank alcohol once in a while. Then I started having pains in my stomach. It turned out to be a hiatal hernia. The doctor forbade caffeine and alcohol. I was also found to have cystic disease of the breasts when I got a routine mammo-gram, and caffeine affects that, too. I got off all alcohol and all caffeine, and the pains in my stomach and breasts went away, and I had no more bumpity-bumping heart. Sorry, Ray.

When you can see the immediate negative effect of certain foods, you are more likely to stay away from them.

The people with bad hearts are in a dangerous position. Sometimes they don't seem to feel anything wrong with their bodies until it's too late. I know Ray can't tell when his blood pressure or blood sugar is up, and he certainly can't feel the cholesterol building up in his veins.

I make a rule in my house. If I cook anything, it's cooked without salt, sugar, or fat. If Ray brings anything he is not supposed to eat into the house (which he does occasionally), I can't stop him, but any food he gets from me is going to be cooked properly. So he eats the right kinds of foods for breakfast, lunch, and dinner, and so do I when we're home. Some things might not be perfect when we go out, but it's about the best we can do.

Cooking the Fat-Free, Salt-Free , Sugar-Free Way

When I give talks to groups in restaurants, the owners often come out to meet me and practically grab my book. They tell me they have people coming in all the time asking for meals cooked without salt, fat, and sugar. Many excellent cooks have no idea what foods contain cholesterol or what is high in sodium. They don't even know how to begin to cook without the fats, salt, and sugar. You need to know which ingredients to use, and how much of certain ingredients can be harmful—or beneficial.

How Much Sodium Is Okay?

I'm always astounded when figuring out how much sodium is in a serving for a recipe. I go, "Hey! What? I didn't put any salt in this, but look at this sodium!" Just think how much there would be if I added salt, or used lots of items containing salt! I asked Vickie Meckel, a dietitian at Northshore Regional Medical Center, a big hospital near where I live, how much sodium one needs to stay healthy. She said the American Heart Association recommends that a healthy adult consume no more than 3,000 milligrams of sodium a day. She also said that doctors usually recommend that people with high blood pressure consume no more than 2,000 milligrams a day, and sometimes less. Some of my entrées contain as much as 300 to 350 milligrams of sodium. That might sound like a lot of sodium, but considering 1 teaspoon of salt has a horrifying 2,132 milligrams of sodium, 300 for a big main serving of something doesn't sound so bad.

Every time you use salt in a dish, the sodium content goes sky high. Instead of salt, use juice concentrates, red rosé wine, and other wines, vinegar, beer, and spices and herbs.

How Much Fat Do We Need?

People always tell me that if you don't eat at least three teaspoons of oil or some kind of fat a day you aren't getting enough fat. I think if you look at the nutrient values at the end of each of the recipes in this book, you will be hard-pressed to find a recipe that does not contain fat, even though I add no oils, grease, margarine, butter, or anything you could think of as fat, except in a few recipes where I use a nonstick spray.

So you are eating some fat whether you add three teaspoons of oil a day to your diet or not.

The American Heart Association says that no more than 30 percent of your calories should come from fat. The Pritikin Program says that no more than 10 percent of your calories should come from fat.

The point is, cave men could not go down to a store and buy cooking oil or margarine; they obtained the fats they needed from whatever foods they ate, without adding any more. You can, too.

Instead of using melted margarine or butter to get moisture into a dish, you can use chicken, beef, or vegetable stock, water, wine, fruit juices, and watery vegetables, such as zucchini. I use nonfat sprays only when absolutely necessary, and no oils, margarine, butter, or other animal fats.

What About Sugar?

I don't think I have to tell you that eating too much ice cream and cake made with refined sugar will make you fat,

and you won't get much nutrition out of it to boot. I don't think I have to tell you diabetics that eating refined sugar can cause your blood sugar and insulin levels to rise. Also, I'm sure you don't want to come home from the dentist and say, "Hey Mom! I've got four cavities and gum disease!" I've even read articles by nutritionists that say too much refined sugar can cause mood changes (usually lethargy and depression—who needs that?) and sodium retention.

Good news! You can make lots of sweets and goodies right out of this book, and you don't have to use refined sugar of any kind. You can use fruits and fruit juices and get the same results.

Get Acquainted with Herbs and Spices

I've always used herbs and spices because my mama did, and I think I've explored their exotic flavors more thoroughly than she did. So I'm surprised when someone who has my cookbook says she didn't cook this and she didn't cook that because she didn't have this herb or spice. What do most people have? Salt and pepper. Come on now! If you look in your kitchen cabinet right now, is that all you'll find? If so, you need to take a trip to the grocery and get yourself a collection of herbs and spices.

My kids tell me most people don't buy herbs and spices because they are expensive. I suppose that's true. Saffron, which I use in several recipes in this book, is very expensive, I'll admit, maybe over $6.00 for .03 ounces. In many stores you have to ask for it because the shopkeepers are afraid to keep it out on the shelves where people can steal it. But that .03 ounces will be enough to make every recipe containing saffron in this book, and you will still have some left over. Some people say saffron doesn't last over a few months, but that's not true. I've used saffron that was over a year old and it was just fine.

One way to keep dried herbs and spices fresher is to put the containers into something airtight and store them in the freezer. Especially chili powder. Weevils love chili powder. They do the Mexican hat dance when they find themselves a bottle or can of chili powder. Incidentally, you can get salt-free chili powder. Just check all the different ingredients on the backs of the containers when you go to buy it.

You will notice I don't use fresh herbs. That's because I can't find a convenient local source. I've tried to grow them and they all die on me. I've had some house plants for 15 years, but I can't grow one fresh herb, not even thyme or parsley. It's too hot for them down South.

If you want to use fresh herbs, use about three times as much as dried ones. In some cases, like parsley and basil, you need even more. Frankly, I can't guarantee how these recipes will come out if you substitute fresh herbs because I haven't tried them. My son Guillaume, who is an excellent cook, says, "Mom, when I can use salt and oil, I experiment with other people's recipes. With your recipes, I make them exactly like you have them because I know they won't come out right if I don't." I wouldn't fool around with these recipes, especially the first time you make them, because they are finely tuned for ultimate flavor and texture. I'm not trying to brag—it's just that I've experimented with these recipes over and over until I got them just right.

Here is a complete list of every herb and spice you will find in the recipes in this book in the order of the most used to the least used. If you can't afford to buy them all at one time, just buy two or three a week.

Cayenne pepper	Basil	Celery seeds
Red pepper flakes	Cumin (cumino)	Dill weed
Garlic powder	Oregano	Cloves
Onion flakes	Chili powder	Cinnamon
Parsley flakes	Turmeric	Allspice
Thyme	Paprika	Mace
Bay leaves	Curry powder	Tarragon
Sage	Mustard seeds	Dried chives
Marjoram	Coriander	Caraway seeds
Saffron	Dill seeds	

Staples You Will Need

People sometimes tell me, "I don't stock all those ingredients you use in your book." Of course you don't. You can't possibly have everything you need for every recipe. That goes for any cookbook you buy. I don't have everything for every recipe in my books either. I decide what I want to cook for a few days or a week, and take my book to the grocery store or I make a list of what I will need for each recipe, shop for each item, and then I have what I need. It's as simple as that. But there are some things you will want to keep on hand so you can get right to the fun of cooking:

Oat bran
Cornmeal
All-purpose flour
Whole wheat flour
Bromated bread flour
Cornstarch
Rapid rise yeast
Baking soda
Low-sodium baking powder
Elbow macaroni (whole wheat and/or semolina)
Instant brown rice
Thin spaghetti (whole wheat and/or semolina)
Whole wheat bread
Evaporated skimmed milk
Sapsago cheese
1% low-fat cottage cheese
Jumbo eggs
Polaner® All Fruit spreadable fruit
Poiret® Pear and Apple spread
Frozen apple juice concentrate
No-salt canned tomatoes
No-salt tomato paste
No-salt tomato sauce
Celery
Green peppers
Yellow or white onions
Irish potatoes
Chuck wagon frozen corn
Unflavored gelatin powder
Vinegar (apple cider and some fancier kinds if you like)
Low-sodium soy or tamari sauce
Tabasco sauce
Inexpensive red hot sauce, such as Crystal or Louisiana
Red Rosé wine
Vanilla extract
Nonstick cooking spray
Apple pectin powder

Oat Bran

I was using oat bran before most people ever heard of it. Whether or not it reduces cholesterol is not important.

What is important is that it's high in fiber and makes wonderful muffins. You can put it in bread dough, too. It's nice and light and good tasting.

When you go to the store you will see a variety of oat bran products. Some of the oat bran cereals are not just plain oat bran. Some of them are flakes and other things. Quaker does put out a hot cereal that is just plain oat bran. By mistake, I once bought an oat bran hot cereal put out by Nabisco, but I didn't notice it was a multi-grain hot cereal. It has some barley flakes and wheat bran in it, and it's a little coarser than plain oat bran. If you do that, don't throw it away, it will work just fine for the muffin recipes. You can often buy oat bran in bulk in health food stores and natural food co-ops.

Bromated Bread Flour

Use bromated bread flour for bread or pizza. Pillsbury and Gold Medal bromated bread flours are fine. The labels will say something like "bread flour" or "better for bread," and will have the word bromated printed on the package.

Bromated flour is simply unbleached white flour to which is added potassium bromate, which increases the protein and enhances gluten development in bread dough. Very little, if any, of the potassium bromate is even absorbed by the body. So it's nothing to get excited about. Honest to God Pizza (page 50) or Dr. Vanselow's Rye Bread (page 127) will not have the proper texture (light, not like a rock) without using bromated bread flour.

Whole Wheat Flour and Unbleached White Flour

Most of the time you should try to use whole wheat flour, but sometimes a recipe won't come out right if you do. When that happens, it is perfectly all right to use unbleached white flour. In many recipes I add a little oat bran to unbleached white flour to give it some more fiber. But don't get yourself all hung up. It's no big deal to use unbleached white flour. Just eat more vegetables to get extra fiber.

Whole Wheat Bread

You aren't going to find a commercial whole wheat bread that does not contain some salt, and most contain some honey or molasses. Every now and then you find one, like Pritikin Bread, that is sweetened with fruit. Get that kind if you can find it. You aren't going to be using that much bread anyway. I buy a loaf, stick it in the freezer, and pull off what few slices I need, then put the rest back in the freezer. A loaf might last me six months. In small amounts like that, the honey or molasses is nothing to fret about, unless you are a diabetic, in which case you should check with your doctor.

Low-Sodium Baking Powder

There are several brands of low-sodium baking powder. I usually use Featherweight brand. You can find it at the supermarket in the diet section. A health food store will usually carry it, too.

Tabasco and Red Hot Sauces

Tabasco sauce is very hot and has a distinct flavor of its own. Some recipes need that special flavor. Crystal, Louisiana hot sauce, and some other less expensive hot sauces are better for some recipes because they are not quite as hot as Tabasco sauce. While they keep a distinctive red pepper flavor, they have more vinegar, which is what some recipes need.

When you squirt red hot sauces on for extra flavor after you have everything on your plate, figure that you are adding about 8 mg of sodium per 1/4 teaspoon.

Sapsago Cheese and 1% Low-Fat Cottage Cheese

People ask me if it is okay to eat the low-fat cheeses, such as part-skim mozzarella and low-fat cheddar. No, it isn't, not if you want to really cut your fat intake. Those cheeses still have too much fat in them.

The only cheeses I know about that really have a very low fat content are sapsago cheese, 1% low-fat cottage cheese, and some kind of hoop cheese (not the yellow kind, but one that looks like cottage cheese).

Sapsago cheese is a hard green cheese from Switzerland flavored with melilot, a kind of clover. I understand that in California where people are super health-conscious, you can get sapsago in every grocery. In Wisconsin, where there is a large Swiss population, I understand you can find sapsago most everywhere. If you can't find it locally, contact the distributor: Otto Roth, 14 Empire Blvd., Moonachie, NJ 07074 (tel: 201-440-3600).

Sapsago cheese is a dead ringer for Parmesan cheese (which is too fatty). But do not bite it. A lady working in a bookstore said to me recently, "That sapsago is terrible. I took one bite, and yuck!" If you got a hunk of ungrated Parmesan cheese and took a bite, how do you think that would taste? Right! About the same as sapsago. But grate sapsago and what happens? It tastes great.

The nutrient values for 1 tablespoon of sapsago cheese are 13.5 calories; 1.80 g protein; 0 g fat; 0 g saturated fat; 0 mg cholesterol; 0 g carbohydrates; 100.6 mg sodium; 0 g fiber.

Why Jumbo Eggs?

I use jumbo eggs in all recipes containing egg whites, simply because they have bigger, fluffier whites. They make the recipes come out better. If you can't find them, extra large eggs will do just about as well. Don't go smaller than the extra large eggs.

Apple Pectin Powder

Apple pectin powder, not tablets, is wonderful for making the jellies in this book. It is the one item you will probably have to get at your health food store. The kind I get is salt-free and starch-free with no sugar added. It's put out by the Solgar Co., Inc. (Lynbrook, NY 11563) and is distributed nationally. (If you can't find it at your local health food store, you can call the company at 1-800-645-2246 and they will direct you to a nearby source.)

Low-Sodium Tamari or Soy Sauce

Low-sodium tamari sauce or low-sodium soy sauce are interchangeable. If you can't find the low-sodium varieties, just use half the amount of the regular sauces. In other words, if the recipe calls for 2 teaspoons of low-sodium soy or tamari sauce, just use 1 teaspoon of the high-sodium variety. Add 1 teaspoon of water for the teaspoon of sauce you are not adding. The sodium content and taste will be about the same.

Red Rosé Wine

Red rosé tastes best in cooking. Gallo puts out a good one.

Instant Brown Rice

In some recipes I use instant brown rice. Minute brand puts out a terrific one and Arrowhead Mills puts one out, too. It is nothing but brown rice, nothing added or subtracted. It cooks up in an absolutely foolproof way. I think it tastes better than regular brown rice. I suggest regular brown rice in some recipes for the purists, but if you haven't tried the instant, please do; you can't go wrong with it. You can find Minute brand at the supermarket and Arrowhead Mills at the health food store. If you can't find Minute brand you can call toll free for information: 1-800-431-1003.

A 1/3-cup serving of instant brown rice contains 80 calories; 2 g protein; .66 g fat; 0 mg cholesterol; 17.3 g carbohydrates; 3.3 mg sodium; 1.3 g fiber. I couldn't find any information on the saturated fat.

Canned Tomatoes and Tomato Paste and Sauce

With any canned tomato product, if you can't find the no-salt variety, you can substitute ones containing salt.

Chuck Wagon Corn

Chuck wagon frozen corn is simply a mixture of whole kernel corn, green pepper, sweet red bell pepper, chopped onion, and sometimes chopped tomato. I find it convenient for making all sorts of dishes. If you can't find it, use 1 part whole kernel corn, 1 part frozen chopped green peppers, and 1 part frozen chopped onions. Add to that about half a medium-size tomato, chopped, and some chopped sweet red bell pepper. If you can't find frozen green peppers and onions, use fresh.

Green Peppers

My sister-in-law who was raised close to the Texas border thinks green peppers are some kind of Mexican peppers, but that's not what I'm talking about when I say green pepper. The green peppers I'm talking about are sweet and not hot at all. Some people call them bell peppers, some call them sweet bell peppers.

Fruit Spreads

You can get wonderful fruit spreads made with nothing but fruit. One brand is Polaner All Fruit Spreadable Fruit, which comes in all varieties. You can find it at grocery and health food stores. Another is Poiret fruit spread, made from pears and apples, which you can find at health food stores.

What To Do If You Can't Find a Specified Package Size

Some canned foods are like candy bars, they keep getting smaller. Do you remember when a nickel candy bar was a regular-size candy bar? At first the manufacturers started making the candy bars smaller, then they started charging more and making the regular size again. Well, the same thing is happening to evaporated skim milk. It used to come in 13-ounce cans, now it comes in 12-ounce cans. Some tomatoes still come in 16-ounce cans, but I see some now in 14-ounce cans. I've found that no matter what size can those items come in, I just use it in the recipe as is and the recipe comes out the same.

Equipment

Get yourself a really good, heavy-duty food processor. I like Cuisinart brand because it is strong enough to knead bread dough. You will also need a blender and an electric mixer. You're going into the business of serious cooking.

I love my slow cooker, too. It frees me up to go out all day if I have to. I use a 5-quart Rival brand. The pot is ceramic and lifts out of the metal electric part. That makes it easy to wash, easy to put in the microwave if I need to, and easy to put in the refrigerator to store or to cool a soup or stew for degreasing.

I like to have several glass measuring cups, in all different sizes. I mix in them and cook in them, as well as use them for measuring. They do very well in the microwave because they are glass and the handles make them easy to lift. I also have a set of metal measuring cups.

I have two sets of measuring spoons, mainly because I don't feel like having to wash and dry spoons while I'm putting a recipe together. Try to find sets that have a 1/8 teaspoon measure.

I own two sets of Silver Stone® coated pots and pans so I can have at least two frying pans, two 5-quart soup pots, and an array of smaller saucepans. I buy inexpensive sets, so when they get beat up, I don't mind replacing them.

Other items you will need are a chopping board, a good set of knives, a hand grater that has small holes for grating sapsago cheese, wooden spoons, a colander, salad dressing bottle, nonstick muffin tins (miniature and large), two large nonstick baking pans, two 9-inch by 13-inch baking dishes, two 8-inch square baking dishes, two 1-1/2-quart casserole dishes, two nonstick bread pans, one large roasting pan with cover, salad bowl, two flan pans, a potato masher, a large kitchen spoon and fork, custard cups, food scale, plastic wrap, zippered plastic bags, and aluminum foil.

Of course, all this is pretty basic; I'm sure you have most of these things in your kitchen.

Cooking Techniques

Some people ask me if it takes me longer to cook the way I do. If you would compare it to opening up a TV dinner, yes, it takes longer. But if you cook from scratch anyway, it won't take you any longer.

Cooking Without Fats

Naturally, since you can't use any oil or grease, you are going to have to learn how to cook without it. You are also going to be doing some serious degreasing of stews, soups, and things like that. I'll start with sauteing.

Sauteing Without Oil—First you need nonstick pots. You will not need chicken stock or water or anything wet to saute with. Liquids will only interfere with the caramelizing process that you get from the natural sugars in the vegetables. Liquids only cause steam; you might as well just boil whatever it is you're trying to saute.

After chopping your vegetables, just toss them into the nonstick pan or pot and turn the heat on. When the vegetables begin to sizzle, stir with a wooden spoon, turning the vegetables over, tossing them some, until they are a little bit brown around the edges and look a little shiny. Then add whatever liquid you need.

When sauteing meats, just put them in the nonstick pan or pot, turn the heat on, and stir and move the pieces around, turning them over until the meat looks brown. In the case of chicken, just get some parts brown.

Degreasing—When you make stocks, gravies, stews, or soups, you will probably have some grease floating on top. If you are in a hurry, just spoon off as much grease as possible, then take a lettuce or cabbage leaf and skim the surface with it to pick up more grease.

Another way to degrease hot liquids is to let them cool, then put them in the refrigerator for several hours, or overnight. The grease hardens on top and you can just lift it off.

The quick way to degrease hamburger meat is to put a paper towel in the pan with the meat when it is almost browned, and stir the paper towel around with meat as it finishes browning. I usually have to use three or four towels to get all the grease out.

A more conventional way to degrease hamburger meat is to brown it, then drain the meat first in a colander, then on paper towels, and pat with more paper towels. Wipe or wash the grease out of the pan. I usually skip the colander part and just use a lot of paper towels so I don't have to wash the colander. Lazy me.

Using Nonstick Spray—Usually, I go ahead and use a nonstick spray, even in nonstick bread pans and muffin tins. There are so few calories in the sprays that I'd rather use them than take a chance my baked goods won't come out of the pans. I've found that if pans are brand new or in extremely good shape, I don't need to use nonstick spray. You should decide for yourself if you think you need a spray.

Pyrex® puts out nonstick glass baking dishes and I've found they work very well. But if I'm cooking something with flour or other starchy foods, I'll usually spray the dish.

Rinsing Salted Canned Goods

Some products such as canned crab, shrimp, and hominy are packed in salted water. If you rinse them twice in cold water, you can get rid of a tremendous amount of the salt and sodium. In fact, with the canned shrimp, crab, or clams you can reduce each can from about 1,410 mg of sodium to about 177 mg, according to information that appeared on a can of crabs I purchased.

To drain a salted canned item, open the can, hold your hand over the top and turn it over; let the liquid drain through your fingers. Fill the can with water with the product still in it; drain again. With canned shrimp, crab, or clams, repeat the process once more.

When I figured out the sodium values for rinsed, canned foods, I assumed the sodium was the same as for cooked, unsalted products. For example, rinsed canned shrimp would have the same sodium as unsalted boiled shrimp.

Don't Omit Ingredients

My cousin, third once-removed, told me she made my Crawfish Étouffée from my first cookbook. I asked, "Well, how did it turn out?" "Umm, okay," she said without much enthusiasm. That answer disturbed me so I started asking questions. It turned out that she didn't include the 4 teaspoons of apple juice concentrate required in the recipe because they didn't seem very important to her. But believe me, the difference between that little bit of juice concentrate and none was the difference between "Wonderful!" and "Umm, okay." If a recipe calls for 1 teaspoon of salt, would you leave it out and expect the dish to taste good? Of course you wouldn't!

Every little thing, down to 1/16 teaspoon of something in the recipes in this book is there because it is absolutely needed. You don't have much leeway when you can't add salt and butter or margarine to taste, so you have to take advantage of every taste-enhancing trick you have available.

Chopping

Sometimes a food processor is really necessary, otherwise you will spend all day in the kitchen. On the other hand, if a recipe calls for something, like celery for instance, to be chopped by hand, please do chop it by hand, as it will make a big difference in texture and taste.

Putting the Dishes Together

When you follow the recipes, you need to follow the exact order as to when each ingredient is added. In other words, if a recipe says cook certain vegetables first, then add fish and cook some more, don't think if you put all the vegetables and fish in at the same time and cook it all together that the dish will come out tasting good. It might be a disaster.

Decoding Nutritive Values

At the end of each recipe you will find a breakdown of nutritive values for each serving. The information was derived using *The Food Processor II, Nutrition Analysis System* computer software from ESHA Research (PO Box 13028, Salem, OR 97309), which is based on the most recent USDA data, and from product manufacturers. I also consulted the USDA's *Nutritive Value of Foods, Home and Garden Bulletin 72*. Keep in mind that the nutrient

data should be viewed as a guide and not as an exact representation of the nutrient values of each and every food. Many recipes, for example, call for an onion or a green pepper, and the exact values of these will vary depending on size. Where possible, in cooked dishes, I have used cooked instead of raw values for foods. Also, I have rounded off all nutrient values to the nearest whole number, except in the case of calories and sodium, in which case I rounded off to the nearest five.

The abbreviation *g* stands for grams, *mg* stands for milligrams, *tr* stands for trace (less than 1 mg), and *NA* stands for not available, where information on an ingredient could not be determined. I did not include the nutritive values for the water used in cooking, as water contains different minerals and chemicals in different locations.

To figure some values you might have to do a little arithmetic depending on what you're trying to measure, so here's a chart that might help.

Equivalents

1 quart	=	4 cups
1 cup	=	8 fluid ounces
	=	1/2 pint
	=	16 tablespoons
5 tablespoons		
+ 1 teaspoon	=	1/3 cup
4 tablespoons	=	1/4 cup
1 tablespoon	=	3 teaspoons
2 tablespoons	=	1 fluid ounce
1 pound	=	16 ounces
3.57 ounces	=	100 grams
1 ounce	=	28.35 grams

Exchanges

You may be on a diet that counts exchanges instead of calories. For the most part, I think the exchange system works well if the foods are not mixed together like when you are eating an apple all by itself, or drinking a cup of milk by itself, or eating a piece of meat all by itself.

Different diets count amounts a little differently sometimes, but for the most part 1/3 cup cooked brown rice is considered 1 bread exchange and 1/2 cup of mashed potatoes is considered 1 bread exchange, 1/4 cup low-fat cottage cheese is considered a dairy exchange, 1 small apple is considered 1 fruit exchange, and so on. When I cooked up all these recipes, I kept exchanges in mind. For instance, when I used low-fat cottage cheese and made something amounting to 6 servings, I used 1-1/2 cups of cottage cheese; that would work out to 1 dairy exchange for each serving. Here is the exchange list which lists many of the foods you will be eating.

Complex Carbohydrate Exchanges
(Each portion provides approximately 80 calories.)

Vegetables

Beans, dried cooked—1/3 cup
Beans, lima, fresh—1/2 cup
Chestnuts—6
Corn, kernels—1/2 cup
Corn on the cob—6 inches long
Corn, popped, no oil or salt added—3 cups
Hominy—1/2 cup
Lentils, cooked—1/3 cup
Parsnips—2/3 cups (1 small)
Peas, black-eyes, split cooked—1/3 cup
Peas, fresh—1/2 cup
Potato, white, baked—1 (2-inch diameter)
Potato, white, mashed—1/2 cup
Potato, sweet—1/3 cup
Pumpkin, cooked—3/4 cup
Squash, winter—3/4 cup
Yams, baked—1/3 cup

Breads and Crackers (whole grain: wheat, rye, or sourdough)

Bagel, water—1/2
Bread, whole wheat, rye, sourdough—1 slice
Breadsticks—2 (4 inches long)
Bun, hamburger, whole wheat—1/2
Bun, hot dog, whole wheat—1/2
English muffin—1/2
Matzo, plain—3/4 ounce
Pita, whole wheat—1/2 of a 6-inch pocket
Rice cakes—3/4 ounce
Rice crackers—3/4 ounce

Roll, whole wheat rye, sourdough—1 (2-inch diameter)
Rye crackers, no salt—4
Tortilla, corn—1 (6-inch diameter)

Flours

Arrowroot—2 tablespoons
Buckwheat flour—3 tablespoons
Cornmeal—3 tablespoons
Cornstarch—2 tablespoons
Matzo meal—3 tablespoons
Potato flour—2-1/2 tablespoons
Rice flour—3 tablespoons
Rye flour, dark—4 tablespoons
Whole wheat flour—3 tablespoons

Grains, Cereals, and Pasta

Barley, cooked—1/2 cup
Cornmeal, dry—2-1/2 tablespoons
Cracked wheat (bulgar), cooked—1/2 cup
Flake cereal—1/2 cup
Nugget cereal—3 tablespoons
Grits, cooked—1/2 cup
Kasha (buckwheat groats), cooked—1/3 cup
Macaroni, whole wheat—1/2 cup
Noodles, rice, cooked—1/2 cup
Noodles, whole wheat, cooked—1/2 cup
Oatmeal, cooked—1/2 cup
Pasta, enriched white, cooked—1/2 cup
Rice, brown, cooked—1/3 cup
Rice, wild, cooked—1/2 cup
Rye cereal, cooked—1/2 cup
Wheat biscuit cereal—1 large
  biscuit or spoon-size—1/2 cup
Steel-cut oats, cooked—1/2 cup

Vegetable Exchanges
(Each portion equals 1 cup of raw or 1/2 cup of cooked vegetables, and provides approximately 25 calories.)

Artichoke, whole base, and ends of leaves (1 small)
Asparagus
Beans, green or yellow

Beets
Bok choy
Broccoli
Brussels sprouts
Cabbage
Carrots (1 medium)
Cauliflower
Celery
Celery root
Cilantro
Chayote (mirliton)
Chicory
Chilies
Chinese cabbage
Chives
Coriander (cilantro)
Cucumber
Eggplant
Endive
Escarole
Greens, beet, collard, chard
Jerusalem artichokes
Jicama
Kale
Leeks
Lettuce
Lima beans, baby (1/4 cup)
Mint
Mushrooms
Okra
Onions, all types
Parsley
Pea pods, Chinese
Peppers, red and green
Pimento
Radishes
Romaine lettuce
Rhubarb
Rutabagas
Shallots
Spinach
Sprouts, assorted
Squash (zucchini, spaghetti, summer)
Tomato (1 medium)

Tomatoes canned in juice, unsalted
Tomato juice, unsalted (2/3 cup)
Tomato paste, unsalted (3 tablespoons)
Tomato sauce, unsalted
Vegetable juice, unsalted (2/3 cup)
Water chestnuts (4 medium)
Watercress

Fruit Exchanges
**(Fresh, dried, frozen, or canned with sugar or syrup.
Each portion provides approximately 60 calories.)**

Apple—1 small (2-inch diameter)
Apple juice or cider—1/3 cup
Applesauce, unsweetened—1/2 cup
Apricots, fresh—4 medium
Apricots, dried—7 halves
Banana—1/2 medium
Berries, boysenberries, blackberries,
    raspberries, blueberries—3/4 cup
Cantaloupe—1/3 (5-inch diameter)
Cherries—12 large
Cranberries, unsweetened—1 cup
Crenshaw melon—2-inch wedge
Dates—2 1/2 medium
Date sugar—1 tablespoon
Figs, fresh—2 (2-inch diameter)
Fruit cocktail—1/2 cup
Fruit juice concentrate—2 tablespoons (1 ounce)
Grapefruit—1/2 medium
Grapefruit juice—1/2 cup
Grapes—15 small
Grapejuice—1/3 cup
Guava—1 1/2
Honeydew melon—1/8 medium
Kiwi—1 large
Kumquats—5
Lemon juice—1/2 cup
Lime juice—1/2 cup
Loquats—13
Mandarin oranges—3/4 cup
Mango—1/2 small
Nectarine—1 (1 1/2-inch diameter)

Orange—1 (2 1/2-inch diameter)
Orange juice—1/2 cup
Papaya—1 cup
Passionfruit—1
Passionfruit juice—1/3 cup
Peach—1 (2 3/4-inch diameter)
Pear—1 small
Persimmon, native—2 medium
Pineapple, fresh—3/4 cup
Pineapple, canned without sugar—1/3 cup
Pineapple juice—1/2 cup
Plantain—1/2 small
Plums—2 (2-inch diameter)
Pomegranate—1/2
Prunes, fresh—2 medium
Prunes, dried—3
Prune juice—1/3 cup
Raisins—2 tablespoons
Strawberries—1 1/4 cups
Tangerine—2 (2 1/2-inch diameter)
Watermelon—1 1/4 cups

Dairy Exchanges
(Each portion contains approximately 90 calories and is 1 % fat or less by weight, 15 % of calories or less from fat.)

Nonfat milk—8 ounces
Nonfat buttermilk—8 ounces
Nonfat yogurt—6 ounces
Evaporated skim milk—4 ounces
Dry-curd cottage cheese or hoop cheese—2 ounces
1% or less low-fat cottage cheese—2 ounces
Nonfat powdered milk—1/3 cup

8 ounces = 1 cup, 6 ounces = 3/4 cup, 4 ounces = 1/2 cup, 2 ounces = 1/4 cup.

High Protein Exchanges
(Each portion provides approximately 35 to 55 calories per ounce. High-protein exchanges are controlled because of their fat and cholesterol content. Although soybeans and tofu do not contain any cholesterol, they are higher in fat than any other legumes; 40 to 50 percent of their calories come from fat. You may select soybeans or tofu in place of fish, fowl, or meat on a no-fat diet.)

In the chart on the next page, note the total fat, cholesterol, and calorie contents, as well as the percentage of calories from fat in 3-1/2-ounce cooked servings of the foods. Shrimp is recommended in 2-ounce portions.

Meat or Fish (3 1/2 ounces cooked)	Fat (g)	Chol. (mg)	Calories	% Calories from Fat
Abalone	0.3	54	49	4.0
Lobster, northern	0.6	72	98	5.4
Pike	0.9	50	113	7.0
Flounder	1.0	46	129	7.0
Cod, Atlantic	0.9	55	105	7.4
Haddock	0.9	74	112	7.5
Sole	0.8	42	68	10.0
Scallops	1.4	52	112	11.0
Clams	2.0	67	148	12.0
Red Snapper, mixed species	1.7	47	128	12.1
Crab, Alaskan king	1.5	53	97	14.0
Tuna, white, water-packed	2.5	42	136	16.0
Turkey, white meat	3.2	69	157	18.0
Sea bass	2.6	53	124	19.0
Halibut	2.9	41	140	19.0
Chicken, white meat	3.6	85	165	20.0
Oysters	2.2	50	90	22.0
Mussels, blue	4.5	56	172	23.0
Trout	4.3	74	151	26.0
Beef, top round	5.4	84	184	26.0
Pork, tenderloin, lean only	4.8	93	166	26.1
Swordfish	5.1	50	155	30.0
Beef, flank, lean only	7.3	90	195	34.0
Lamb, lean leg	7.0	93	184	34.0
Salmon, sockeye	11.0	81	178	61.0
Sardines, Pacific, water packed, unsalted	12.0	81	178	61.0
Shrimp	1.1	133	99	9.8
Crayfish	1.4	178	114	10.7
Chicken, dark, without skin	9.7	93	205	43.0
T-bone steak, lean	10.4	80	214	44.0
Veal, rump and round	11.2	101	215	46.0
Turkey, dark, without skin	11.5	89	221	47.0
Pork loin, top	14.9	94	258	52.0
Beef, lean ground, broiled	17.6	101	280	57.0
Beef, chuck (pot roast), fat and lean	24.4	99	337	65.0

Serving Sizes

Item	Raw Weight	Serving Size	Cooked Weight (edible portion)
Chicken breast	5 oz	1	3 1/2 oz
Clams (in shell)	36 oz	16	3 1/2 oz
Mussels (in shell)	15 oz	33	3 1/2 oz
Oysters (raw)	4 oz	7	
Scallops	4 oz	18-20	3 1/2 oz
Shrimp, boiled, medium-size		9	2 oz
Soybeans, cooked (37 calories/oz)		2/3 cup	
Tofu (21 calories/oz)		6 oz	
Ultra low-fat cheese (less than 34% of calories fat, 67 calories/oz)		2 oz	

Miscellaneous Foods

In addition to the exchanges, here are recommendations for the following food items:

Item	Quantity	Calories
Egg whites	7/week	16 each
Garlic	As desired	Negligible
Gelatin, plain	1 oz/week (4 envelopes)	95/oz
Horseradish, prepared (no salt added)	1 Tbsp/day	7/Tbsp
Sapsago cheese (green)	1-2 Tbsp/week	20/Tbsp
Seeds (as seasoning only)	Less than 1/8 tsp/day	Negligible
Soy sauce (low-sodium)	1 tsp/day	Negligible
Teas: selected herbal	Moderate amount	Negligible
Unprocessed bran	1-3 Tbsp/day as needed	9/Tbsp

Source: U.S.D.A. Handbooks 8-5, 1979; 8-10, 1983; 8-13, 1986; 8-15, 1987

How To Use These Charts

If your doctor puts you on a 1,000-calorie-a-day diet, you may be told to eat 6 complex carbohydrate servings (starchy foods such as beans, corn, potatoes, cereals, and rice), 12 vegetable servings, 3 fruit servings, and 2 dairy servings. You may be allowed only 3 ounces of meat, fish, or poultry a week; on those days count the meat as a dairy serving.

If you are put on a maintainence diet of 2,000 calories a day, you may be told to eat 18 servings of complex carbohydrates, 15 vegetable servings, 5 fruit servings (of which 1 should be citrus), 2 dairy servings (or 1 dairy serving if meat is eaten that day). You may be allowed 3 to 4 ounces of meat, poultry, or fish a day, not to exceed 1-1/2 pounds a week. You may be told to limit shrimp, crab, crayfish (crawfish), and lobster servings to 1-3/4 ounces cooked weight per day because of their high cholesterol content.

If you look at these charts, you will see how large the servings are for each item. As you plan out your foods for the day, check the recipes you plan to use, as a single recipe may contain, for example, 2 milk servings or 2 fruit servings.

Note to diabetics: If exchanges get too complicated for you to figure out in the different recipes, ask your doctor if you can go by the nutritional values at the end of the recipes to tabulate how many grams of carbohydrates, protein, fat, and calories you are getting every day.

2

Dips, Tidbits, and Snacks

Everyone needs some treats and no one is expecting you to go through life without them—hence this chapter on dips, tidbits, and snacks.

Catfish Nuggets

Yield: 60 nuggets

Great for parties. Serve with toothpicks and a bowl of Piquante Sauce (page 150), Horseradish Sauce (page 151), or ketchup, if you want to cheat.

1/2 cup yellow cornmeal
1/16 teaspoon cayenne pepper
1/2 teaspoon crumbled or powdered thyme
1/2 teaspoon ground sage
6 catfish fillets measuring about 6 inches by 3 inches (30 ounces)
Water

Preheat the oven to 400°F. Spray a nonstick cookie sheet with nonstick spray.

In a plastic or paper bag combine the cornmeal, pepper, thyme, and sage. Shake the bag to mix the spices. Cut the catfish into bite-size pieces.

Place the fish in a colander, rinse, and drain. Don't dry the fish. Place a few pieces at a time in the bag with the cornmeal. Shake to coat. Place each piece, not touching, on the cookie sheet.

Bake on the top rack of the oven for 20 to 25 minutes until lightly brown. Turn once if they look like they won't stick when you run a spatula under the pieces. If they appear to be sticking, though, leave them alone. They will be fine. Serve the fish brown side up on a plate around a container of sauce. Each serving will contain about 1/2 ounce.

Per nugget: 40 calories; 5 g protein; 1 g fat; tr saturated fat; 16 mg cholesterol; 2 g carbohydrates; 20 mg sodium; tr fiber

Shrimp Tidbits

Yield: 40 tidbits

This is very nice for a party. Serve with toothpicks and a bowl of Horseradish Sauce (page 151), Piquante Sauce (page 150), or ketchup, if you want to cheat a little.

1 pound large fresh peeled shrimp (2 pounds if weighed unpeeled)
1 cup yellow cornmeal
1/4 teaspoon marjoram
1/4 teaspoon crumbled or powdered thyme
1/4 teaspoon cayenne pepper
1/4 teaspoon ground sage

Wash the unpeeled shrimp and peel. Take out the veins. Do not wash after they are peeled.

Combine in a plastic or paper bag the cornmeal, marjoram, thyme, cayenne pepper, and sage. Shake well to mix.

Spray a nonstick pan with nonstick spray. Throw a few shrimp at a time into the bag with the seasoned cornmeal and shake to coat. Place the shrimp, not touching, on the pan. Place on the middle rack of the oven and set the temperature at 400°F. Bake for 15 minutes. Serve immediately. Each shrimp will weigh less than 1/4 ounce.

Per shrimp: 25 calories; 3 g protein; tr fat; tr saturated fat; 17 mg cholesterol; 3 g carbohydrates; 15 mg sodium; tr fiber

Pickled Shrimp

Yield: About 20-24 servings

Pickled Shrimp makes a nice hors d'oeuvre and is not terribly difficult to make. The first time I made them, I offered some to my husband and he ate the whole platter, including the onions, which he said were delicious. I only got to taste one shrimp. (No, you're not supposed to eat the whole platter.)

Shrimp

6 cups water
1 medium-size onion, quartered (do not peel)
1 teaspoon no-salt chili powder
2 tablespoons apple cider vinegar
1 lemon, halved
6 medium-size garlic cloves (do not peel)
1/4 teaspoon dried red pepper flakes
1/3 bag commercial crab boil or 1/3 recipe for
    Homemade Crab Boil (page 156)
1 pound unpeeled large shrimp, heads on (about 20
    to 24 shrimp)

Pickling Juice

7/8 cup apple cider vinegar
1 cup water
3/4 cup apple juice concentrate
1/2 teaspoon dried red pepper flakes
1 medium-size red onion, sliced in rings

Combine the water, quartered onion, chili powder, vinegar, lemon, garlic, and red pepper flakes in a 3-quart pot. If you use commercial crab boil, make a bag of cheesecloth for it as you would for Homemade Crab Boil. Drop the bag into the pot. Cover and turn the heat on high. When the pot comes to a rolling boil, boil for about 10 minutes, or until the onion is tender.

Add the unpeeled shrimp. Cover. When the water returns to a boil, remove the pot from the heat and let it sit for 10 to 12 minutes. Remove the shrimp to a colander, but reserve 1/2 cup of the cooking liquid. Discard the rest. Let the shrimp cool.

To prepare the pickling juice, combine the vinegar, water, juice concentrate, pepper, and sliced onion, and set aside.

After the shrimp have cooled, peel and de-vein them, but leave the little red tails on. Drop them into the pickling juice. Add 1/2 cup of the reserved cooking liquid. Refrigerate for at least 2 hours.

Drain the shrimp and serve on a small platter with the onion rings, and, if you like, a container of Horseradish Sauce (page 151) for dipping in the center. Each shrimp will weigh less than 1/4 ounce. One pound of unpeeled shrimp will yield a half pound peeled.

Per shrimp with onion: 20 calories; 3 g protein; tr fat; tr saturated fat; 28 mg cholesterol; 1 g carbohydrates; 35 mg sodium; tr fiber. Nutritive values of crab boil and pickling juice are negligible.

Asparagus Sandwiches

Yield: 18 sandwiches

9 slices whole wheat bread, crusts removed
1/2 cup Dill Dip
1 (14-1/2-ounce) can cut asparagus spears, drained
Fresh parsley
Cherry tomatoes

Place a slice of bread on a board and roll a rolling pin over it to flatten it. Spread the bread with 1 tablespoon Dill Dip. Place 3 or 4 asparagus pieces in a line on one end of the slice of bread. Roll that end over the asparagus. Place more asparagus on the bread and continue rolling. Place a sprig of parsley at each end (let the parsley stick out a little). Roll the sandwich all the way up. Cut the roll in half to make two sandwiches. Place the sandwiches seam side down on a serving platter. Continue to do the same with the remaining slices of bread. Decorate the platter with cherry tomatoes and more parsley.

Per sandwich without parsley and tomatoes: 50 calories; 3 g protein; 1 g fat; tr saturated fat; tr cholesterol; 9 g carbohydrates; 190 mg sodium; 2 g fiber

Dill Dip

Yield: 1/2 cup

1/2 cup low-fat cottage cheese
1 teaspoon finely chopped onion
1 teaspoon apple juice concentrate
1/8 teaspoon dill weed
1/8 teaspoon Tabasco sauce

Process all the ingredients in a blender or food processor. This doesn't keep well for long periods in the refrigerator.

Per tablespoon: 10 calories; 2 g protein; tr fat; tr saturated fat; 1 mg cholesterol; 1 g carbohydrates; 60 mg sodium; tr fiber

Bean Dip

Yield: 2 cups

2 cups cold cooked Quick and Easy Pinto Beans (page 92)
2 very small onions or 1/2 large onion, quartered
1 fresh jalapeño pepper
2 teaspoons red hot sauce (not Tabasco)
1 tablespoon apple cider vinegar
1 teaspoon garlic powder
1/4 cup raisins
1 teaspoon paprika
Juice of 1 lemon

Combine all the ingredients in a food processor and blend until smooth. Serve with Toasted Tortilla Chips.

Per tablespoon without chips: 20 calories; 1 g protein; tr fat; tr saturated fat; 0 mg cholesterol; 5 g carbohydrates; 5 mg sodium; tr fiber

Toasted Tortilla Chips

Yield: 48 chips

Place 12 fresh or frozen soft corn tortillas on the racks of the oven and set the temperature at 350°F. Bake for 3 to 5 minutes. Watch the tortillas on the bottom rack carefully. They will be done very quickly. I set my oven timer for 2 minutes, and look at them, then set the timer for each minute after that if they aren't done. When the tortillas are crisp, remove them from the oven and break into 4 chips each.

Per chip: 15 calories; .5 g protein; tr fat; tr saturated fat; 0 mg cholesterol; 3 g carbohydrates; tr sodium; 1 g fiber

Artichoke Balls

Yield: 48 balls

Artichoke balls are especially nice party fare. I add a little meat to give them flavor and body.

1 (14-ounce) can artichoke hearts, rinsed
3 ounces very lean ground top round beef steak
2 cups Grape-Nuts® cereal
1/4 teaspoon dried oregano
1/4 teaspoon garlic powder
1/16 teaspoon cumin
1/8 teaspoon dried basil
1/2 teaspoon dried parsley
1/8 teaspoon cayenne pepper
3 tablespoons sapsago cheese
4 jumbo egg whites, lightly beaten
3 tablespoons dry vermouth
1 teaspoon red hot sauce (not Tabasco)
1/4 baked banana (page 148)

Preheat the oven to 400°F. Spray two 9-inch by 13-inch baking dishes with nonstick spray.

Drain the artichoke hearts very well. Set aside.

Saute the meat in a nonstick frying pan by turning it over and over until brown. Drain on paper towels and pat with more paper towels to remove grease.

While the meat is browning, pour the Grape-Nuts into a food processor fitted with a cutting blade and process until you have very fine crumbs.

In a large mixing bowl, combine the crumbs, oregano, garlic, cumin, basil, parsley, cayenne pepper, and sapsago cheese. Set aside.

Place the artichoke hearts in the food processor and pulse 6 or 7 times. You don't want to grind them too much. Combine the chopped artichokes and meat with the crumbs.

In another small bowl, combine the egg whites, vermouth, hot sauce, and banana and its baking liquid. Beat lightly with a fork. Combine the mixture very well with the artichoke mixture.

Form bite-size balls and place them (not touching) in the baking dishes. Cover the baking dishes with aluminum foil and place on the middle and top racks of the oven for 15 minutes. Eat hot, or let cool covered to serve at room temperature, or refrigerate and serve ice cold. Each ball will contain 0.07 ounces of meat.

Per artichoke ball: 35 calories; 2 g protein; tr fat; tr saturated fat; 2 mg cholesterol; 6 g carbohydrates; 60 mg sodium; 1 g fiber

Stuffed Artichoke Bottoms

Yield: 5 snacks

1 (7-ounce) can artichoke bottoms, rinsed
3 to 4 radishes, thinly sliced (do not peel)
5 tablespoons low-fat cottage cheese
2 teaspoons finely chopped onion
1/8 teaspoon Tabasco sauce

Line the cup of each artichoke bottom with as many slices of radish that will fit. If they hang over the sides, that's all right.

Mix the cottage cheese, onion, and Tabasco sauce in a small bowl. Place a dollop of the mixture on top of each artichoke bottom, giving an equal amount to each bottom.

Cut some of the slices of radishes in half, like half-moons, and push as many as you like, red skin side up, into the cottage cheese mixture. The more radishes the better with this recipe.

Serve as hors d'oeuvres or as a little something extra and decorative on a dinner plate.

Per snack: 30 calories; 3 g protein; tr fat; tr saturated fat; 1 mg cholesterol; 4 g carbohydrates; 80 mg sodium; 3 g fiber

Pickled Okra

Yield: 1 quart

This is a New Orleans favorite, where so many people have okra growing in abundance in their yards. It makes a very nice snack. Or you can place a couple of okra on top of a salad for a spicy touch, or serve it alongside roast beef. Use the youngest, smallest okra you can find.

Okra

2 quarts water
1 pound fresh okra (about 4 cups, or 32 pods)

Pickling Juice

1 cup water
7/8 cup apple cider vinegar
1 garlic clove
1/4 teaspoon red pepper flakes
1 cinnamon stick
1/2 teaspoon mustard seeds
1 bay leaf, broken into several pieces
1 teaspoon coriander seeds
17 whole allspice berries
4 cloves

Bring 2 quarts of water to a rapid boil in a 5-quart soup pot. Toss in the okra and cover the pot. Boil for 5 minutes. Pour the okra immediately into a colander and drain. While you are cooking the okra, make the pickling juice.

Microwave Directions

Pour the water and vinegar into a 1-quart container. Add the garlic, pepper, cinnamon, mustard seeds, bay leaf, coriander seeds, allspice, and cloves. Microwave, uncovered, on high for 4 minutes, then simmer at 50% power for 8 minutes. Let cool.

Stove Top Directions

Pour the water and vinegar into a 1-1/2-quart or 2-quart pot. Add the garlic, pepper, cinnamon, mustard seeds, bay leaf, coriander seeds, allspice, and cloves. Cover, bring to a boil, then simmer for 8 minutes. Let cool.

Lift the cooked okra one at a time, into a 1-quart jar with tongs. If you don't have tongs, use a fork, but be careful not to break the okra. Pour the cooled pickling juice into the jar over the okra. If you have too much juice, lift out all the spices and put them in the jar with the okra. Use the extra juice for salad dressing. Cover the jar and refrigerate. The okra is better if you let it sit for at least a day, but if you can't wait, it is plenty spicy as soon as it is cold. Be sure to lift the okra out of the jar with tongs or a fork so you don't contaminate the liquid with your fingers.

Per okra: 5 calories; tr protein; tr fat; tr saturated fat; 0 mg cholesterol; 1 g carbohydrates; 1 mg sodium; tr fiber. Nutritive value of pickling juice is negligible.

Note

See Zucchini Squares on page 108 for a lovely hors d'oeuvre, and page 82 for a delicious oyster dip.

3

Soups

We New Orleanians just love our soup. Soups are not only delicious—they provide an easy way to consume a variety of vegetables without feeling like a rabbit. Also, sometimes people will eat vegetables they don't like if they are mixed into a soup. My husband, Ray, wouldn't eat okra by itself for a million dollars. (On second thought, he might force himself.) But when I give him gumbo made with okra, or callaloo, a Caribbean dish, he loves it.

If you have been avoiding certain vegetables that you know you should be eating, try them in soup, and get all your vitamins and minerals, plus lots of fiber in a delicious way. Unless otherwise noted, each serving measures about 1 cup.

Stock from Uncooked Turkey or Chicken

Chicken or turkey stock can be made from raw or roasted turkey or chicken.

1 to 2 pounds turkey or chicken parts (1 or 2 turkey wings; or 2 chicken backs, 2 necks and 4 wing tips)
2 carrots
1 large onion, quartered
2 celery ribs, including leaves
Water

Take any parts of raw turkey or chicken and put them in a 5-quart soup pot with the carrots, onion, and celery. Fill the pot with water. Bring the pot to a boil, then reduce the heat to a simmer. Simmer for about 5 hours. If you need especially strong stock, simmer the stock longer, until much of the liquid has evaporated. If you need stock in a hurry, cook at a fast boil uncovered for 20 to 25 minutes. When the liquid is cool, remove the meat and bones, and vegetables. Chill the liquid in the refrigerator until the grease hardens on top. Remove the grease.

Pick the cooked meat off the bones and use it to make dishes requiring cooked chicken or turkey meat.

Per 1-cup serving: 40 calories; 5 g protein; 1 g fat; tr saturated fat; tr cholesterol; 1 g carbohydrates; 10 mg sodium; 0 g fiber. This information assumes that homemade stock is similar in value to degreased, canned, no-salt chicken stock. The nutritive values of this stock will vary according to its strength.

Stock from Roasted Chicken or Turkey

I've found over the years that the stock made from the leftover bones of roasted chickens or turkey breasts is far superior to that made from raw chicken or turkey. You can use the stock of the roasted birds for any recipes in this book requiring stock.

To roast a chicken, skin it, sprinkle it with 1/4 plus 1/8 teaspoon garlic powder, 1/8 teaspoon cayenne pepper, and 1-1/2 tablespoons dried minced onion, in that order. For a roasted turkey breast, follow the recipe on page 65.

Microwave Directions

Bake the chicken, uncovered, at 80% power or on roast for 30 to 40 minutes. With a sharp knife, pierce the chicken in the very meaty part of the thigh near where it is connected to the back. If any red juice comes out, cook the chicken for 5 to 6 minutes longer.

Oven Directions

Bake the chicken for 1 hour at 350°F with an aluminum foil tent over the chicken. When the legs are loose and easy to lift up and down, the chicken is done. Just to make sure, pierce the meaty part of the thigh near where it is connected to the back. If any red or pink juice runs out, bake the chicken a little longer.

After the chicken is roasted, you will have drippings in the bottom of the pan. After the turkey breast is roasted, you will have some leftover gravy, maybe. Save any drippings or gravy in the refrigerator and degrease. Place leftover bones in a large pot with any remaining drippings or gravy. Fill the pot with water and simmer for 5 to 6 hours. For especially strong stock, simmer the meat and bones longer, until the liquid has evaporated quite a bit. Remove the bones and meat and refrigerate the stock. Remove any grease. You will have a beautifully seasoned stock which will enhance any dish using chicken or turkey stock in this book.

Pick the cooked chicken or turkey off the bones and save for recipes needing turkey or chicken meat.

Per 1-cup serving: 40 calories; 5 g protein; 1 g fat; tr saturated fat; tr cholesterol; 1 g carbohydrates; 10 mg sodium; 0 g fiber. This information assumes that homemade stock is similar in value to degreased, canned, no-salt chicken stock. The nutritive values of this stock will vary according to its strength.

Chicken Tomato Soup

Yield: 12 servings

2 quarts chicken stock (page 24)
1 cup diced cooked white meat chicken
2 large onions, chopped
1 celery rib, chopped
3 large tomatoes, chopped
1 large green pepper, chopped
1 large carrot, chopped
1/4 teaspoon cayenne pepper
1/2 cup chopped fresh parsley

Slow Cooker Directions

Combine all the ingredients in a 5-quart slow cooker, except the parsley. Set on high and cook for 4-1/2 hours. Add the parsley. Cook for 20 minutes more.

Stove Top Directions

Combine all ingredients in a 5-quart soup pot. Bring to a boil, then simmer covered until all the vegetables are tender, about 2 hours.

Per serving: 60 calories; 7 g protein; 2 g fat; tr saturated fat; 10 mg cholesterol; 4 g carbohydrates; 25 mg sodium; 1 g fiber

Tomato Soup Scramble

Yield: 6 servings

I'd been thinking about how to make an interesting tomato soup, and adding scrambled eggs not only gives interest, but body too. The beer and pepper give it pizzazz.

6 jumbo egg whites
1 (12-ounce) can nonalcoholic or alcoholic beer
1 large onion, cut in rings
1 (16-ounce) can whole peeled no-salt tomatoes
7 to 8 medium-size fresh mushrooms, sliced
2 teaspoons dried sweet green pepper
1/2 teaspoon dried celery flakes
1 teaspoon dried parsley
1/4 teaspoon cayenne pepper
1 bay leaf
2 tablespoons apple juice concentrate

Crack the egg whites into a nonstick 5-quart soup pot. Turn the heat on high and scramble the eggs when they begin to turn white. Remove them to a separate bowl. Pour the beer into the pot. Add the onion rings and cover. Bring to a boil, then reduce the heat to medium-low.

In the meantime, drain the juice from the canned tomatoes into the pot. Place the tomatoes in a bowl and chop them. Add them and their remaining juice to the pot. Add the mushrooms, green pepper, celery flakes, parsley, cayenne pepper, bay leaf, and juice concentrate. Simmer for 15 minutes, covered. Add the egg whites and break them up. Cover and simmer for 5 to 10 minutes, until the onions are tender yet crisp. Serve hot.

Per serving: 70 calories; 5 g protein; tr fat; tr saturated fat; 0 mg cholesterol; 10 g carbohydrates; 71 mg sodium; 2 g fiber

Bouillabaisse New Orleans Style

Yield: 4 servings

Bouillabaisse, pronounced boo-ya-baze, means something like stop boiling. In other words, the fish in this soup is not supposed to be overcooked. My husband and I have eaten bouillabaisse in three different settings: in New Orleans, then in St. Raphael, which is a town on the Mediterranean a bit west of Cannes on the French Riviera, and in Brussels, Belgium.

The restaurant in Brussels was a fancy one with beautiful displays of boiled seafood on mountains of ice and carts of gorgeous desserts. It was in the very festive restaurant section of Brussels right off Galeries St. Hubert, which is Europe's oldest covered shopping arcade. A lovely restaurant it was, on quaint and narrow Petit rue de Bouchers, but unfortunately the bouillabaisse tasted like canned cream of tomato soup with a few pieces of lobster and shrimp tossed in.

The bouillabaisse in St. Raphael had a brown broth base. It was heavenly. The fish was cooked separately and served on a platter with mussels. The pot of soup was served to one side. They merely placed the fish in the soup bowl and poured the broth over it. Then they placed a large toasted crouton on top, and atop that, rouille sauce, which is totally forbidden to dieters. It's like homemade mayonnaise with saffron, garlic, pepper, a little yellow mustard, lemon juice, and salt mixed in. Oh, the mussels were eaten separately as an appetizer.

Ordinarily, New Orleans bouillabaisse has a tomato broth, and the fish are cooked for a while along with onions, then removed. After that the soup is made, and the fish pieces are returned to the broth at the last minute to finish cooking.

For bouillabaisse made in Marseilles, where it was first created, and in other Mediterranean areas, perch and sturgeon are usually used together. Bouillabaisse always has to be made with at least two different kinds of fish, one kind that is firm-fleshed, and another kind which has flesh that flakes easily when cooked.

New Orleans bouillabaisse calls for a combination of redfish and red snapper. However, when I created the recipe for this book, I couldn't find any redfish (their scarcity is due to the popular craze of blackening them), so I substituted speckled trout for the redfish. You could use other fish such as cod, orange roughy, or flounder.

Soup

2-1/2 cups finely chopped onions
1/4 cup finely chopped celery
1 cup red rosé wine
4 cups chicken stock from roasted chicken (page 24)
1/4 cup finely chopped fresh parsley
1 medium-size carrot, finely chopped
1 (16-ounce) can no-salt tomatoes, chopped (save the juice)
1 large fresh tomato, chopped
2 bay leaves
1 teaspoon crumbled or powdered thyme
1/8 teaspoon cayenne pepper
1/8 teaspoon powdered allspice
2 garlic cloves, chopped
1 tablespoon apple juice concentrate
1/4 teaspoon powdered saffron or threads, packed tightly
4 teaspoons low-sodium tamari or soy sauce
6 tablespoons water
Juice of 2 lemons
1/2 teaspoon garlic powder
1/8 teaspoon cayenne pepper
1/2 pound speckled trout fillets
1/2 pound red snapper fillets
1/4 cup water

Topping

3 slices commercial whole wheat bread, trimmed and diced
4 tablespoons sapsago cheese

Combine the onions and celery in a 5-quart non-stick soup pot and saute over high heat by tossing them over and over until the onions look a little bit transparent and brown around the edges. Reduce the heat and add the rosé, chicken stock, parsley, carrots, tomatoes and juice, bay leaves, thyme, cayenne pepper, allspice, garlic, and juice concentrate. Bring the pot to a boil; then cover, reduce the heat, and simmer for 1 hour, or until the onions and carrots are soft. Stir occasionally. Add the saffron during the last 15 minutes.

About 30 minutes before the soup is ready, start cooking the fish. Make a sauce by combining in a cup the soy or tamari sauce, the 6 tablespoons water, lemon juice, garlic powder, and remaining cayenne pepper. Cut the fish into 2-1/2-inch pieces. Pour 2 tablespoons of the sauce into a nonstick frying pan and turn the heat on high. When the sauce starts to sizzle, add half the fish. Turn it over to coat it with the sauce. Cook for about 3 minutes on one side. Pour 2 tablespoons of the sauce over, and turn the fish over. Cook for about 3 minutes on the second side. The fish should look brown. If it doesn't, keep cooking it, turning it over and over until it is brown. Remove it to a bowl. Pour another 2 tablespoons of the sauce into the pan and add the rest of the fish. Brown it as you did the first batch. Remove it to the bowl.

Pour any extra sauce into the pan, plus 1/4 cup of water. Mix it around and let it sizzle uncovered until the liquid thickens and begins to look like a butter sauce. Pour it into the soup. Place the fish in the soup pot and simmer for about 10 minutes, covered.

To serve, ladle the soup and fish into soup bowls. Sprinkle untoasted diced whole wheat bread on top of each serving. Sprinkle 1 tablespoon sapsago cheese over the bread. Serve immediately. Each serving contains 4 ounces of fish.

Per serving without saffron: 390 calories; 36 g protein; 6 g fat; 2 g saturated fat; 69 mg cholesterol; 41 g carbohydrates; 554 mg sodium; 7 g fiber. Nutritive values of saffron are not available.

Clam and Tuna Chowder

Yield: 11 servings

1 large Irish potato, diced
1 large carrot, sliced
1-1/2 cups chopped celery (include a few leaves)
Water
1/4 teaspoon dried red pepper flakes
1 tablespoon dried parsley
1/4 cup white Bordeaux wine
1 (6-1/2-ounce) can minced clams, rinsed
1 (6-1/2-ounce) can water-packed tuna, drained
1 (12-ounce) can evaporated skim milk

Combine the potato, carrot, and celery in a 3-quart pot. Cover the vegetables with water. Cover the pot and bring to a boil. Uncover and boil for 5 minutes over high heat. Add the parsley, wine, clams, and tuna. Cover, cook for 2 minutes over medium heat. Add the milk and heat through. Serve hot.

Per serving: 80 calories; 10 g protein; tr fat; tr saturated fat; 16 mg cholesterol; 8 g carbohydrates; 120 mg sodium; 1 g fiber

Bouillabaisse St. Raphael

Yield: About 7 servings

I cook this almost exactly as the bouillabaisse was cooked in St. Raphael on the French Riviera. I do, however, put the fish into the soup pot for a few minutes to add flavor. It has a golden brown broth, rather than the red broth of the New Orleans Style Bouillabaisse.

Soup

1 large onion, finely chopped by hand
4 celery ribs, finely chopped by hand
1/4 cup whole wheat flour
4 cups chicken stock from roasted chicken (page 24)
1-1/2 cups red rosé wine
1 large carrot finely chopped (in a food processor, if possible)
1/2 cup chopped celery leaves
1/8 teaspoon powdered allspice
1/4 teaspoon saffron powder or threads, tightly packed
1/2 teaspoon dried red pepper flakes
1 tablespoon dried parsley
2 tablespoons apple juice concentrate
4 teaspoons low-sodium soy or tamari sauce
1/2 cup water
Juice of 2 lemons
1/2 teaspoon garlic powder
1/2 pound cod
1/2 pound orange roughy
1-1/2 teaspoons dried parsley

Topping

3-3/4 slices commercial untoasted whole wheat bread, trimmed and diced
7 tablespoons sapsago cheese

Combine the onions and celery in a 5-quart non-stick soup pot and saute over high heat by tossing them over and over until the onions look a little bit transparent and brown around the edges. Add the flour and continue tossing and stirring until the flour looks a little bit brown. Reduce the heat and add the chicken stock, 1 cup of the rosé, the carrot, celery leaves, allspice, saffron, red pepper flakes, parsley, and juice concentrate. Bring the pot to a boil; then cover and reduce the heat and simmer for 1 hour, or until the onions and carrots are soft. Stir occasionally.

About 30 minutes before the soup is ready, start cooking the fish. Make a sauce by combining in a cup the soy or tamari sauce, 1/2 cup water, the lemon juice, and the garlic powder. Cut the fish into 2-1/2-inch pieces. Pour 2 tablespoons of the sauce into a nonstick frying pan and turn the heat on high. When the sauce starts to sizzle, add half the fish. Turn it over to coat it with the sauce. Cook for about 3 minutes on one side. Pour 2 tablespoons of the sauce over, and turn the fish over. Sprinkle with a little more than 1/2 teaspoon of parsley. Cook for about 3 minutes on the second side. The cod will probably start falling apart, but that's all right. Just keep cooking it and turning it over. Orange roughy and cod don't brown very much but will be done. Remove the fish to a bowl. Pour 2 more tablespoons of sauce into the pan and add the rest of the fish. Cook it as you did the first batch, adding the rest of the parsley. Remove it to the bowl. Pour any extra sauce into the pan, plus the remaining 1/2 cup of rosé. Mix it around and let it sizzle, uncovered, until the liquid reduces by about half. Pour it into the soup. Place the fish in the soup pot and simmer for about 10 minutes, covered.

Ladle the soup and fish into soup bowls. Sprinkle untoasted diced whole wheat bread on top of each serving. Sprinkle 1 tablespoon sapsago cheese over the bread and serve. There will be a little over 2 ounces of fish in each 1-cup serving.

Per serving without saffron: 210 calories; 20 g protein; 2 g fat; 1 g saturated fat; 28 mg cholesterol; 19 g carbohydrates; 390 mg sodium; 3 g fiber. Nutritive values of saffron are not available.

Quick and Easy Seafood Gumbo

Yield: 14 servings

New Orleans-style seafood gumbo can be an all-day project if you have to catch crabs, clean them, chop all the ingredients, saute everything, and make chicken stock. One night, I was pressed for time, but I had frozen or canned ingredients for gumbo in the house. I thought, what the heck, I'm just going to dump everything in and let it go. I was amazed. It turned out great! It took a while to cook, but the preparation time was reduced to 20 minutes, if that. Of course, I had chicken stock already made and stored in the freezer.

And all you Cajuns out there? Did I write this recipe to give yaw'll a heart attack? No! Even without sauteing anything it came out delicious.

2 cups frozen diced onions
1 cup frozen diced green peppers
1-1/2 cups frozen diced celery
5 cups frozen sliced or cut okra (20-ounce package)
6 cups water
3 tablespoons whole wheat flour
4 cups chicken stock from roasted chicken (page 24)
3 bay leaves
1 tablespoon dried parsley
1/2 teaspoon cayenne pepper
2 teaspoons garlic powder
2 teaspoons crumbled or powdered thyme
5 tablespoons apple juice concentrate
1/2 cup red rosé wine
2 (6-1/2-ounce) cans claw or white crabmeat, rinsed
2 (4-1/2-ounce) cans shrimp, rinsed
1 pint fresh unwashed oysters and juice, or 1 (8-ounce) can oysters, rinsed, or 1 (6-ounce) can clams, rinsed
Instant brown rice or white rice

In a 5-quart soup pot, combine the onions, green peppers, celery, okra, and 5-1/4 cups of the water.

Pour the flour into a blender. Add the remaining 3/4 cup water and blend. When the mixture is perfectly smooth, mix it slowly into the pot with the vegetables. Add chicken stock. Turn the heat on high and bring to a boil. Reduce the heat to a simmer, and simmer for 1 hour uncovered, stirring occasionally. After 1 hour, add the bay leaves, parsley, cayenne pepper, garlic powder, thyme, juice concentrate, rosé, crab, shrimp, and oysters and oyster juice, if they are fresh oysters. Simmer for 30 minutes, uncovered, stirring occasionally.

Let sit for 30 minutes with the heat off, then reheat. Or better yet, when cool, refrigerate for 4 or 5 hours, then reheat. Letting the gumbo sit allows the flavors to mingle, and it is much better. Each 1-cup serving will contain 2 to 2-1/2 ounces of seafood. Serve in a soup bowl over 1/3 cup of rice.

Per 1-cup serving, soup only: 105 calories; 9 g protein; 1 g fat; tr saturated fat; 40 mg cholesterol; 13 g carbohydrates; 95 mg sodium; 3 g fiber

Per serving with rice: 185 calories; 11 g protein; 2 g fat; tr saturated fat; 40 mg cholesterol; 31 g carbohydrates; 105 mg sodium; 4 g fiber

Gombo aux Herbes

Yield: 14 servings

I always thought this was spelled "gombo zab," because that's exactly the way it's pronounced. Some people in New Orleans spell it "gombo zhebes," and my 82-year-old cousin, Muriel, who speaks French, says it's spelled "gombo zherbes." Everyone in New Orleans has his or her idea about this and there's no convincing any of them differently. William de Marigny Hyland, an attorney and historian for St. Bernard Parish, who is also an expert in French, says none of the versions are correct (French); all are "Créolisms." This is typical for New Orleanians. However, Mr. Hyland said since the 1901 *Times-Picayune Créole Cookbook*, which is the Bible of Créole cookbooks, calls it "Gombo aux Herbes," I should entitle it that. Do you know that I lay awake at night worrying about things like this? Why? Because I'm a typical New Orleanian. What else do New Orleanians have to worry about?

Gombo aux Herbes is made from at least seven green leaf vegetables for good luck, and when I was a child, we always ate it after midnight mass on Christmas Eve at what we called Reveillon (Rev-ee-yon). Now, the *Times-Picayune Créole Cookbook* says people in New Orleans used to eat this on Good Friday, but without the meat. I've never heard that—and when did they eat it *with* meat? However, New Orleans is composed of different nationalities, mostly French, Italian, Irish, German, and African, and it wasn't until the era of television that we began discovering each other, and then it took us at least 25 or 30 years to get to know each other. So maybe eating "gombo zab" on Good Friday is Irish, or German, or something other than French. I had never heard of eating blackeyed peas (for luck) and cabbage (for money) on New Year's Day either, until I married my husband who had a half-German mother. Now, though, you find cabbage and black-eyed peas on sale in big displays in every grocery in New Orleans right before New Year's Day, and no one would be caught New Year's Day not eating them, with corned beef (page 41), of course.

I use just the lean part of a rib-eye steak to make Gombo aux Herbes, and I'd suggest not using a tough cut.

If you can't find fresh greens, use frozen greens. If you can't find radish greens, substitute watercress, or some other greens, but not beet greens as they will muddy the green color with red. Also, when you prepare your greens, be sure to remove the center veins of the leaves because they will be too tough for this soup.

9 ounces very lean beef steak, cubed small
1 large yellow onion, chopped
8 to 12 scallions, including the green, chopped (1 bunch)
9 cups water
1-1/2 cups chopped green cabbage (1/4 cabbage)
1/4 cup chopped radish greens
2 cups chopped spinach
1-1/2 cups chopped fresh parsley (1 bunch)
1-1/4 cups chopped turnip greens
1-1/4 cups chopped collard greens
2 cups chopped lettuce (any kind)
2 cups chopped mustard greens
10 whole allspice berries
1 whole clove
1 large bay leaf
1 teaspoon crumbled or powdered thyme
1 teaspoon dried marjoram
1/2 teaspoon dried red pepper flakes
1/4 teaspoon garlic powder
3 tablespoons apple juice concentrate
1 tablespoon red hot sauce (not Tabasco)
9 ounces cooked or raw white meat chicken, cubed
1 large carrot, sliced
1-1/2 teaspoon dry vermouth
9-1/4 cups cooked brown rice

Brown the meat in a nonstick 5-quart pot. Remove the pot from the heat, then remove the meat to a bowl. Just blot any grease out of the pot with paper towels, leaving the brown drippings. Return the pot to high heat and saute the onion and scallions tossing them over and over until the edges of the onion are brown. Quickly add 2 cups of the water; reduce the heat to medium-low. Add the chopped vegetables to the pot as it simmers, along with the remaining 7 cups of water.

Take an 8-inch square piece of cheesecloth (you can buy cheesecloth in the automotive section of the grocery) and cut a narrow strip off one side to make a tie. Put the allspice berries, clove, and bay leaf in the center of the cloth. Gather the cloth up around the spices and tie it to make a bag. Cut off any excess cloth. Drop the bag into the center of the soup and push it to almost the bottom. Add the thyme, marjoram, red pepper flakes, garlic powder, juice concentrate, red hot sauce, and browned meat. Increase the heat to high and bring the pot to a boil, then reduce the heat to low and let simmer for 1 hour, uncovered.

Now, I know what I'm going to tell you next isn't going to make much sense, but it's necessary. First, and very important, remove the spice bag and reserve it. Place a colander over another 5-quart soup pot. Pour the cooked vegetables into the colander and reserve the liquid. Pick out the chunks of meat and reserve. Now, place about half the cooked vegetables in a food processor and process until almost as fine as baby food. You can do this in a blender, too, but you will have to add a little of the reserved cooking liquid.

Put all the meat, all the vegetables (including the puréed vegetables), the reserved spice bag, and the cubed chicken (if the chicken is raw, sprinkle it lightly with a little garlic powder, onion powder, and cayenne pepper) into the pot with the reserved cooking liquid. Add the carrot. Simmer for 1 hour, uncovered, or until the carrot is tender. Add the vermouth during the last 15 minutes.

Serve in soup bowls with 1/3 cup brown rice in each. Some people like a few drops of vinegar in their gumbo. I do. Eat a few spoonfuls before you add anything. It takes a while for the taste to come through. Each 1-cup serving of soup will contain 1-1/4 ounces of meat.

Per serving, including rice: 160 calories; 14 g protein; 3 g fat; 1 g saturated fat; 30 mg cholesterol; 20 g carbohydrates; 50 mg sodium; 3 g fiber

Po-man's Gumbo

Yield: 13 servings

One cold day Ray said he wanted gumbo for dinner. Well, I went out to the bayou and checked the crab traps, but no crabs, just a couple of perch. Crabs just don't like to get caught in cold weather, never did, probably never will. I checked the freezer and there was not one shrimp to be found, and no oysters, either. Then I saw I didn't even have a bag of frozen okra. But Ray still insisted he wanted gumbo. Well, I wasn't about to go riding all the way to town searching up crabs, shrimp, oysters, and okra. I searched my refrigerator and pantry instead. I made gumbo with canned tomatoes, onions, celery, zucchini, tuna fish, and canned clams—and Ray never knew the difference. I made it again later, and didn't even have any zucchini, so I substituted more celery. It was just as good. I called this Po-man's Gumbo.

Filé is a powdered herb made of sassafras leaves. Back in the late 1700s and early 1800s you would see Choctaw Indians sitting on the wooden banquettes in what is now the French Quarter in New Orleans, selling the leaves from baskets. If you decide to use filé for your gumbo, be sure you use the commerical kind and don't go grinding up your own sassafras leaves. The untreated leaves contain safferole, which is suspected of causing cancer in animals. The safferole is removed from the commercial filé.

2-1/2 cups chopped onion
6 celery ribs and as many leaves as you can get, chopped
1 medium-size zucchini, chopped (or substitute 2 celery ribs, chopped)
1 (16-ounce) can whole peeled no-salt tomatoes
1 (12-ounce) can nonalchoholic or alcoholic beer
1/4 cup apple juice concentrate
1 cup water
6 tablespoons whole wheat flour

4 cups chicken or turkey stock (page 24)
1 (6-1/2) ounce can minced clams, rinsed
1 (6-1/2) ounce can water-packed tuna, drained
3 bay leaves
2 tablespoons chopped fresh garlic
1/4 teaspoon cayenne pepper
2 teaspoons crumbled or powdered thyme
2 tablespoons dried parsley
4-1/3 cups instant brown rice
2 teaspoons filé per bowl (optional)

Place the onion in a dry nonstick 5-quart soup pot. Turn the heat on high, and saute by tossing the onion over and over until it looks a little transparent and brown around the edges. Remove the pan from the heat. Add the celery, zucchini, and the canned tomatoes with their liquid. Break up the tomatoes in the pot. Add the beer.

Combine the juice concentrate, water, and flour in the blender. Blend until smooth. Add to the soup pot. Add the chicken stock. (No, you do not need to brown the flour. It works better this way for this recipe; don't worry, everything will turn out the right color.) Add the clams, tuna, bay leaves, garlic, and cayenne pepper.

Stir and cover the pot. Bring to a boil, then simmer for 1 hour, stirring occasionally. After 1 hour, add the thyme and parsley. Simmer, covered, for 1 more hour. Stir occasionally.

Serve hot in individual bowls over 1/3 cup cooked instant brown rice. Add filé to each bowl if you like it. Each 1-cup serving of gumbo contains 1 ounce of fish.

Per serving, not including rice, filé 125 calories; 11 g protein; 2 g fat; tr saturated fat; 12 mg cholesterol; 14 g carbohydrates; 90 mg sodium; 2 g fiber. Nutritional information pertaining to filé is not available.

Per serving with rice, not including filé: 205 calories; 13 g protein; 3 g fat; tr saturated fat; 12 mg cholesterol; 32 g carbohydrates; 100 mg sodium; 4 g fiber.

Quick Vegetable Soup

Yield: 8 servings

If you are in a hurry and out of soup, this is the soup to make. Chop the onion, turnip, cabbage, and carrot in the food processor. If you don't have any cooked brown rice, you can use broken raw spaghetti.

1 medium-size onion, chopped
1 medium-size turnip, peeled and chopped
1-1/2 cups chopped green cabbage (about 1/4 of a cabbage)
1 medium-sized carrot, chopped
1/3 cup cooked brown rice or 1/3 cup broken raw spaghetti
2/3 cup frozen chuck wagon corn
2/3 cup frozen French-style green beans
1/2 cup water
4 cups roasted chicken or turkey stock (page 24)
6 tablespoons apple juice concentrate
2 tablespoons no-salt tomato paste
1/2 teaspoon cayenne pepper

Microwave Directions

Combine the vegetables in a 5-quart microwave container. Add the rice or spaghetti, corn, green beans, water, stock, juice concentrate, tomato paste, and cayenne pepper. Stir to mix. Cook on high, uncovered, for 25 to 30 minutes, stirring twice, until the vegetables are tender.

Stove Top Directions

Combine the onion, turnip, cabbage, and carrot in a 5-quart soup pot. Add the rice or spaghetti, corn, green beans, water, stock, juice concentrate, tomato paste, and cayenne pepper. Stir to mix. Cover, bring to a boil, then reduce the heat to medium-high and cook for 30 to 40 minutes, stirring a couple of times, until the vegetables are tender.

Per serving: 75 calories; 4 g protein; 1 g fat; tr saturated fat; .5 mg cholesterol; 13 g carbohydrates; 29 mg sodium; 2 g fiber

No-Work Chicken Vegetable Soup

Yield: 16 servings

This is, of course, no work only if you happen to have some chicken stock made from roasted chicken, and some leftover chicken stored away in the freezer. It turns out simply delicious. I make this when I see I am out of soup, and I just don't have any time for chopping vegetables.

9-1/2 cups roasted chicken stock (page 24)
1 (15-ounce or 16-ounce) can no-salt tomato sauce (about 2 cups)
1-1/2 cups frozen chopped onion
1 cup frozen green peas
1-1/2 cups frozen chuck wagon corn
1 cup frozen French-style green beans
1/2 cup chopped cooked white meat chicken
1/4 teaspoon cayenne pepper
1 tablespoon dried parsley
1/2 cup apple juice concentrate
1/2 cup uncooked elbow macaroni (semolina or whole wheat)

Slow Cooker Directions

In a 5-quart slow cooker, combine all the ingredients. Cover and set the temperature on high. Cook for 5 hours. That's all the time it takes, but if it has to simmer longer, it won't hurt.

Stove Top Directions

In a 5-quart soup pot, combine all the ingredients. Cover, bring to a boil, then simmer for about 2 hours. Each serving contains 0.18 ounces of meat.

Per serving: 90 calories; 6 g protein; 1 g fat; tr saturated fat; 5 mg cholesterol; 13 g carbohydrates; 30 mg sodium; 2 g fiber

Callaloo

Yield: About 7 servings

When my husband and I visited the Virgin Islands, I thought this soup was so interesting and delicious I ordered it twice, at Bluebeard's Castle Hotel and at Frenchman's Reef Hotel, both on St. Thomas. Callaloo, for which the soup was named, is really a leafy vegetable that tastes something like spinach. Cooked in the soup, I couldn't tell the difference—if that is what I was eating. I may have been eating callaloo, spinach, or maybe dasheen, which is an Indian kale, because people in the East Caribbean are said to use dasheen in Callaloo. Who knows? Both waiters told me there was spinach in my soup.

Bluebeard's Castle made Callaloo with salt meat. Frenchman's Reef used ham and crabmeat, and spelled this soup Kallaloo. Both used different vegetables. The people from the Caribbean have even more of a "don't worry" attitude than the people from New Orleans. In our hotel on St. Croix, Virgin Islands, the water went off for five hours and the manager just shrugged her shoulders and said, "Don't worry." "But I've got toothpaste in my mouth!" I said. "Look under the sink in the bathroom, there are usually some bottles of water," she said. I looked, and there were two milk jugs of water. So you see, "Don't worry, be happy," as the song says.

Incidentally, if you should read a Jamaican cookbook, you will notice they call allspice berries "pimento"; so don't think they are talking about the soft red peppers you can buy marinated in jars. The soft red peppers are, for the most part, spelled pimientos, though sometimes you see them spelled pimentos, like the berries.

1 large onion, chopped
1 medium-size green pepper, chopped
2-1/2 cups roasted chicken stock (page 24)
1 cup water
1 large yellow crookneck squash, finely chopped (1-1/2 cups)
1 (10-ounce) package frozen finely chopped spinach
1 (10-ounce) package frozen cut okra
1 large bay leaf
1/2 teaspoon dried marjoram
1 teaspoon crumbled or powdered thyme
1/4 teaspoon garlic powder
1/4 teaspoon cayenne pepper or more to taste
2 tablespoons apple juice concentrate
10 whole allspice berries
1 whole clove
1 (6-ounce) can white crabmeat, rinsed
1 tablespoon dried parsley

Combine the onion and green pepper in a 5-quart nonstick soup pot. Turn the heat on high and saute the onion and green pepper by tossing them over and over until the onion pieces look a little brown around the edges and a bit transparent. Add the chicken stock and water. Reduce the heat to a simmer. Add the squash, spinach, okra, bay leaf, marjoram, thyme, garlic powder, cayenne pepper, and juice concentrate.

Place the allspice and clove in the center of a 4-inch square of cheese cloth. Gather the cloth up around the spices, making a little bag, and use a small strip of cheese cloth to tie the bag at the top. Cut off the excess material. Drop the bag in the pot.

Add the crabmeat to the pot. Increase the heat and bring to a boil; then reduce the heat to a simmer and cook, covered, for 2-1/4 hours, stirring occasionally. Add the parsley during the last 30 minutes of cooking. Let stand for 30 minutes. Remove the spice bag, then reheat and serve. Actually, this tastes even better if you refrigerate it overnight and eat it the next day. Callaloo contains less than 1 ounce of crabmeat per 1-cup serving.

Per serving: 85 calories; 9 g protein; 1 g fat; tr saturated fat; 24 mg cholesterol; 11 g carbohydrates; 110 mg sodium; 3 g fiber

Meatballs and Spaghetti Soup

Yield: 14 servings

Eggplant makes this wonderfully hearty soup unusual. This soup tastes even better the next day.

Meatballs

1 pound very lean ground top round beef
2 jumbo egg whites
1/16 teaspoon cayenne pepper
1/4 teaspoon dried oregano
1/16 teaspoon cumin
1/8 teaspoon garlic powder
1 slice commercial or Pritikin whole wheat bread
Water

Soup

6 cups water
2 medium-size onions, chopped
1/4 medium-size cabbage, chopped
1 medium-size eggplant, peeled and finely cubed
1 (15-ounce) can no-salt tomato sauce
1/4 cup red rosé wine
2 teaspoons dried parsley
1/4 teaspoon garlic powder
1/16 teaspoon cumin
1/8 teaspoon cayenne pepper
1/4 teaspoon dried oregano
4 tablespoons apple juice concentrate
4 ounces uncooked whole wheat or semolina spaghetti
Sapsago cheese (optional)

In a large bowl, combine the meat, egg whites, cayenne pepper, oregano, cumin, and garlic powder. Wet the bread with water and squeeze the water out. Break up the bread and mix it in well. Make 21 meatballs and place them in a metal baking pan. Set the oven temperature at 425°F and bake for 30 minutes. Remove the meatballs from the pan and drain on paper towels. Do not wash the baking pan.

Place the meatballs in a 5-quart slow cooker or 5-quart soup pot. Blot the pan the meatballs were in with paper towels to remove the grease, then add 2 cups of water to the pan. With a spatula, scrape up the drippings and combine with the water as much as possible. Return the pan to the oven and bake at 500°F for 10 minutes.

Slow Cooker Directions

Pour the water from the baking pan into the slow cooker. Add the onions, cabbage, eggplant, tomato sauce, rosé, 4 more cups of water, parsley, garlic powder, cumin, cayenne pepper, oregano, and juice concentrate. Break the spaghetti into 1-inch pieces and add to the pot. Cook in the slow cooker, covered, on high for 5 to 6 hours.

Stove Top Directions

Pour the water from the baking pan into the soup pot. Add the onions, cabbage, eggplant, tomato sauce, rosé, 4 more cups of water, parsley, garlic powder, cumin, cayenne pepper, oregano, and juice concentrate. Break the spaghetti into 1-inch pieces and add to the pot. Simmer, covered, for 2 to 3 hours, stirring occasionally. Add water if necessary.

Use a lettuce or cabbage leaf to remove any grease that is beaded up on the top.

Serve 1-1/2 meat balls with each 1-cup serving. Sprinkle 1/2 tablespoon sapsago cheese over the top, if desired. Each 1-cup serving will contain 1-1/17 ounces of meat.

Per serving without sapsago cheese: 120 calories; 12 g protein; 3 g fat; 1 g saturated fat; 27 mg cholesterol; 12 g carbohydrates; 55 mg sodium; 2 g fiber

Per serving with sapsago cheese: 130 calories; 12 g protein; 3 g fat; 1 g saturated fat; 27 mg cholesterol; 12 g carbohydrates; 105 mg sodium; 2 g fiber

Red Bean Soup

Yield: 14 servings

This is a very hearty soup; it will fill you up. And no, you don't need to pre-soak the red beans. Some people say their beans never get soft. That only happens if you do not add enough water to start, or if the beans are very old. A slow cooker is safer and much more convenient for cooking beans than a pot on top of the stove because it eliminates the worry of burning the beans.

1 pound dry red kidney beans (2-2/3 cups)
1 large onion, chopped
2 large carrots, sliced
1/2 medium-size turnip, chopped (do not peel)
3 celery ribs, including leaves, chopped
11 cups water
2 bay leaves
1/4 teaspoon cayenne pepper
2 tablespoons apple juice concentrate
3 tablespoons no-salt tomato paste
1 teaspoon dried thyme
4 teaspoons onion powder

Slow Cooker Method

Combine the beans, onion, carrots, turnip, celery, water, bay leaves, cayenne pepper, juice concentrate, and tomato paste in a 5-quart slow cooker. Cover and cook on high for 5 hours. Add the thyme and onion powder. Cook for 30 minutes more.

Stove Top Directions

When cooking beans on top of the stove, set a timer for every 20 minutes so you will remember to check and stir them. Combine the beans, onion, carrots, turnip, celery, water, bay leaves, cayenne pepper, juice concentrate, and tomato paste in a 5-quart soup pot. Cover and simmer for about 3 hours. Add the thyme and onion powder. Cook for 30 minutes more.

Let the soup cool slightly. Then remove and discard the bay leaves. Purée the soup in the blender until smooth. Reheat a little if needed, or serve immediately. Leftovers can be frozen.

Per serving: 125 calories; 8 g protein; tr fat; tr saturated fat; 0 mg cholesterol; 24 g carbohydrates; 20 mg sodium; 8 g fiber

Zucchini Crab Soup

Yield: 4 servings

This soup is really delicious—colorful, too.

1 medium-size onion, chopped
1 medium-size zucchini, halved the long way and sliced
1 cup chicken stock from raw or roasted chicken (page 24)
1 teaspoon dried parsley
1/8 teaspoon dried red pepper flakes
1 (4-ounce) jar pimiento pieces, chopped
1 (6-ounce) can white crabmeat, rinsed
1 (12-ounce) can evaporated skim milk (1-1/2 cups)

In a 2-quart pot, combine the onion, zucchini, chicken stock, parsley, and red pepper flakes. Cover. Bring to a boil; then cook on high heat for 10 minutes. Remove from the heat. Add the pimiento, crabmeat, and milk. Heat through and serve immediately.

Per serving: 150 calories; 18 g protein; 1 g fat; tr saturated fat; 47 g cholesterol; 16 g carbohydrates; 238 mg sodium; 2 g fiber

Zucchini Corn Chowder

Yield: 7 servings

1 cup frozen diced onion
1 cup frozen whole kernel corn
2 cups sliced zucchini (1 large squash)
2 cups diced raw Irish potatoes
2-1/4 cups chicken stock from raw or roasted chicken (page 24)
1/4 teaspoon dried red pepper flakes
1/2 cup sliced carrot
1 (12-ounce) can evaporated skim milk
1/2 teaspoon dried parsley

Combine the onion, corn, zucchini, potatoes, chicken stock, red pepper flakes, and carrot in a 2-quart pot. Bring to a boil, cover, and cook over medium heat for 15 minutes. Add the milk and parsley and heat. Do not boil.

Per serving: 135 calories; 9 g protein; 1 g fat; tr saturated fat; 2 mg cholesterol; 25 g carbohydrates; 79 mg sodium; 3 g fiber

Cream of Corn Soup

Yield: 4 servings

1 medium-size onion, chopped, or 1 cup frozen chopped onion
1 medium-size carrot, sliced
2 cups frozen chuck wagon corn
1-1/2 cups water
1 (12-ounce) can evaporated skim milk
1/16 teaspoon cayenne pepper

Stove Top Directions

Combine the onion, carrot, corn, and water in a 2-quart pot. Cover, bring to a boil, and boil for 7 or 8 minutes. Add the milk and cayenne pepper and heat through.

Per serving: 130 calories; 9 g protein; tr fat; tr saturated fat; 4 mg cholesterol; 23 g carbohydrates; 120 mg sodium; 3 g fiber

Hominy Bean Soup

Yield: 7 servings

This is a delicious meatless soup, but chicken, beef, or shrimp could be added if desired.

3 cups roasted chicken stock (page 24)
1 (16-1/2-ounce) can golden hominy, rinsed
1 (16-ounce) can whole tomatoes
1 cup frozen or fresh chopped onions
2 cups frozen or fresh speckled butter beans
1 celery rib, coarsely chopped
3 tablespoons apple juice concentrate
1/4 teaspoon cayenne pepper
1 tablespoon dried parsley

Slow Cooker Directions

Pour the chicken stock into the slow cooker. Add the hominy. Add the canned tomatoes with their liquid, cutting up the tomatoes right in the pot. Add the onions, butter beans, celery, juice concentrate, and cayenne pepper. Cover and cook on high for about 5 hours. Stir and test several of the beans to see if they are soft. Cook a little longer if they are not. Add the parsley and cook for 15 minutes longer.

Stove Top Directions

Pour the chicken stock into a 5-quart pot. Add the hominy. Add the tomatoes with their liquid, cutting up the tomatoes right in the pot. Add the onions, butter beans, celery, juice concentrate, and cayenne pepper. Cover and bring to a boil, then reduce the heat to simmer. Cook for 1 hour, stirring occasionally. Stir and test several of the beans to see if they are soft. Cook a little longer if they are not. Add the parsley and cook for 15 minutes longer.

Per serving: 190 calories; 8 g protein; 1 g fat; tr saturated fat; tr cholesterol; 8 g carbohydrates; 40 mg sodium; 6 g fiber

Black-eyed Pea Soup

Yield: 14 servings

This tastes even better if you refrigerate it overnight and eat it the next day. The recipe calls for white chicken meat, but if you choose to mix the white and dark meat, the calories will increase by about 5 per serving, and the cholesterol will increase by about 2 mg per serving.

4 ounces lean ground top round beef steak
6-1/2 cups roasted chicken stock (page 24)
4 ounces cooked chopped white meat chicken
1 medium-size raw sweet potato or yam, cubed (about 2 cups)
4 cups frozen (20-ounce bag) black-eyed peas
2 cups chopped onions
1 medium-size unpeeled raw turnip, cubed
2 cups frozen French-style green beans
1 large carrot, sliced
1/2 cup broken uncooked semolina or whole wheat spaghetti
1/4 cup apple juice concentrate
2 tablespoons low-sodium soy or tamari sauce
1/4 plus 1/8 teaspoon cayenne pepper
2 teaspoons dried parsley

Slow Cooker Directions

In a nonstick frying pan, saute the beef over high heat until it looks cooked. Drain thoroughly on paper towels, then place in a 5-quart slow cooker. Add the chicken stock, chicken, sweet potato, and black-eyed peas. Set the temperature on high and cook covered for 5 hours. Add the onions, turnip, green beans, carrot, spaghetti, juice concentrate, soy sauce, cayenne pepper, and parsley, and cook on high for 1 more hour, or until the onions and carrot are tender. Serve hot.

Stove Top Directions

In a nonstick 5-quart pot, saute the beef over high heat until it looks cooked. Drain thoroughly on paper towels. Return the meat to the pot. Add the chicken stock, chicken, sweet potato, black-eyed peas, onions, turnip, green beans, carrot, spaghetti, juice concentrate, soy sauce, and cayenne pepper. Bring to a boil, then reduce the heat to simmer, cover, and cook for 1 hour. Add the parsley, cook for 15 minutes more, or until the peas and other vegetables are tender.

Each 1-cup serving contains less than 1 ounce of meat. Serve hot.

Per serving: 150 calories; 11 g protein; 2 g fat; 1 g saturated fat; 14 mg cholesterol; 23 g carbohydrates; 100 mg sodium; 6 g fiber

4

Main Dishes with Meat

For the most part, my recipes use meat as additions to other foods, but sometimes it's wonderful to have meat out there by itself, where you can really taste it, so I've included recipes like that too.

In a steak house, I order rib-eye, ask them to take all the fat off before cooking it, eat just a little, then have the rest wrapped up to take home for several meals. It just doesn't pay any more to go into a restaurant and get the all-you-want-to-eat-at-a-certain-price because I can't take anything home and I certainly am not going to eat my money's worth. I wish they would let me get the child's plate where the portions are usually the right size.

Slow Cooker Beef

Yield: 13 servings

A slow cooker is a wonderful way to have roast for dinner and still be able to leave your house for hours. Even if the roast cooks for an hour more than recommended, it will be all right. I slice the mushrooms and mix up the cornstarch, water, juice concentrate, and rosé before I leave home and refrigerate them, so that when I get home, I just have to add them to the pot.

I give two alternative methods for this recipe—one where the meat cooks over 8-1/2 hours, and one that takes 5 hours. Choose the method that best suits your schedule.

3-pound to 3-1/2-pound eye of round or rump roast
1/4 teaspoon cayenne pepper
1/2 teaspoon garlic powder
1/4 cup dried minced onion or onion flakes
2 ribs celery and leaves
2 cups water
3 tablespoons cornstarch
1/4 cup red rosé wine
1 tablespoon apple juice concentrate
2 cups sliced mushrooms
1 tablespoon dried parsley

Defrost the roast slightly if it is frozen, trim off any visible fat, and place it in a 5-quart slow cooker. Even if the roast is still frozen inside, you don't need to defrost it further.

8-1/2 Hour Method

Sprinkle the cayenne pepper, garlic powder, and dried onion over the roast, letting some of the onion fall into the bottom of the pot. Cut the celery ribs in half and place on top. Add 1/2 cup of the water. Cover and turn the setting to low. Cook for 8 hours.

Mix together the cornstarch, the remaining 1-1/2 cups water, rosé, and juice concentrate. Pour it into the pot. Add the mushrooms and parsley, turn the heat to high and cook for another 30 minutes, stirring a few times. The roast should be very tender.

5-Hour Method

Sprinkle the cayenne pepper, garlic powder, and dried onion over the roast, letting some of the onion fall into the bottom of the pot. Cut the celery ribs in half and place on top. Do not add water now. Cover and turn the setting to high. Cook for 4-1/2 hours.

Mix together the cornstarch, water, rosé, and juice concentrate. Pour it into the pot. Add the mushrooms and parsley, and cook for another 30 minutes, stirring a few times. The roast should be very tender.

Remove the roast from the pot to a dish and cover. De-grease the gravy. Serve the roast along with brown or white rice. Pour 1/4 cup of the gravy over each serving of the rice and the meat. My husband adds a few squirts of Tabasco sauce. I like it just as is. Each serving will contain about 4 ounces of meat.

Per serving including gravy: 290 calories; 39 g; 12 g fat; 4 g saturated fat; 116 mg cholesterol; 4 g carbohydrates; 70 g sodium; tr fiber

Easy Corned Beef

Yield: 14 servings

This is a great New Year's Day dish which you can cook a day ahead, reheat, and serve with Cabbage and Potatoes (page 102). Use the juice from the cooked corned beef to cook the Cabbage and Potatoes. I like to cook corned beef in a slow cooker so I can go off and forget it, but you can cook it on top of the stove very easily, too. If you live in Louisiana or some place where you can buy crab boil, this dish is extremely easy to make. If you can't find commercial crab boil, you can make your own.

Serve the corned beef with Horseradish Sauce or Creamy Horseradish (page 151).

3-pound sirloin tip, eye of the round, or rump roast
5 cups water
1 large onion, quartered
1 celery rib, cut in thirds
1/2 cup apple cider vinegar
1/4 cup apple juice concentrate
1 pouch commercial crab boil, or Homemade Crab Boil (page 156)

Slow Cooker Directions

Trim off all visible fat from the roast and place it in a 5-quart slow cooker. Add the water, onion, celery, vinegar, juice concentrate, and bag of crab boil. Cover, cook for 5 hours on high, or until the meat is very tender. Remove 1 cup of liquid and refrigerate it until any grease hardens on top; then remove the grease. Meanwhile, keep the meat warm on a low setting. Reheat the liquid to pour over the meat when served. Slice the roast with an electric knife if you have one.

Stove Top Directions

Trim off all visible fat from the roast and place it in a 5-quart soup pot. Add the water, onion, celery, vinegar, juice concentrate, and bag of crab boil. Cover, bring to a boil, then simmer for 5 hours, or until the meat is very tender. You shouldn't have to add water, but check and maintain the water level at the same height. Add more, if necessary. Remove 1 cup of liquid and refrigerate it until any grease hardens on top; then remove the grease. Meanwhile, keep the meat warm on a simmer. Reheat the liquid to pour over the meat when served. Slice with an electric knife if you have one.

When I cook this on New Year's Eve to eat the next day, I just slice the roast, put it in an ovenproof serving dish and pour the juice over it after it has been degreased. I let it sit in the refrigerator covered that way. On New Year's Day, either I put the whole thing in the microwave covered with plastic wrap for about 10 to 15 minutes on high, or I cover the dish with aluminum foil and reheat at 300°F for about 30 minutes in the oven. Each serving will contain about 3-1/2 ounces of meat.

Per serving, not including seasonings: 185 calories; 28 g protein; 7 g fat; 2 g saturated fat; 67 mg cholesterol; 3 g carbohydrates; 65 mg sodium; tr fiber. Nutrient values for seasonings are negligible.

Boeuf en Brochette

Yield: 4 servings

12 ounces very lean sirloin, filet mignon, or rib-eye steak, cut into bite-size pieces
8 mushrooms, cut in half
2 medium-size onions, quartered and separated
2 medium-size tomatoes, cut in 8 wedges
1 medium-size green pepper or yellow sweet bell pepper, cut in 10 to 12 pieces
4 teaspoons low-sodium soy or tamari sauce
6 tablespoons water
Juice of 2 limes
1/2 teaspoon garlic powder
2 tablespoons apple juice concentrate
1/4 teaspoon cayenne pepper

Spear the meat and vegetables with the skewers, alternating the meat and vegetables. Make sure there is a piece of onion and pepper on either side of the meat.

Make the marinade in a cup by mixing together the soy sauce, water, lime juice, garlic powder, juice concentrate, and cayenne pepper.

Place the skewered meat and vegetables in a flat-bottomed dish. Pour the marinade over the meat and vegetables. Put in the refrigerator to marinate for 2 hours. Baste with the marinade every 30 minutes.

Place the brochettes in a metal baking pan and put it about 4 inches from the heat of the broiler. Reserve the marinade. Turn the setting to broil and broil for 4 minutes. Check a couple of times so you don't scorch the tops of the vegetables.

Turn the brochettes over and baste them with the marinade. Broil for about 5 minutes checking a couple of times until the meat looks nice and brown. Serve immediately. If the meat was totally fat-free, pour some pan juices over. Each serving will contain 3 ounces of meat.

Per serving: 225 calories; 27 g protein; 8 g fat; 3 g saturated fat; 65 mg cholesterol; 12 g carbohydrates; 235 mg sodium; 2 g fiber

Ground Meat Hash

Yield: 6 servings

1 pound very lean ground round beef or flank steak
2 medium-size onions, chopped
1 small green pepper, chopped
5 cups water
4 cups cubed, peeled Irish potatoes
1-1/2 teaspoons crumbled or powdered thyme
2 bay leaves
1/4 teaspoon cayenne pepper or more to taste
1 tablespoon dried parsley or 1/4 cup chopped fresh parsley
2 tablespoons plus 1 teaspoon orange juice concentrate
1 teaspoon red hot sauce (not Tabasco)

Place the ground beef in a nonstick 5-quart pot. Turn the heat on high and saute the meat until it is brown. Drain the meat on paper towels and wipe out the pot with paper towels. Pat the meat with more paper towels.

In the same pot, combine the onions and green pepper. Turn the heat on high and saute by turning the vegetables over and over, until the onions look brown around the edges and a little bit transparent. Add the water, potatoes, meat, thyme, bay leaves, cayenne pepper, parsley, juice concentrate, and hot sauce. Bring to a boil, then reduce the heat to medium and cook uncovered for 45 minutes. Stir every so often, and then stir frequently the last 10 minutes.

Serve hot. Each serving will contain about 2-2/3 ounces of meat.

Per serving: 285 calories; 24 g protein; 6 g fat; 2 g saturated fat; 62 mg cholesterol; 32 g carbohydrates; 60 mg sodium; 3 g fiber

Créole-Style Meat Loaf

Yield: 10 servings

This Créole-style meat loaf comes out just like the meat loaf my mama used to make. My kids love this one. There is no way Créole-Style Meat Loaf is going to be anything but juicy and delicious.

Meat Loaf

2 pounds very lean ground round beef steak
2 raw jumbo egg whites
2 slices Pritikin or commercial whole wheat bread
Water
1/8 teaspoon cayenne pepper
1/2 teaspoon garlic powder
1/4 teaspoon basil
1/4 teaspoon oregano
1/8 teaspoon cumin
1/4 teaspoon marjoram
1/4 baked banana (page 148)
Cooked whole wheat elbow macaroni or spaghetti or brown rice

Sauce

2 cups sliced mushrooms
2 medium-size onions, chopped
1 large green pepper, chopped
3 cups water
1 (12-ounce) can or 1-1/4 cups no-salt tomato paste
1/2 teaspoon garlic powder
1-1/2 teaspoons oregano
1/2 teaspoon basil
1 tablespoon dried parsley or 1/2 cup chopped fresh parsley
1/4 teaspoon cayenne pepper
1/8 teaspoon cumin
2 tablespoons apple juice concentrate
1/4 cup white Chablis

Place the meat in a large bowl and add the egg whites. Wet the bread with water and squeeze the water out of it. Break up the wet bread and add it to the meat and egg whites. Sprinkle in cayenne pepper, garlic powder, basil, oregano, cumin, marjoram, and banana. Mix the meat and seasonings gently with your hands until well blended. Don't try to squeeze the meat to death. That will make the loaf tough.

Place the meat mixture in a 9-inch by 13-inch baking dish and form it gently into a stocky loaf about 8 inches by 4 inches.

Place the loaf in the oven on the middle rack and set the heat on 400°F. Bake for about 25 minutes until brown.

Tip the dish and spoon out any grease that collects. Wipe the dish around the loaf with paper towels to remove any grease left.

To make the sauce, combine the mushrooms, onions, and green pepper in a nonstick frying pan and turn the heat on high. Saute the vegetables, turning them over and over, until the onions look a little transparent and brown around the edges. Remove the pan from the heat and add the water, tomato paste, garlic powder, oregano, basil, parsley, cayenne pepper, cumin, juice concentrate, and Chablis. Stir well, return the pan to the heat, cover, and simmer for 1 hour, checking and stirring every 10 to 15 minutes. Add a little water if the liquid starts to dry out. Pour the sauce over the browned loaf.

Cover the baking dish with aluminum foil and place on the middle rack in the oven. Set the heat on 325°F. Bake for 1 hour, basting occasionally.

Place 1 cup cooked whole wheat elbow macaroni or spaghetti or 2/3 cup brown rice on each plate. Pour the sauce over the pasta or rice and meat. There are 3 ounces of meat in each serving.

Per serving including sauce and macaroni: 495 calories; 33 g protein; 12 g fat; 5 g saturated fat; 79 mg cholesterol; 52 g carbohydrates; 155 mg sodium; 8 g fiber

Grillades and Gravy

Yield: 4 servings

Grillades (pronounced gree-ahds) is an old-time favorite served in New Orleans, usually for breakfast over grits, but it is also eaten for dinner, usually over rice.

3/4 pound round beef steak
1-1/2 cups chopped onions
1 cup chopped green pepper
1/3 cup whole wheat flour
2-2/3 cups water
1 large carrot, sliced
1/8 teaspoon cayenne pepper
1 bay leaf
1/8 teaspoon garlic powder
1/2 teaspoon crumbled or powdered thyme
1 tablespoon apple juice concentrate
2 tablespoons red rosé wine
2-2/3 cups cooked grits or brown or white rice

Remove any fat from the meat, and cut the meat into 1-inch squares. Combine the steak pieces, onion, and green pepper in a nonstick frying pan. Turn the heat on high and saute all together, turning the meat and vegetables over and over until the meat looks brown. Add the flour and toss with the meat and vegetables for about 25 seconds. Add the water, stirring until mixed in well. Add the carrot. Cover and cook over low heat for 2 hours, stirring often. Add a little water if the mixture starts to dry out.

Add the cayenne pepper, bay leaf, garlic powder, thyme, juice concentrate, and rosé. Simmer covered for 30 minutes more, until the meat is very tender. Don't forget to stir every so often.

To serve, place 2/3 cup either grits or rice on each plate, and serve the grillades and gravy over. Each serving will contain 3 ounces of meat.

Per serving with grits: 380 calories; 28 g protein; 12 g fat; 5 g saturated fat; 68 mg cholesterol; 38 g carbohydrates; 75 mg sodium; 6 g fiber

Grillades Rouge

Yield: 3 servings

1/2 pound lean, thinly sliced top round beef steak
1 large onion, chopped
1 large green pepper, chopped
1 (12-ounce) can no-salt tomato paste (1-1/2 cups)
2-1/2 cups water
1 cup red rosé wine
1 large bay leaf
1 teaspoon crumbled or powdered dried thyme
1-1/2 teaspoons dried or 3 tablespoons chopped fresh parsley
1/4 teaspoon cayenne pepper
1-1/2 teaspoons apple juice concentrate
2 cups cooked brown or white rice

Remove any fat from the meat and cut the meat into 1-inch squares. Place it in a nonstick 5-quart pot and saute over high heat by turning the meat over and over until it looks fairly brown. Add the onion and green pepper and continue to stir until the vegetables begin to brown. Put your nose over the pot; the aroma will turn from slightly sour to almost smoky. When the aroma changes, stir for just about 25 seconds more.

Remove the pot from the heat. Add the tomato paste, water, rosé, bay leaf, thyme, parsley, cayenne pepper, and juice concentrate. Stir well. Cover, bring to a boil, then reduce the heat to the lowest setting. Cook for 3 hours, until the meat is tender. Stir every now and then. You shouldn't need more water, but if the mixture looks dry, add just a little.

To serve, place 2/3 cup of rice on each plate and ladle the Grillades Rouge over. Each serving will contain about 2-2/3 ounces of meat.

Per serving including rice: 485 calories; 32 g protein; 10 g fat; 3 g saturated fat; 72 mg cholesterol; 57 g carbohydrates; 125 g sodium; 8 g fiber

Hamburger

Yield: 2 servings

7 ounces very lean ground top round beef or flank steak
2 tablespoons finely grated carrot
1/16 teaspoon cayenne pepper
1/8 teaspoon dried parsley
1/8 teaspoon garlic powder

Mix the ground meat with the carrot, cayenne pepper, parsley, and garlic powder. Form the mixture into 2 patties and place them in a nonstick frying pan. Turn the heat on high and fry for 5 minutes after the meat starts to sizzle. Turn the patties over and reduce the heat to medium-low. Turn the patties often to keep down the smoke. Cook for about 15 minutes total.

Barbara's Cabbage Relish (page 152) is good served on the side. Each serving will contain 3-1/2 ounces of meat.

Per serving: 195 calories; 28 g protein; 8 g fat; 3 g saturated fat; 82 mg cholesterol; 1 g carbohydrates; 65 mg sodium; tr fiber

Mexican Corn Bread

Yield: 12 servings

1 pound lean ground top round beef or flank steak
1 large onion, chopped
1 large green pepper, chopped
1-1/2 cups yellow cornmeal
2 tablespoons no-salt chili powder
1 tablespoon low-sodium baking powder
1/2 baked banana (page 148)
3/4 cup apple juice concentrate
3/4 cup water
4 jumbo egg whites, beaten until just foamy
2 (4-ounce) cans whole peeled green chilies, drained
1 cup frozen chuck wagon corn

Preheat the oven to 400°F.

In a nonstick frying pan, brown the ground beef over high heat. Remove it to paper towels to drain, and pat with more paper towels.

Wipe the pan clean of grease with more paper towels. Add the onion and green pepper and saute over high heat, tossing them over and over until the onions are a little bit transparent and brown around the edges. Remove from the heat.

In a large mixing bowl, combine the cornmeal, chili powder, and baking powder. Mix together the banana and its juices, juice concentrate, and water, and add to the bowl. Add the egg whites. Mix well. Add the chilies and corn. Mix. Add the onion, green pepper, and ground meat, and mix well.

Unless you have a nonstick 9-inch by 13-inch baking pan, spray the pan with nonstick spray. Pour the batter into the pan. Even out the mixture by shaking the pan from side to side. Place the baking pan or dish on the middle rack and bake uncovered for 20 to 25 minutes, or until a toothpick inserted into the center comes out clean.

Remove from the oven and let sit for 10 minutes. Each serving will contain about 1-1/3 ounces of meat. Serve topped with Piquante Sauce (page 150).

Per serving: 195 calories; 14 g protein; 4 g fat; 1 g saturated fat; 31 g cholesterol; 25 g carbohydrates; 145 g sodium; 2 g fiber

Salisbury Steak

Yield: 5 servings

My mother taught me how to make Salisbury steak. When I want meat with a delicious gravy and don't have a lot of time to make something complicated, Salisbury steak is a quick and tasty answer. It takes about 30 minutes to cook, but you can do other things while it simmers.

5 (3-1/2 ounce) patties very lean ground top round beef or flank steak
1/8 teaspoon cayenne pepper
2 cups water
1/2 cup red rosé wine
1 tablespoon apple juice concentrate
1 teaspoon red hot sauce (not Tabasco)
1 very large onion or 2 medium-size onions, sliced in rings
1 tablespoon cornstarch

Place the meat patties in a nonstick frying pan and sprinkle with cayenne pepper. Turn the heat to high. Leave the pan uncovered to brown the meat. Turn the meat over once or twice while browning, until it looks quite brown on both sides. Remove the patties to a plate. Pour out any grease that formed in the pan and wipe the pan clean with paper towels.

Return the meat to the pan. Reduce the heat to medium-low. Add the water, rosé, juice concentrate, and hot sauce. Distribute the onion rings over the patties. Cover and cook for about 25 minutes, moving the meat around occasionally, but don't turn it over. You want the onions to stay on top. At the end of 25 minutes, uncover. Sprinkle the cornstarch over the tops of the patties, then turn them over and move them around in the pan to mix the cornstarch smoothly into the liquid. Cook uncovered for 10 minutes more over medium-high heat, stirring frequently.

Serve with brown rice. The gravy and onions over the rice taste wonderful! Each serving will contain 3-1/2 ounces of meat.

Per serving without rice: 300 calories; 25 g protein; 14 g fat; 5 g saturated fat; 86 mg cholesterol; 4 g carbohydrates; 80 mg sodium; tr fiber

Variation

Green Pepper Steak. Before browning the meat, cut 1 large green pepper into long slices, and chop 1 large onion. Saute the onion and green pepper together in a nonstick pan until the onion pieces look a bit transparent and brown around the edges. Remove the onion and green pepper from the pan and reserve them. Then brown the meat patties as above. Distribute the sauteed onion and green pepper over the meat patties instead of the onion rings and finish cooking as above.

Per serving without rice: 305 calories; 25 g protein; 13 g fat; 5 g saturated fat; 86 mg cholesterol; 5 g carbohydrates; 80 mg sodium; tr fiber

Cajun-Style Shepherd's Pie

Yield: 4 servings

When my husband and I were last in London, we stopped to eat lunch at an outdoor café not a half block from the bridge that crosses the Thames, linking the Tower of London on one side, and Parliament, Westminster Abbey and Big Ben on the other. As we sat there watching the boats slide by, taking in the ancient castle walls of the Tower of London across the river, we ate shepherd's pie. I liked the concept, but I just had to "Cajunize" it when I came home.

4 medium-to-large Irish potatoes, peeled
1 large carrot, sliced
Water
6 ounces very lean ground round beef or flank
  steak
1 cup chopped onion
1 cup chopped green peppers
About 1/4 cup skim milk
1/2 teaspoon dried basil
1-1/2 teaspoons dried parsley
1 tablespoon onion powder
1/8 plus 1/16 teaspoon cayenne pepper
1 cup frozen or fresh green peas
2 tablespoons sapsago cheese

Cover the potatoes with water and boil over high heat until tender when pierced with a sharp knife, about 25 minutes. Drain and set aside.

Microwave Directions

Pour 1/4 cup water into a narrow high-sided 3-cup container and cover. Microwave on high for 25 seconds. Add the carrots, cover, and microwave on high for 5 minutes. Drain, reserving the cooking liquid, and set both the liquid and carrots aside.

Stove Top Directions

Pour 1/2 cup water into a 1-quart saucepan and bring to a boil over high heat. Add the carrots, cover tightly, return to a boil, and cook for 5 minutes, until tender. Watch carefully. Drain, reserving the cooking liquid. Set both the carrots and liquid aside.

While the potatoes and carrots are cooking, saute the ground meat in a nonstick frying pan, stirring until nice and brown. Remove the meat from the pan, then drain it on paper towels, and pat with paper towels to get out all the grease. Wipe out the pan with paper towels. Add the onions and green pepper to the pan. Turn the heat on high and saute the vegetables, tossing them over and over until the onion looks brown around the edges and a little transparent. Remove the pan from the heat and set aside.

Mash the potatoes with enough milk to make them creamy. Add the basil, parsley, onion powder, 1/8 teaspoon cayenne pepper, and the reserved cooking liquid from the carrots.

In the frying pan, combine the meat, carrots, onions, green pepper, peas, and the remaining 1/16 teaspoon of cayenne pepper.

In a 8-inch square nonstick casserole dish or pan, layer half the potato mixture, then all of the meat mixture, then the remaining potato mixture. Sprinkle sapsago cheese on top. Bake on the middle rack of the oven for 35 minutes at 350°F. Then broil for 3 minutes to brown the top, watching carefully not to burn.

Cooked spinach is nice on the side. Each serving will contain about 1-1/2 ounces of meat.

Per serving: 275 calories; 18 g protein; 4 g fat; 1 g saturated fat; 35 mg cholesterol; 41 g carbohydrates; 140 mg sodium; 6 g fiber

Enchilada Casserole

Yield: 8 servings

I've served this dish at several garden club luncheons and have received beaucoup compliments on it. No one realizes this is a healthy, low-cal dish.

I chop the cauliflower, carrots, celery, yellow squash, zucchini, mushrooms, and cucumbers in a food processor, measuring them after they are chopped, to end up with 4 cups of finely chopped vegetables. The onion and green pepper I chop by hand. (Hint: When chopping the vegetables, I keep a soup pot handy. After measuring the vegetables, I put the extras in the soup pot and make vegetable soup at the same time I am making this casserole. I just add whatever else I need to complete the soup.)

1/2 cup finely chopped cauliflower
1 cup finely chopped carrots
1/2 cup finely chopped celery
1/2 cup finely chopped yellow squash
1/2 cup finely chopped zucchini squash
1/2 cup finely chopped mushrooms
1/2 cup peeled and finely chopped cucumbers
2-1/2 cups water
9 ounces very lean ground top round beef or flank
   steak
1 large onion, chopped
1/2 large green pepper, chopped
1 (12-ounce) can no-salt tomato paste
1/4 cup no-salt chili powder
1/4 teaspoon garlic powder
1/8 teaspoon cayenne pepper
12 fresh or frozen soft corn tortillas
1 (24-ounce) carton low-fat cottage cheese
1 (4-ounce) can whole, roasted, peeled mild green
   chili peppers, rinsed
1 very large or 2 medium-size onions, chopped
1 teaspoon Tabasco sauce
1 tablespoon skim milk
2 tomatoes, chopped

Microwave Directions

Combine the cauliflower, carrots, celery, yellow squash, zucchini, mushrooms, and cucumbers in a 1-1/2-quart to 2-quart container. Add 1/2 cup of the water and cover. Microwave on high for 7 to 8 minutes, until the vegetables are tender-crisp. Drain, reserving the cooking liquid. Toss the vegetables together, mixing them well.

Stove Top Directions

Combine the cauliflower, carrots, celery, yellow squash, zucchini, mushrooms, and cucumbers in a 1-1/2-quart to 2-quart pot. Add 1/2 cup of the water and cover. Bring to a boil and cook for 5 to 7 minutes until the vegetables are tender-crisp. Drain, reserving the cooking liquid. Toss the vegetables together, mixing them well.

Saute the ground beef in a nonstick frying pan over high heat, stirring and breaking up the pieces until the meat is brown. Remove the beef from the frying pan to a plate lined with paper towels to drain away the grease. Pat with more paper towels.

Wipe any grease out of the pan with paper towels. Add the onion and green pepper to the pan and saute, turning them over and over until the onion looks transparent and the edges begin to brown. Remove the pan from the heat. (If you don't, when you add the tomato paste it will bubble and spit all over the place.) Add 1 cup of the water, the reserved cooking liquid, and tomato paste. Add the remaining 1 cup of water to the tomato paste can and stir to dissolve the paste adhering to the can. Add the water from the can. Stir well, then add the chili powder, garlic powder, and cayenne pepper. Cover and cook on a low heat for about 30 minutes, stirring occasionally, until the vegetables are tender. Add a little water if the mixture becomes too dry or thick.

In the meantime, stack the tortillas and cut them into approximately 1-inch squares. This makes it easier to serve the casserole after it is cooked.

In a 9-inch by 13-inch baking dish, layer the sauce, then the tortillas, then the cooked vegetables, then half the low-fat cottage cheese, then the sauce again, then the tortillas, then the remaining sauce. (Hint: When layering the sauce, it's hard to judge exactly 1/3 of the sauce for each layer, so be rather skimpy with the sauce on the bottom layer, saving the most sauce for the top layer.) Cut the chili peppers in strips and decorate the top of the casserole. Cover the casserole with aluminum foil and place it on the middle rack of the oven. Set the temperature at 350°F and bake for 30 minutes.

To make the topping, combine the remaining half-carton of cottage cheese, 2 tablespoons of the chopped onion, the Tabasco sauce, and skim milk in a blender or food processor. Blend or process until the mixture is very smooth.

Spread the topping evenly over the cooked hot casserole. Sprinkle the remaining chopped onions and chopped tomatoes all over the top. Serve immediately in squares. Each serving will contain about 1-1/8 ounces of meat.

Per serving: 325 calories; 25 g protein; 10 g fat; 3 g saturated fat; 31 mg cholesterol; 40 g carbohydrates; 565 mg sodium; 9 g fiber

Eggplant Sorrento

Yield: 4 servings

Something about this pasta dish reminds me of the quaint mountainside town of Sorrento, Italy, which sits on a sunny spot on the Mediterranean Sea directly across the water from the Isle of Capri. Perhaps it's the fragrance of the oregano, cumin, basil, and tomato. It is said that smells last longer in our memories than any other sensual experience. The taste of this eggplant dish just brings me back to that magical little town.

4 ounces very lean ground top round beef or flank steak
1 large onion, chopped
1 large green pepper, chopped
1 (15-ounce) can no-salt tomato sauce
1 cup water
1/4 teaspoon garlic powder
1-1/2 teaspoons dried oregano
1/4 teaspoon dried red pepper flakes
1/2 teaspoon dried basil
1/4 teaspoon cumin
1 large eggplant
6 ounces uncooked semolina or whole wheat spaghetti (about 2 cups cooked)
4 tablespoons sapsago cheese

Brown the ground beef in a nonstick 5-quart pot over high heat, then remove it from the pot and drain on paper towels. Pat with more paper towels.

Wipe out any grease that formed in the pot. Add the onion and green pepper and saute over high heat by tossing the vegetables over and over, until the onions look transparent and a little brown around the edges. Remove the pot from the heat and add the tomato sauce. Rinse the tomato sauce can with 1 cup of water, and add the rinse water to the pot. Add the garlic powder, oregano, red pepper flakes, basil, and cumin. Stir and set the pot over medium-low heat. Cover.

Peel the eggplant and cut it into 1-inch cubes. Add to the pot, cover, and cook over low heat for about 45 minutes, stirring occasionally.

About 25 minutes before the eggplant is cooked, heat the water for the spaghetti. When it comes to a rolling boil, throw in the spaghetti. If it is semolina spaghetti, cook for about 10 minutes. Cook whole wheat spaghetti for about 15 minutes. Drain the spaghetti. Set aside.

When the eggplant is very tender, chop it up a little more with the edge of a spoon, then add the spaghetti to the pot and mix all together.

Serve immediately. You don't need any vegetables on the side with this. Sprinkle 1 tablespoon of grated sapsago cheese over each serving. Each serving will contain about 1 ounce of meat.

Per serving with spaghetti and cheese: 230 calories; 15 g protein; 3 g fat; 1 g saturated fat; 23 mg cholesterol; 34 g carbohydrates; 150 mg sodium; 5 g fiber

Honest-to-God Pizza

Yield: 10 servings

I had to make this dough five times with different methods and flours before I got it right. So don't go worrying about why I use this and why I use that. Just be glad it wasn't you who had to throw away five pizzas before getting a good one. I've made this pizza several times since just to be sure the recipe works.

Just to get you into the mood, I'll tell you a story. Have you ever heard of Huey Long? He was Governor of Louisiana back in the 1930s and he was famous for getting what he wanted. The way he did it was to look at things differently. He wanted to build a football stadium at Louisiana State University, and the only money available was tagged for a dormitory. The Louisiana legislature told him no way was that money going to be used for a stadium, it had to be used for a dormitory. You know what Huey did? He built a dormitory in the shape of a doughnut, put seats up and down the inside of the doughnut, and left just enough land in the middle large enough for a football field. That dormitory was and still is the LSU stadium, and yes, students still sleep in the rooms around the sides. Sometimes you just have to go another way around.

My husband, who never eats pizza crust, said he loved this crust and ate every bit.

Suggestion: Start the dough first, then immediately make the filling and refrigerate it until you are ready to bake the pie. For insurance, I give directions for weighing the pie down, but you should know that each time I've made the pie, it hasn't puffed. Be sure you use bromated bread flour.

Pizza Dough

4 cups bromated white flour
3 envelopes (3 tablespoons) "rapid rise" dry baker's yeast
2 cups tepid water

Meat Sauce

12 ounces very lean ground top round beef or flank steak
1 medium-size onion, chopped
1/2 large green pepper, chopped
1/2 cup red rosé wine
1 (12-ounce) can no-salt tomato paste
1 cup water
1/2 teaspoon dried oregano
1/8 teaspoon cayenne pepper
1 teaspoon dried parsley
1/8 teaspoon dried basil
1/4 teaspoon garlic powder

Topping

1 (12-ounce) carton low-fat cottage cheese
2 tablespoons grated sapsago cheese
1/2 cup chopped onion
1 cup sliced fresh mushrooms
1/2 large green pepper, cut in strips
1 (4-ounce) jar pimientos, cut in strips

Measure the flour into a large bowl and add the yeast. Mix well. Make a hole in the center of the flour and pour in the water. Mix with a spoon to blend in the water; then, if still dry, with one hand, turn the dough over and over in the bowl, poking your fingers into it to distribute the water more evenly. But don't squeeze the dough hard. Be gentle. Mostly just poke your fingers and thumb into it. If the dough still looks dry after turning and poking about 15 or 16 times, pour 1 tablespoon of water over it, and pick up the rest of the flour in the bowl with the dough. Then, if there is still flour in the bottom of the bowl, add another tablespoon of water and mix in. The dough might also be sticky or slick, but don't worry, just let it be. Do not, under any circumstance, add more flour. Lightly flour a zippered-type, gallon-size plastic bag, place the dough in it, and squeeze out all the air. Zipper the bag

5

Main Dishes with Poultry

At first I thought a 3-1/2 or 4-ounce portion of chicken or turkey would not be worth eating, but over the years this size portion seems quite normal. Now I nearly faint when I go into a restaurant and see an order of half a good-sized chicken on someone's plate.

I think you will be surprised at the traditional-sounding recipes in this book. You don't have to stop living just because you cook a little differently. Eat and enjoy. And think of all the money you will save!

Poulet Sauce Blanc

Yield: 4 servings

I just couldn't resist giving this recipe a fancy name. It's just chicken in white gravy, the kind that Mississippians pour over biscuits, except that this gravy tastes a whole lot better. I really think the chicken tastes better in white gravy than sausage, which is usually used. I ate white gravy only one time, from a hotel breakfast buffet in Natchez, and I was completely turned off—but maybe that hotel chef was a lousy cook. I liked the idea of the white gravy, though, so I've been trying to come up with a good one for five or six years now. My husband said this one is excellent.

You can pour the chicken and gravy over whole wheat toast or Corn Bread (page 126) for a delicious main meal. You could even pour this over spaghetti. This recipe is much easier to make in a microwave than on top of the stove.

1 large onion, sliced in rings
1 cup strong roasted chicken stock (page 24)
3 tablespoons cornstarch
1/4 baked banana (page 148)
1/4 teaspoon cayenne pepper
1/2 teaspoon dried parsley
1/4 teaspoon crumbled or powdered thyme
1/4 teaspoon dried sage

8 ounces chopped cooked white meat chicken
1 (12-ounce) can evaporated skim milk
8 pieces of commercial whole wheat or Pritikin toast
Paprika

Microwave Directions

Place the onion rings in a 2-quart microwave dish. Mix the chicken stock with the cornstarch until perfectly smooth, and add it to the onion rings. Cover. Microwave on high for 2 minutes. Stir. Cover and microwave on high for 5 minutes. Stir. Cover and microwave on high for 3 minutes. The onions should be cooked and the liquid thickened; if not, microwave for another 2 minutes. Mash the baked banana. Add the cayenne pepper, banana and its juices, parsley, thyme, and sage. Mix well. Add the chicken and mix. Add the milk and mix. Cover and microwave on high for 5 minutes.

Stove Top Directions

Combine the onion and chicken stock, cayenne pepper, parsley, thyme, and sage, in a medium-size sauce pan. Bring to a boil, cover and cook on high heat for 5 minutes. Remove from the heat. Combine the milk, banana, and cornstarch in a blender. Blend until smooth. Add the milk mixture and chicken to the pot. Return the pot to the heat, cover and cook over medium heat, stirring all the time for 3 minutes, or until the mixture thickens.

To serve, pour the sauce over whole wheat toast, giving each person 2 pieces of toast and 1 cup of sauce. Sprinkle paprika on for color. Each serving will contain 2 ounces of chicken.

Per serving with toast: 385 calories; 33 g protein; 6 g fat; 2 g saturated fat; 51 g cholesterol; 51 g carbohydrates; 600 g sodium; 6 g fiber

Chicken in Wine Sauce

Yield: 4 servings

How's this for an American dish? Tarragon and nectarines, no less. I think it's positively yuppie-Californian. You have to wear Gucci shoes to eat this.

1 cup red rosé wine
1/4 teaspoon dried tarragon
1/4 teaspoon garlic powder
1/8 teaspoon cayenne pepper
11 tablespoons apple juice concentrate
2 tablespoons dried onion flakes
4 chicken breasts, skinned
4 tablespoons cornstarch
2 nectarines, sliced (do not peel)

Combine the rosé, tarragon, garlic, cayenne pepper, juice concentrate, and onion flakes in an 8-inch square baking dish. Place the chicken breasts, meat side down in the mixture. Place in the refrigerator for at least an hour to marinate. You can leave it much longer, until you are ready to cook it, if you like.

When you are ready to cook, remove the chicken to another dish, and add the cornstarch to the marinade. Stir until the cornstarch is smooth. Add the nectarines, distributing them evenly in the baking dish. Place the chicken breasts, meat side down into the marinade.

Place in the microwave oven and cook uncovered on high for 20 minutes. Move the chicken around to stir the sauce. Cook on high for 5 minutes, still uncovered. Let sit for 5 minutes.

Serve meat side up with the sauce and nectarines on top. What class. Each serving will contain about 3-1/2 ounces of chicken.

Per serving: 345 calories; 32 g protein; 5 g fat; 1 g saturated; 84 mg cholesterol; 33 g carbohydrates; 90 g sodium; 2 g fiber

Slow Cooker Chicken Dinner

Yield: 6 servings

This makes a delicious one-dish meal. It can cook for an hour longer than the 3-1/2 hours required by the recipe.

3 chicken breasts, bones in, skinned, cut in half
1/4 teaspoon garlic powder
2 tablespoons dried onion flakes
1/4 teaspoon cayenne pepper
3 large carrots, in chunks
2 cups sliced mushrooms
1 teaspoon dried celery flakes
1 tablespoon dried green peppers
2 cups sliced Irish potatoes
1/4 cup red rosé wine
1 tablespoon dried parsley
1 (15-1/2-ounce) can no-salt cut green beans, drained

Place the chicken in a 5-quart slow cooker. Sprinkle the garlic powder over, then the onion, then the cayenne pepper. Toss in the carrots, then the mushrooms on top of the carrots. Sprinkle the dried celery over the carrots, then the green pepper. Toss in the potato slices. Pour the rosé over all the potatoes. Sprinkle the potatoes with the parsley. Cover and cook on high for 3-1/2 hours. During the last half hour, toss in the green beans. Each serving will contain 1-3/4 ounces of chicken.

Per serving: 175 calories; 15 g protein; 2 g fat; .5 g saturated fat; 33 mg cholesterol; 23 g carbohydrates; 45 mg sodium; 4 g fiber

Slow Cooker Chicken Cacciatore

Yield: 4 servings

If you want to cook something delicious yet simple to put together, this recipe is a breeze. The hardest thing to do is skin the chicken. My husband asks me to cook this all the time. He loves it, and he thinks I've been chopping and cooking all day.

4 chicken breasts, skinned
1/4 teaspoon garlic powder
1/16 teaspoon cumin
2-1/2 tablespoons minced dried onion
1/4 teaspoon dried red pepper flakes
1/8 teaspoon dried basil
2 teaspoons dried celery flakes
1 teaspoon dried oregano
2 tablespoons dried chopped green pepper
1 tablespoon dried parsley flakes
3 (8-ounce) cans no-salt tomato sauce
1 cup water
3 tablespoons cornstarch
2 tablespoons apple juice concentrate
1/4 cup red rosé wine
4 cups cooked spaghetti, whole wheat or semolina
  (about 12 ounces uncooked)
4 tablespoons sapsago cheese

Place 2 pieces of the chicken in a 5-quart slow cooker. Sprinkle on half of the garlic powder, cumin, onion, pepper, basil, celery, oregano, green pepper, and parsley. Place the other 2 pieces of chicken on top of the others. Sprinkle on the remaining garlic powder, cumin, onion, pepper, basil, celery, oregano, green pepper, and parsley. Cover, turn the heat on high, and cook for 3 hours.

Pour the tomato sauce over the chicken. Add the water to 1 can, then pour the water from can to can to get all the tomato sauce left in the cans. To the last can full of water, add the cornstarch and mix it into the water until it is smooth. Pour the mixture around the sides of the chicken pieces, not on top of them. Pour the juice concentrate and rosé around the sides of the

chicken also. Cover and cook for 3 more hours. Stir once or twice.

To serve, pour the tomato sauce over cooked spaghetti and serve the chicken on the side. Sprinkle a tablespoon of sapsago cheese over each serving. Each serving will contain about 3-1/2 ounces of chicken.

Per serving with spaghetti and cheese: 455 calories; 40 g protein; 5 g fat; 1 g saturated fat; 76 g cholesterol; 58 g carbohydrates; 210 mg sodium; 5 g fiber

Brunswick Stew

Yield: 10 servings

I really like lima beans in this, but it is very hard to find any without salt in them. Salt-free speckled butter beans are easier to find and make a good substitute.

15 ounces cooked or raw diced white meat chicken
1 (16-ounce) can peeled no-salt tomatoes
1-1/2 cups frozen or fresh diced onions
3 cups frozen lima or speckled butter beans
3 cups frozen whole kernel corn
1-1/2 cups diced raw Irish potatoes
3 cups strong chicken stock (page 24)
1/4 teaspoon cayenne pepper
1/4 cup red rosé wine
1 tablespoon apple juice concentrate
1 cup fresh Pritikin or commercial whole wheat
  bread crumbs

Combine the chicken, tomatoes, onions, beans, corn, potatoes, chicken stock, cayenne pepper, and rosé in a 5-quart pot. Break up the tomatoes with the edge of your spoon. Bring to a boil and cook uncovered over a medium heat for 30 to 40 minutes, or until the potatoes and onions are tender. Stir occasionally. Add the juice concentrate during the last 10 minutes of cooking. Make the bread crumbs in a food processor or blender. Add the bread crumbs just before serving. Serve hot. Each serving will contain 1-1/2 ounces of chicken.

Per serving: 250 calories; 21 g protein; 3 g fat; 1 g saturated fat; 36 mg cholesterol; 35 g carbohydrates; 100 mg sodium; 8 g fiber

Chicken R. B.

Yield: 4 servings

My son R. B. was furious when he realized I hadn't mentioned him in my first cookbook. It was an oversight, of course, so I named this recipe after him. R. B. (Raymond Benton) is a very good cook himself. He says he is because he raised himself and cooked for himself all his life. That's not exactly true. But I did let all my boys cook a lot. I figured they should know how. I have to say, when R. B.'s friends give a party, they always ask him to make his special dishes.

Chicken R. B. is a spaghetti-chicken casserole. You can get the spaghetti cooking some time in the middle of the chicken preparation and have it ready to mix with the sauce. I do love angel hair spaghetti with this, but any very thin spaghetti will do, including whole wheat spaghetti.

4 chicken breasts, skinned
1/8 teaspoon garlic powder
1/16 teaspoon cayenne pepper
1 medium-size carrot, sliced
1 medium-size green pepper, sliced
1 cup sliced fresh mushrooms, sliced
1 celery rib, chopped
1-1/3 cups skim milk
2 tablespoons whole wheat flour
1/4 teaspoon dried red pepper flakes
1 teaspoon dried oregano
1/2 teaspoon dried basil
1/4 teaspoon garlic powder
1 teaspoon onion powder
1 tablespoon dried parsley
1 (4-ounce) jar chopped pimientos and juice
1 cup fresh or frozen green peas (rinsed if frozen)
4 cups cooked very thin (angel hair) spaghetti
1 medium-size zucchini, sliced
2 tablespoons sapsago cheese

Place the chicken in a 9-inch by 13-inch baking dish. Sprinkle it with the garlic powder and cayenne pepper. Place the baking dish on the middle rack of the oven and set the temperature at 400°F. Bake for 25 minutes, turning the chicken once. Remove the chicken to another dish and set aside. Wipe out any grease that formed in the baking dish, and set the dish aside.

Combine the carrot, green pepper, mushrooms, and celery in a nonstick frying pan. Turn the heat on high, and saute the vegetables by tossing them over and over, until the green peppers develop a very nice aroma and look shiny. Remove the pan from the heat.

To make the sauce, pour 5 tablespoons of the milk into a cup. Add the whole wheat flour, and mix until there are no lumps. Pour the rest of the milk into the cup and mix well with the flour. Set aside.

Return the pan with the vegetables in it to a medium heat. Add the milk-flour mixture to the pan, plus the red pepper flakes, oregano, basil, garlic powder, onion powder, parsley, and pimientos. Cook and stir until the mixture bubbles. Add the peas. Remove the pan from the heat and set aside.

Preheat the oven to 350°F.

Cook the spaghetti in plenty of boiling water until tender, drain it, and then combine it with the sauce in the frying pan. Now layer half the spaghetti-sauce mixture in the bottom of the 9-inch by 13-inch baking dish. Layer the raw zucchini slices over. Layer the chicken over the zucchini slices. Top with the remaining spaghetti.

Cover the dish with aluminum foil and place it on the middle rack of the oven. Bake for 30 minutes. Serve hot and sprinkle 1/2 tablespoon of sapsago cheese over each serving. Each serving should contain about 3-1/2 ounces of chicken.

Per serving: 490 calories; 46 g protein; 6 g fat; 2 g saturated fat; 85 mg cholesterol; 61 g carbohydrates; 235 mg sodium; 8 g fiber

Poulet à la Green Store

Yield: 4 servings

St. Bernard Parish, which abuts New Orleans, is a place where the residents do not adjust well to change. For example, the Spaniards or Isleños (don't dare call them Hispanics), whose ancestors came from the Canary Islands between 1779 and 1785, still fly the Spanish flag over their shrimp boats at the annual blessing of the fleet. Juan Carlos, King of Spain, even comes to visit them occasionally. A war-like people, they speak Spanish and live in the past, as if the pirate Jean Lafitte were still helping Andrew Jackson to win the Battle of New Orleans, which was fought in St. Bernard in 1815. Other residents with historic ancestors won't put up with change either. There are Cajuns whose predecessors arrived as exiles from Nova Scotia in 1755, and Frenchmen whose predecessors arrived from France during the early 1700s and planted indigo on large plantations. Every one of these people will talk to you about their ancestors almost in the present tense.

My son Guillaume and I were passing through historic St. Bernard Parish on our way to Pointe à la Hache to go to the Plaquemines Parish Courthouse. We wanted to find records of a French ancestor's riverside plantation which was burned by the British before the Battle of New Orleans.

Guillaume said, "Mom, we have to turn left at The Green Store to get to Pointe à la Hache" (pronounced hash by the locals). Then he told me this story: It seems the grocery store at the crossroads, which has belonged to the same family for about 100 years, was always painted green. Everyone in St. Bernard would tell travelers who were trying to find their way to Pointe à la Hache to turn left at the green store. About two or three years ago, the owner painted the store brown. Well, it caused such havoc and confusion, no one could find their way to Pointe à la Hache because the St. Bernardians kept telling everyone to turn left at

the green store, which was now brown. The owner, in order to restore peace to St. Bernard Parish, repainted his store green, an electric green now. Even though it was never the actual name of the store, he has painted in black building-size letters on the side of the store: **THE GREEN STORE.** I just had to name a recipe in honor of St. Bernard Parish's Green Store.

Chicken

1 medium-size zucchini, sliced, or 1 medium-size cucumber, peeled and sliced
2 celery ribs, chopped
1 medium-size onion, chopped
1-1/2 cups chopped cooked white meat chicken
1/2 cup roasted chicken stock (page 24)

Sauce

1-1/2 cups roasted chicken stock (page 24)
1/4 teaspoon garlic powder
1/8 teaspoon cayenne pepper
1-1/2 teaspoons onion powder
1/2 teaspoon crumbled or powdered thyme
1/2 teaspoon crumbled or powdered sage
1 cup sliced mushrooms
1 medium-size ripe tomato, chopped
1 cup chopped celery
2 tablespoons apple juice concentrate
2 tablespoons unbleached flour

Stove Top Directions for the Sauce

Pour the 1-1/2 cups chicken stock into a medium-size saucepan. Add the garlic powder, cayenne pepper, onion powder, thyme, sage, mushrooms, tomato, celery, and juice concentrate. Cover and bring to a boil. Turn the heat to low and simmer covered for 5 minutes. Stir every now and then. Add the flour by sprinkling it over the mixture a tablespoon at a time and mixing thoroughly after each addition. Cook uncovered for 2 minutes over low heat, stirring constantly.

Microwave Directions

In a 1-1/2-quart baking dish, layer the zucchini, celery, onion, and chicken. Add 1/2 cup chicken stock. Cover and microwave for 8 minutes on high.

Pour the sauce over the cooked layered vegetables and chicken in the casserole dish. Cover the casserole and cook for 5 minutes on high.

Oven Directions for Chicken and Sauce

Layer the zucchini, 2 chopped celery ribs, onion, chicken, the remaining cup of chopped celery, mushrooms and tomato in a 1-1/2-quart casserole dish.

Pour all of the chicken stock into a small bowl or large measuring cup. Mix in the garlic powder, cayenne pepper, onion powder, thyme, and sage. Add the juice concentrate. Mix in the flour, 1 tablespoon at a time, until well blended. Pour the mixture over the vegetables and chicken in the casserole. Cover and bake at 350°F for 45 minutes, and then let it sit in the oven for 15 minutes with the oven off.

Serve hot over fluffy, cooked brown rice, over whole wheat toast, or whole wheat spaghetti. Each serving will contain about 2 ounces of chicken.

Per serving without rice, toast, or spaghetti: 175 calories; 21 g protein; 3 g fat; 1 g saturated fat; 44 mg cholesterol; 15 g carbohydrates; 90 mg sodium; 3 g fiber

Chicken on Toast

Yield: 4 servings

1 medium-size onion, chopped
1/2 medium-size green pepper, chopped
1/2 medium-size sweet red bell pepper, chopped (substitute a 4-ounce jar of pimientos and juice if sweet red bell peppers are unavailable)
2 cups roasted chicken stock (page 24)
1 teaspoon crumbled or powdered thyme
1/8 teaspoon garlic powder
1 tablespoon dried parsley
1/2 cup sliced fresh mushrooms
3 tablespoons apple juice concentrate
1/4 teaspoon red hot sauce (not Tabasco)
1/2 cup Chicken Gravy Base (page 149) or water
2 cups cooked white meat chicken (12 ounces)
5 tablespoons whole wheat flour
8 slices toasted Pritikin or commercial whole wheat bread

Combine the onion, green pepper, sweet red pepper, chicken stock, thyme, garlic powder, parsley, mushrooms, juice concentrate, red hot sauce, and gravy base or water in a 2-quart saucepan. Cover and cook over medium heat for 10 minutes. Add the chicken. Cover and cook over medium heat 5 minutes. Remove the pan from the heat.

Place the flour in a 2-cup container. Remove 1 cup of the liquid and slowly add it to the flour, stirring and blending it until the mixture is smooth. Add the mixture to the saucepan. Place the pan over medium heat. Cook, stirring constantly, until the mixture thickens, 3 or 4 minutes. Serve immediately over toast. Each serving will contain 3 ounces of chicken.

Per serving: 425 calories; 39 g protein; 8 g fat; 2 g saturated fat; 72 mg cholesterol; 51 g carbohydrates; 525 mg sodium; 8 g fiber

Chicken Fricassée

Yield: 4 servings

Chicken Fricassée is a favorite old New Orleans Créole dish. I suspect its origins are Caribbean because I was served practically the same dish called by the same name in Jamaica. *Fricassée* is a French word, meaning hash, so perhaps this recipe was created on Martinique or Haiti, which were French possessions. The white coffee and sugar cane planters (including several of my ancestors) on St. Domingue (Haiti) fled for their lives, many with just the clothes on their backs, to Cuba and other islands during the slave rebellion in the late 1700s. They lost their plantations and beautiful homes forever. Many French people (my family) as well as Africans, both free men and slaves, came to New Orleans from St. Domingue in the early 1800s.

One of my ancestors, Guillaume Hubert, brought 20 slaves who were loyal to him from St. Domingue. One of them, Lapalu, was responsible for saving Guillaume's life by hiding him in the jungle, then getting him off the island. For doing that, Lapalu is written up as a hero in Kendal's *History of New Orleans*. Lapalu's wife, or one of the other black women in Guillaume's household, probably brought the recipe for Chicken Fricassée with her from St. Domingue. The recipe was passed down from one generation to the next.

4 chicken breasts, skinned
1 large green pepper, chopped
2 medium-size onions, chopped
1-1/4 cups sliced mushrooms
2 celery ribs, chopped
4 cups water
2 cups cubed zucchini (1 medium-size to large zucchini)
3/4 cup coarsely chopped fresh parsley
1 bay leaf
1 teaspoon crumbled or powdered thyme
1/2 teaspoon dried sage
1/4 teaspoon cayenne pepper
5 tablespoons apple juice concentrate
2 tablespoons dry vermouth
Cooked brown rice

Place about half the chicken pieces in a 5-quart nonstick pot to just cover the bottom of the pot with no pieces touching, and turn the heat on high. Saute until lightly brown, moving the pieces often and turning them over. Remove the pieces from the pot and add the rest of the chicken. Saute as you did the first pieces. If the pot starts to smoke, reduce the heat. When the chicken pieces are brown, remove from the pot; turn off the heat and wipe any grease that has formed out of the pot.

In the same pot, combine the green pepper and onion. Turn the heat on high and saute the vegetables, turning them over and over, until the onion is a little brown around the edges and somewhat transparent. Add the mushrooms and celery; continue sauteing until the mushrooms are dark and limp. Reduce the heat. Add the water, zucchini, parsley, bay leaf, thyme, sage, cayenne pepper, juice concentrate, and vermouth. Stir. Return the chicken to the pot. Add more water, enough to almost cover the chicken. Cover, turn the heat to low. Simmer for 1-1/2 hours, stirring occasionally.

Serve the chicken over 1/3-cup portions of cooked brown rice. Each serving contains about 3-1/2 ounces of chicken.

Per serving with rice: 315 calories; 33 g protein; 5 g fat; 1 g saturated fat; 76 mg cholesterol; 33 g carbohydrates; 100 mg sodium; 4 g fiber

Chicken Alexander

Yield: 5 servings

Chicken Alexander is named after my youngest son Alex. Alex is very health-conscious. He's a long-distance runner, lifts weights, and takes after his mother. He likes to cook good food for himself in college.

2 cups roasted chicken stock (page 24)
1 medium-size onion, chopped
1 medium-size zucchini, diced
1 medium-size carrot, diced
1/4 cup chopped green pepper
1 tablespoon dried celery flakes
1/8 teaspoon cayenne pepper
1/16 teaspoon dried marjoram
1/16 teaspoon powdered cumin
1/8 teaspoon dried sage
1/4 teaspoon plus 1/8 teaspoon crumbled or
   powdered thyme
1/4 cup cornstarch
1 (12-ounce or 13-ounce) can evaporated skim milk
1-1/2 cups cooked diced white meat chicken
5 cups cooked whole wheat spaghetti or elbow
   macaroni

In a 1-1/2-quart pot, combine the chicken stock, onion, zucchini, carrot, green pepper, celery flakes, cayenne pepper, marjoram, cumin, sage, and thyme, and bring to a boil. Continue to boil over medium heat, uncovered, for 15 minutes. Remove the pot from the heat. Add the the cornstarch to the milk, a little at a time, blending it and smoothing out any lumps. Add the milk mixture and chicken to the pot and place it over medium heat. Cook, stirring constantly, for 2 to 4 minutes until the mixture is thickened.

Serve immediately over cooked elbow macaroni or spaghetti. Use 1 cup of cooked pasta per serving. Each serving will contain about 1-3/5 ounces of chicken.

Per serving with macaroni: 385 calories; 29 g protein; 4 g fat; 1 g saturated fat; 39 mg cholesterol; 59 g carbohydrates; 135 mg sodium; 4 g fiber

Arroz con Pollo

Yield: 3 servings

3 chicken legs or chicken breasts or a mixture
1 medium-size onion, chopped
1 medium-size green pepper, chopped
1 cup uncooked brown rice
1-1/2 cups sliced mushrooms
2 cups roasted chicken stock (page 24)
1/4 cup apple juice concentrate
1/4 teaspoon cumin
1/4 teaspoon dried oregano
1/4 teaspoon garlic powder
1/4 teaspoon cayenne pepper
1/4 teaspoon saffron, ground or threads
1 tablespoon dry vermouth
1 cup frozen or fresh green peas
1 (4-ounce) jar chopped pimientos

Skin the chicken pieces and cut at the joints if you use legs. Place the chicken pieces in a 5-quart nonstick pot. Turn the heat on high and saute the chicken, turning it over occasionally and moving it about until it gets brown in some areas. Remove the chicken to a plate and wipe out any grease that has formed in the pot. Add the onion, green pepper, and rice. Over high heat, stir to brown the vegetables and rice. Keep stirring until the rice begins to look lighter in color. Add the mushrooms and stir until they look wilted. Remove the pot from the heat.

Add the chicken stock, juice concentrate, cumin, oregano, garlic powder, cayenne pepper, saffron, vermouth, peas, and chopped pimientos. Return the chicken to the pot and mix all the ingredients together. Place the pot on high heat until the liquid begins to boil. Reduce the heat to low immediately. Cover and cook over low heat for 1 hour. Turn the heat off and let the pot sit covered for 20 minutes. Serve hot. Each serving will contain about 3-1/2 ounces of chicken.

Per serving, using dark and light meat: 505 calories; 37 g protein; 10 g fat; 3 g saturated fat; 83 mg cholesterol; 65 g carbohydrates; 95 mg sodium; 5 g fiber

Kiwi Chicken and Rice

Yield: 4 servings

Use Kiwi Dressing (page 120) to make the sauce for this tasty sweet and sour chicken dish.

1/4 cup uncooked wild rice
3/4 cup uncooked brown rice
2 cups water
3/4 cup Kiwi Dressing (page 120)
4 chicken breasts, skinned and deboned
1/4 teaspoon garlic powder
1/4 teaspoon onion powder
1/8 teaspoon cayenne pepper

Microwave Directions

Mix the wild rice and brown rice in a 2-quart microwave container and add the water. Cover and microwave on high for 5 minutes. Then microwave on low or 50% power for 40 minutes. Set aside with the cover on.

Make the Kiwi Dressing and set aside unrefrigerated.

Place the chicken breasts in an 8-inch square baking dish. Sprinkle with the garlic powder, onion powder, and cayenne pepper. Cover and microwave on high for 6 minutes. Check to see if the chicken is still pink inside by slitting with a knife in a small section. If still pink, microwave on high for 2 minutes more and check for pinkness again. If still pink, 1 more minute on high ought to finish cooking it. When the chicken meat is white throughout, pour the Kiwi Dressing over each piece. Cover and microwave on high for 1-1/2 minutes.

Stove Top and Oven Directions

Mix the wild rice and brown rice in a 2-quart pot and add the water. Bring to a boil, cover, reduce the heat to low, and let cook for 40 minutes. Remove from the heat and let sit covered for at least 15 minutes.

Make the Kiwi Dressing and set aside unrefrigerated.

Place the chicken breasts in an 8-inch square baking dish and sprinkle with the garlic powder, onion power, and cayenne pepper. Cover the dish with aluminum foil and slit the foil in several places to let steam out. Set the oven temperature at 450ºF and bake for 25 minutes. Pour the Kiwi Dressing over the chicken, cover and bake for 5 minutes more.

Place a chicken breast on each plate. Pour the Kiwi Dressing from the baking dish over the chicken. Serve 3/4 cup of rice on each plate in the pool of dressing that forms around each chicken breast. Each serving will contain about 3-1/2 ounces of chicken. Serve a green vegetable, such as steamed broccoli, on the side. Leftover rice can be frozen and saved for another meal.

Per serving with rice: 355 calories; 32 g protein; 5 g fat; 1 g saturated fat; 76 mg cholesterol; 44 g carbohydrates; 75 g sodium; 2 g fiber

Roasted Turkey Breast

Yield: 14 servings

You can buy turkey breasts these days. I'm not talking about turkey roll, or pressed turkey. I'm talking about the whole breast which has been cut from the turkey and still has the bone in it. It's very nice for company or just for the convenience.

6-pound turkey breast
1/4 plus 1/16 teaspoon garlic powder
1/16 teaspoon cayenne pepper
1/4 teaspoon dried ground sage
3 cups water
1/2 cup chicken or turkey stock (page 24)
2 cups or more Chicken or Turkey Gravy Base
  (optional) (page 149)
1 tablespoon cornstarch
1/8 teaspoon crumbled or powdered thyme
1/8 teaspoon dried ground sage

Defrost the breast just enough so you can remove the skin and fat. Remove the skin and fat. Put the breast in a roasting pan. Sprinkle the breast with garlic powder, cayenne pepper, and 1/4 teaspoon of the sage. That's all. Any more spices and you won't be able to taste the turkey. Cover the breast (but not the whole pan) with an aluminum foil tent. Place on the middle rack of a conventional oven. Turn the temperature to 350°F. Roast undisturbed for 1 hour. Then add 1 cup of water to the pan. Roast for another hour. Baste the turkey breast with some of the chicken or turkey stock and add another cup of water to the pan. Cover with the tent. Roast for another hour. Baste again, using all the remaining chicken stock, and add 1 more cup of water. Cover, roast for 30 minutes. Roast for 3-1/2 hours in all.

Remove the breast from the pan to a platter and keep covered and warm. To make the gravy, see if any grease is floating in the roasting pan. It probably won't be much. Remove it with a spoon and get the last little bit by running a lettuce or cabbage leaf over the top. Repeat if necessary. Sprinkle the cornstarch over the liquid left in the pan, and mix well to work out any lumps. Add the thyme and the remaining 1/8 teaspoon of sage. Heat the gravy in the oven at 400°F for about 5 or 6 minutes until the cornstarch thickens the gravy. Stir 2 or 3 times. If you have some Chicken or Turkey Gravy Base, heat it and add it to the gravy. That way you will have beaucoup gravy. Each serving will contain about 3-1/3 ounces of turkey.

Turkey per serving: 155 calories; 28 g protein; 3 g fat; 1 g saturated fat; 69 mg cholesterol; tr carbohydrates; 65 mg sodium; tr fiber. Nutritive values for turkey gravy not available.

Turkey Hash

Yield: 6 servings

What to do with the holiday turkey carcass after making turkey stock from it? Make a wonderful hash, of course.

1 turkey carcass (to yield 3-1/2 cups stock plus 2
    cups chopped white meat)
Water
1 medium-size onion, chopped
1 large green pepper, chopped
1-1/2 cups sliced fresh mushrooms
1 large carrot, sliced
4 medium-size Irish potatoes, cubed (3 cups)
1 cup chopped fresh parsley
1/4 teaspoon garlic powder
1/4 teaspoon dried ground sage
1/2 teaspoon powdered or crumbled thyme
1 bay leaf
1 teaspoon red hot sauce (not Tabasco)
1 tablespoon apple juice concentrate
1/4 teaspoon cayenne pepper
1 tablespoon cornstarch

Make turkey stock by immersing the turkey carcass in a large pot of water. Boil uncovered over medium heat for about 3 hours. Remove the carcass and refrigerate; chill the stock until the grease hardens on top. Remove the grease. Measure out 3-1/2 cups of stock and freeze the rest for future use. Pick all the meat off the carcass. Measure 14 ounces (2 cups) of it and cube it. Freeze the rest of the meat.

Place the onion and green pepper in a 5-quart nonstick pot. Turn the heat on high and saute the vegetables by turning them over and over until the onions begin to look transparent and brown around the edges. Add the mushrooms and continue sauteing until the mushrooms look limp. Reduce the heat to low. Add the turkey stock, carrot, and potatoes. Increase the heat to high and bring to a boil. Turn the heat to medium and cook uncovered for 25 minutes. Add the parsley, garlic powder, sage, thyme, bay leaf, hot sauce, juice concentrate, and cayenne pepper. Mix well. Sprinkle the cornstarch over the top and mix it in well. Cook uncovered for 15 minutes more over medium heat. Stir occasionally. The gravy should be slightly thick and the liquid should be reduced enough that you can eat this on a plate (as opposed to in a bowl). Cook longer to reduce the liquid if necessary. Serve hot.

This freezes well. Each serving will contain about 2 ounces of meat.

Per serving: 190 calories; 18 g protein; 2 g fat; .5 g saturated fat; 32 mg cholesterol; 26 g carbohydrates; 45 g sodium; 3 g fiber

6

Main Dishes with Fish and Seafood

This introduction is mainly written for the people in my hometown of New Orleans who will see the words "fish fillets" all through this chapter. I never saw "fillet" spelled that way either, until recently, but you have to understand that this book goes all over the world and the rest of the world spells "filet" as fillet (and sometimes pronounces it fill-it). That's what a fillet is, a filet. Note to the rest of the world: filet is pronounced filé (fee-lay) as in gumbo, and if I asked a fishmonger in New Orleans to fillet my fish, he would ask, "Fill it with what?"

When you leave New Orleans, it's like going to the moon. Why, you can't even find crawfish once you get 50 miles away from Louisiana, except in gourmet stores, where I'm sure they must feel extremely uncomfortable. On the other hand, they probably feel safe, away from all "coonasses," which is an affectionate term mainly for Cajuns but has been adopted by native Louisianians as well. You've heard that joke, haven't you?

All these baby crawfish were sunning themselves on the edge of the water in the Atchafalaya Swamp when they saw something big coming. They screamed, "Mama! Mama! Something big's comin'!"

The crawfish mama said, "Don't worry 'bout that, that's just a dog. He won't hurt you."

"Oh," said the little crawfish.

Later the baby crawfish saw something else big coming. "Mama! Mama!" they screamed again. "Something big's comin'!"

"Don't worry 'bout that," the crawfish mama said. "That's just an old horse, he won't hurt you."

"Oh," said the baby crawfish.

Later the baby crawfish saw something else big coming. The babies screamed, "Mama! Mama! Something big's comin'!"

"Run for your lives!" the crawfish mama yelled, pushing all her babies into the water. "That's a coonass. He'll eat anything!"

Redfish and Shrimp in Saffron Sauce

Yield: 3 servings

You can use any flaky, white-fleshed fish for this. Try to avoid any that are strong-tasting. This dish should be very delicate. You can substitute lobster for the shrimp. The sauce tastes rich, much like a sauce you'd find with pasta and shrimp dishes in restaurants.

1 small white onion, finely chopped
2 tablespoons finely chopped fresh garlic
1/2 cup red rosé wine
1 cup chicken stock (page 24), divided
3 tablespoons apple juice concentrate
1/2 teaspoon saffron, threads or powder
1/8 plus 1/16 teaspoon cayenne pepper
1/8 teaspoon crumbled or powdered thyme
8 ounces redfish fillets
2 tablespoons cornstarch
5 ounces fresh peeled shrimp (about 10 to 12 large shrimp)
3 cups cooked angel hair spaghetti
6 teaspoons sapsago cheese

Combine the onion, garlic, rosé, 1/2 cup of the chicken stock, the juice concentrate, saffron, cayenne pepper, and thyme in a 1-1/2-quart pot. Bring to a boil, then simmer covered for 15 minutes.

Cut the fish into 1/2-inch strips, cutting across the short part of the fillet. Set aside.

Mix the cornstarch with the remaining 1/2 cup of chicken stock until very smooth. Add the cornstarch mixture to the pot and mix well. Add the fish and the shrimp. Cover and simmer for 15 minutes, stirring at 5 minute intervals.

Serve over the spaghetti (1 cup per serving). Sprinkle 2 teaspoons sapsago cheese over each serving.

Per serving, not including saffron: 430 calories; 35 g protein; 3 g fat; 1 g saturated fat; 100 mg cholesterol; 54 g carbohydrates; 335 mg sodium; 3 g fiber. Nutritive values for saffron not available.

Redfish Bouilli

Yield: 4 servings

Bouilli (pronounced boo-yee) means boiled in French, so this is really boiled redfish, but boiled gently.

1/2 cup strong roasted chicken stock (page 24)
1/2 cup white Chablis
1 tablespoon apple juice concentrate
1 medium-size onion, chopped
1/2 medium-size green pepper, chopped
1 celery rib, chopped
1 large ripe tomato, hand chopped
1 bay leaf
1/4 teaspoon garlic powder
1/2 teaspoon crumbled or powdered thyme
1/2 teaspoon onion powder
1/2 teaspoon saffron powder or threads, tightly packed
1 teaspoon dried parsley
1/8 teaspoon dried red pepper flakes
4 (3-1/2-ounce) redfish or mahi mahi fillets

Combine all the ingredients, except the fish, in a saucepan. Bring to a boil, then cover and reduce the heat to low for 15 minutes, stirring occasionally, until the vegetables are tender. Spoon half the cooked vegetables and liquid into a 1-1/2-quart baking dish. On top of the liquid and vegetables, place the redfish fillets. Then spoon the rest of the cooked vegetables and liquid over the fish. Cover the dish and bake on the top shelf of the oven for 40 minutes at 350°F.

Serve over cooked angel hair spaghetti (or the smallest semolina spaghetti you can find) with green peas on the side. Each serving will contain 3-1/2 ounces of fish.

Per serving without spaghetti, saffron: 150 calories; 22 g protein; 2 g fat; tr saturated fat; 37 mg cholesterol; 6 g carbohydrates; 80 mg sodium; 1 g fiber. Nutritive values for saffron not available.

Easy Oven-Fried Catfish

Yield: 6 servings

This recipe is great with catfish. It's easier to prepare than the oven-fried catfish in my first book. I like to use small catfish. If you go to a fishmonger and see large, steak-like-looking pieces of catfish, don't get them. They are liable to be strong tasting. The best catfish are the whole ones that are no longer than 12 inches, tail to head.

1/2 cup yellow cornmeal
1/16 teaspoon cayenne pepper
1/2 teaspoon crumbled or powdered thyme
1/2 teaspoon ground sage
3 (7-ounce to 8-ounce) catfish (skinned and cleaned) or trout
Water

Preheat the oven to 400°F. Spray a large nonstick baking pan with nonstick spray.

In a plastic or paper bag, combine the cornmeal, cayenne pepper, thyme, and sage. Shake the bag to mix the spices. Cut each catfish in half making the tail ends longer, since the part nearest the head has more meat. You're aiming to have about 3-1/2 ounces of meat per serving, not including the bones. Rinse the pieces one at a time under cold water. Leaving them wet, place them one at a time in the bag with the cornmeal mixture. Shake to coat. Place each piece on the pan.

Bake the fish on the top rack of the oven for 20 to 25 minutes until lightly brown. Turn once if they don't stick when you run a spatula under the pieces. If they appear to be sticking, though, leave them alone. They will be fine. Just serve them brown side up. Serve with fresh lemon wedges. Each piece will have about 3-1/3 ounces of meat.

Per serving: 175 calories; 22 g protein; 5 g fat; 1 g saturated fat; 66 mg cholesterol; 9 g carbohydrates; 70 mg sodium; 1 g fiber

Catfish Bonfouca

Yield: 6 servings

What's Bonfouca? It's the name of the bayou where I live. We catch more catfish than any other fish.

1 large onion, halved and sliced in half rings
1/2 medium-size green pepper, chopped
3 cups cubed fresh tomatoes (3 to 4 tomatoes)
3 cups cubed eggplant
1 medium-size carrot, sliced
2 tablespoons dry vermouth
1 tablespoon low-sodium tamari or soy sauce
1/8 teaspoon cayenne pepper
1/4 teaspoon dried basil
1 teaspoon dried parsley
1/8 teaspoon garlic powder
1-1/2 pounds whole catfish (3 medium-size catfish)
4 cups cooked spaghetti (whole wheat or semolina)
A few drops Tabasco or red hot sauce (optional)

Combine the onion and green pepper in a nonstick frying pan and saute. Add the tomatoes, eggplant, carrot, vermouth, tamari, cayenne pepper, basil, parsley, and garlic powder. Cover. Cook for 20 minutes, stirring occasionally, breaking up the eggplant and tomatoes as they cook.

In the meantime, cut the catfish in half. Place in a 9-inch by 13-inch baking dish. Pour the cooked vegetables over the fish. Cover with aluminum foil and place on the middle rack of the oven. Set the temperature to 350°F and bake for about 40 minutes, or until the flesh of the fish is flaky and white.

While the fish is cooking, cook the spaghetti in plenty of boiling water until just tender. Drain. Place a piece of fish on each plate along with 1 cup of spaghetti. Ladle the cooked vegetables and juice in the baking dish over both the fish and spaghetti. Pass the Tabasco or red hot sauce to squirt a few drops over each serving.

Per serving without hot sauce: 310 calories; 27 g protein; 6 g fat; 1 g saturated fat; 66 mg cholesterol; 36 g carbohydrates; 170 mg sodium; 5 g fiber

Bronzed Catfish Guillaume

Yield: 2 servings

My son Guillaume, who's in college at Louisiana State University, wanted the recipe. I was so flattered that I named the dish after him.

2 teaspoons low-sodium tamari or soy sauce
3 tablespoons water
Juice of 1 medium-size lemon or 2 tablespoons
frozen concentrated pure lemon juice
1/4 teaspoon garlic powder
1/8 teaspoon cayenne pepper
2 (4-ounce) catfish fillets or trout
1/2 teaspoon dried parsley
1/4 cup water

For the sauce, mix the tamari, the 3 tablespoons of water, the lemon juice, the garlic powder, and the cayenne pepper in a small container. Pour 2 tablespoons of the sauce in a nonstick pan. Turn the heat on high. When the sauce begins to steam, add the fillets, then turn them over to coat them with sauce. Shake the pan back and forth, sliding the fillets around. Leave space between the fillets, and turn them often. After cooking for 3 minutes, add 2 more tablespoons of sauce and sprinkle the parsley over. Continue to cook for 3 minutes more, shaking the pan and turning the fish. Add any extra sauce to the pan as the fish cooks. Press on the fish with the edge of your spatula. When the fish is so tender you can cut right through it with the spatula, it's done.

Remove the fish to a warm plate and cover. Add 1/4 cup of water to the pan and deglaze the juices over high heat moving the juices back and forth in the pan with the spatula. When the juices have reduced by about half and look like a nice butter sauce, pour over the fish. If you double this recipe, do not double the 1/4 cup of water for the sauce.

Per serving: 140 calories; 22 g protein; 5 g fat; 1 g saturated fat; 66 g cholesterol; 2 g carbohydrates; 245 mg sodium; tr fiber

Mahi Mahi, Jamaican-Style

Yield: 6 servings

When my husband and I were last in Jamaica, having lunch in the lovely beach-front, open-air dining area of our hotel, we were served mahi mahi (called dolphin in the Caribbean) cooked with a wonderful curry sauce. I added baked bananas as a side dish. Please don't skip making them. They really bring out the flavor of the whole dish.

You can get dolphin or mahi mahi at big supermarkets now most everywhere (don't worry—they aren't the kind of dolphins that look like Flipper). If you can't find mahi mahi, swordfish, shark, or any fish that has rather heavy, flaky white meat will do.

Fish

1-1/2 pounds mahi mahi fillets
1-1/2 tablespoons fresh lemon juice
1/4 teaspoon garlic powder

Baked Bananas

3 very ripe bananas
2 tablespoons water

1 medium-size onion, chopped
1 large green pepper, cut in long, narrow strips
1-1/2 cups water
1/2 cup red rosé wine
2 tablespoons apple juice concentrate
4 garlic cloves, chopped
2 tablespoons curry powder
2 large tomatoes, sliced in narrow wedges
1/8 to 1/4 teaspoon cayenne pepper (optional)
4 cups cooked instant brown rice

Skin the mahi mahi fillets by cutting with a sharp knife under the skin and working your way back until you get the skin off. Cut the fish into 6 equal sections. Line an 8-inch square baking dish with aluminum foil, leaving extra foil to fold over the fish. Place the fish on the foil. Sprinkle the lemon juice over, then the garlic powder. Cut slices off the squeezed lemons and place pulp side down over the fish. Fold the foil loosely over the fish. Set the fish in the refrigerator and get the bananas ready to bake.

Peel the bananas and cut in half across the short part of the banana, leaving their full thickness. Place the halves in a nonstick baking pan. Sprinkle 2 tablespoons of water over the halves. Cover the pan with foil. (If you plan to freeze extra servings of mahi mahi—the recipe makes 6—just put as many banana halves as you wish to eat in a pan and add 1 teaspoon of water for each half.)

Put the bananas and the fish in the oven and set the temperature at 350°F. Bake for about 35 minutes, or until the fish is flaky and white.

While the fish and bananas are cooking, combine the onion and green pepper in a nonstick 5-quart pot. Saute by tossing the vegetables over and over until the onion becomes somewhat transparent and a little brown around the edges. Add the 1-1/2 cups water. Turn the heat to medium. Add the rosé and juice concentrate. Add the garlic and curry powder and mix in. Add the tomatoes. Cover and cook for about 15 minutes, or until the tomatoes and onion are tender. Stir occasionally.

When the fish is done, pick it up out of the baking dish in the aluminum foil, holding the top edges of the foil around the fish. Carefully pour any juice from the fish into the pot with the vegetables. Mix it in. Taste. If the curry powder contains no pepper, add cayenne pepper to taste. Reheat the sauce if necessary.

Serve 2/3 cup instant brown rice on each plate. Place 1 piece of fish over the rice on each place. Serve the sauce over the fish. Place a banana half on each plate, and some of the baking liquid from the pan over each serving of banana.

Per serving with rice, sauce, and banana: 400 calories; 28 g protein; 7 g fat; 1 g saturated fat; 44 mg cholesterol; 56 g carbohydrates; 120 mg sodium; 5 g fiber

Grouper Jus Rouge

Yield: 4 servings

Grouper is a large, sweet-tasting fish caught in Louisiana and other warm waters. Redfish or sheepshead, two other large fishes, can be substituted for this. Any other fish that has delicate, flaky, white meat would also be good in this recipe. It is very nice if you can get the fish with the head and tail on because the head gives a lot of juice and flavor to the gravy. But if you can find only fillets, that's all right. Tuna and salmon are much too heavy for this dish.

4-1/2 pound grouper, weighed unscaled, with the head and tail on, or 12 to 16 ounces grouper fillets
1 cup strong roasted chicken stock (page 24)
1/2 cup red rosé wine
3 tablespoons apple juice concentrate
1-1/2 cups chopped onion
1-1/2 cups chopped celery
1 cup chopped green pepper
2 teaspoons dried parsley
1 teaspoon crumbled or powdered thyme
1/8 teaspoon cayenne pepper
1/2 teaspoon garlic powder
1/4 teaspoon ground bay leaf or 1 large bay leaf
1 (16-ounce) can no-salt tomato sauce
1 tablespoon low-sodium tamari or soy sauce (optional)

If you have a whole fish with the head, place it in a 9-inch by 13-inch baking dish. If you have 4 fillets, place them in an 8-inch square baking dish. Pour 1/2 cup of the chicken stock, and all of the rosé and juice concentrate over the fish. Sprinkle the onions, celery, and green pepper over the fish and into the liquid around it. Sprinkle the parsley, thyme, cayenne pepper, garlic powder, and ground bay leaf over the vegetables and fish, and into the liquid. If you have whole bay leaf, place it in the liquid. Pour the tomato sauce over the fish and into the liquid in the dish. Leave the tomato sauce on top of the fish alone. Pour the remaining 1/2 cup of chicken stock into the can which contained the tomato sauce and mix it well with the remaining tomato sauce stuck to the can. Add the stock-tomato sauce mixture in the can to the liquid in the dish. Do not pour it over the fish.

Cover the dish; I use aluminum foil. Place the dish on the bottom rack of the oven and set the temperature at 350°F. Bake for about 1 hour. Check after 30 minutes and baste lightly, trying not to wash the tomato sauce off the fish. Taste the sauce. If you don't think it has enough taste, add the tamari. Serve with brown or white rice, pouring the gravy over the rice. If you have fish with the bones in, divide it in 4. Each serving will weigh about 8 ounces; however, they will in reality be only about 3-1/2 to 4 ounces of meat.

Per serving with tamari, but without rice: 240 calories; 29 g protein; 1 g fat; .5 g saturated fat; 42 mg cholesterol; 23 g carbohydrates; 275 mg sodium; 4 g fiber

Sheepshead Supper

Yield: 3 servings

No! Not a real sheep's head. A sheepshead is a big fish with nice, white, delicate meat. Some people boil the fish in seafood seasoning and use it instead of crabmeat because the texture is so similar. Try to have your fishmonger scale and gut the sheepshead for you. If not, I guarantee that when you scale it yourself, you will end up with scales on your kitchen ceiling, curtains, and hidden behind various objects for years to come. Leave the head and tail on the fish. A large flounder, or some other large fish that has flaky white meat, can be substituted for the sheepshead.

2-1/2-pound sheepshead, weighed ungutted and unscaled, head on
5 celery ribs with leaves, chopped coarsely
6 broccoli spears, stems sliced and broken florets
3 medium-size Irish potatoes, peeled and cut in half lengthwise
1 carrot, cut in 6 pieces
1-1/2 cups chicken stock from uncooked or roasted chicken (page 24)
1/4 cup red rosé wine
2 tablespoons apple juice concentrate
1 medium-size onion, sliced in rings
1/2 teaspoon dried parsley
1/4 teaspoon garlic powder
1/4 teaspoon cayenne pepper

Microwave Directions

Defrost the fish if it is frozen. I wouldn't suggest doing it in the microwave because you will probably end up cooking it.

Combine the celery, broccoli, potatoes, and carrot in a 9-inch by 13-inch baking dish. Mix the chicken stock, rosé, and juice concentrate, and pour the mixture over the vegetables. Cover (use plastic wrap, if the dish has no cover) and cook on high 20 minutes, rotating once. Test *all* the potatoes with a sharp knife to see if they are soft. If not, cook on high for 5 minutes more, or until soft.

Place the fish in the dish and rearrange the vegetables to fit. Cover the fish with the onion rings. Baste everything with the pan juices. Sprinkle the parsley, garlic powder, and cayenne pepper over the fish and vegetables. Cover (use a fresh piece of plastic wrap, if that's what you are using) and cook for 11 minutes on high. Flake the fish with a fork in a small area to see if the fish is flaky and white. If not, cook for 2 or 3 minutes more. Let sit covered for 10 minutes, then serve.

Oven Directions

Defrost the fish if it is frozen.

Spread the celery on the bottom of a 9-inch by 13-inch baking dish. Set the fish in the dish on top of the celery. Surround the fish with the broccoli, potatoes, and carrot. Sprinkle the parsley over just the fish. Place the onion rings over the fish. Now sprinkle the cayenne pepper and garlic powder over everything.

In a small bowl, mix together the chicken stock, rosé, and juice concentrate. Pour around the fish, not on top, being careful not to wash the seasonings off the fish. Cover the whole dish with aluminum foil and place on the middle rack of the oven. Set the temperature at 375°F and bake for 1 hour and 10 minutes. This will make tons of juice, so save the juice for use as fish stock. Each person will be served about 3-1/2 ounces of fish.

Per serving: 380 calories; 35 g protein; 3 g fat; 1 g saturated fat; 37 mg cholesterol; 55 g carbohydrates; 230 mg sodium; 14 g fiber

Poached Sheepshead

Yield: 4 servings

This is a tasty dish flavored with the spices of crab boil. If you don't want to bother making your own, you can buy packaged crab boil. Have your fishmonger scale and gut the sheepshead for you and tell him to leave the head on.

2-1/2 quarts water
1 pouch prepared salt-free crab boil or Homemade
    Crab Boil (page 156)
1 tablespoon salt-free chili powder
1/2 cup apple cider vinegar
1 large onion, peeled and quartered
2 celery ribs, cut in halves
1/4 cup apple juice concentrate
2-1/2-pound sheepshead, weighed head on, unscaled
    and ungutted
1 lemon

Pour the water into a roasting pan that just fits the fish nicely. In other words, not too large a pan. Add the pouch of crab boil, chili powder, vinegar, onion, celery, and juice concentrate. Bring the mixture to a boil uncovered on top of the stove. Reduce the heat to medium and simmer uncovered for 35 minutes. Put the fish in the pan. If you need more water to cover the fish, add it, but as little as is possible. Simmer the fish uncovered over medium-high heat for 20 minutes. Turn off the heat and squeeze the lemon over the fish and cooking liquid. Drop the peels into the liquid. Let sit for 30 minutes to marinate.

If the fish is still hot enough, serve immediately. If the fish has cooled too much, heat gently until just hot enough. Place on a platter. Serve with more lemon wedges and Horseradish Sauce (page 151) if desired. Warn diners to watch for small bones. There will be about 3-1/2 ounces of fish per serving.

Per serving: 150 calories; 21 g protein; 2 g fat; tr saturated fat; 37 mg cholesterol; 13 g carbohydrate; 90 mg sodium; 1 g fiber

Easy Oven-Fried Shark

Yield: 5 servings

Shark! Well, we might as well eat them before they eat us, don't you think? And believe it or not, they are just as delicious to us as we are to them. Nice, tender, white boneless meat. What more could we ask? Use flounder if you must substitute. The secret is to cut the fish into small pieces. Also, don't use a big shark. If the fish is over 3 feet long, it won't be as tasty.

1 pound shark steak, about 3/4 inch thick
1/2 cup yellow cornmeal
1/16 teaspoon cayenne pepper
1/2 teaspoon crumbled or powdered thyme
1/2 teaspoon dried ground sage
Water

Cut the steak across the grain into 1/2-inch-wide slices. In a plastic or paper bag, mix the cornmeal, cayenne pepper, thyme, and sage. Wet the fish with water, a few pieces at a time, and shake in the cornmeal mixture. Place the pieces on a nonstick baking pan or cookie sheet on the middle rack in the oven. Turn the oven temperature to 425°F and bake for 25 minutes. Don't turn the fish.

Serve the fish brown side up with lemon wedges. Serve ketchup, too, if you can afford to cheat a little, otherwise serve Piquante Sauce (page 150). Each serving will contain a little over 3 ounces of shark.

Per serving: 135 calories; 18 g protein; 1 g fat; tr saturated fat; 44 mg cholesterol; 11 g carbohydrates; 75 mg sodium; 1 g fiber

Spaghetti with Petite Jaws

Yield: 4 servings

The "petite jaws" are sliced baby shark. Don't faint at the amount of garlic in this. Cooked whole this way, it develops a delicate buttery taste and texture. Cook the spaghetti while you prepare the fish.

2 cups cooked spaghetti (use whole wheat if you like)
4 teaspoons low-sodium soy or tamari sauce
6 tablespoons water
Juice of 2 lemons
1/4 teaspoon cayenne pepper
1 pound baby shark steak, cut about 1 inch thick
8 large fresh garlic cloves
1/2 teaspoon dried parsley
2 tablespoons cornstarch
1 cup water
1 tablespoon dry vermouth
2 tablespoons apple juice concentrate
2 tablespoons sapsago cheese

While the water heats for the spaghetti, make a sauce by mixing together the soy or tamari sauce, 6 tablespoons water, the lemon juice, and cayenne pepper. Set aside.

Slice the shark against the grain into 8 pieces. Set aside. Peel the garlic.

Pour 2 tablespoons of the sauce into a nonstick frying pan. Turn the heat to high. Add half the shark and all of the garlic. When the pan starts to sizzle, tilt it back and forth to distribute the sauce. Turn the shark over to coat with the sauce. Gently move the fish around in the pan from time to time, and turn them over occasionally. Keep the pieces from touching each other. After cooking for 3 minutes, add 2 more tablespoons of sauce, and sprinkle half the parsley over the fish. Turn the fish over. Continue to cook for 3 minutes more, tilting the pan, sliding the fish back and forth. Remove the fish to a plate; pour the rest of the sauce in the pan and add the remaining fish pieces. Cook exactly as you did the first batch. Do not remove the garlic from the pan—continue to cook it along with the second batch of fish. Remove the pan from the heat and return the first batch of cooked fish to the pan.

The water for the spaghetti should be boiling now. Throw in the spaghetti and stir. Cook semolina spaghetti for about 10 minutes, whole wheat spaghetti for about 15 minutes.

In another small container, combine the cornstarch with the remaining 1 cup water. Stir until smooth. Add the vermouth and juice concentrate. Stir. Pour the mixture over the fish. Place the pan of fish over low heat. Cover and cook for 6 to 7 minutes, until the juice in the pan is thickened. Keep warm until the spaghetti is done.

Drain the spaghetti. Place the spaghetti on a large platter. Place the fish pieces and garlic around the spaghetti. Pour the juice from the pan over the spaghetti. Serve with grated sapsago cheese to sprinkle over. Each serving will contain 4 ounces of shark.

Per serving: 255 calories; 28 g protein; 2 g fat; tr saturated fat; 54 mg cholesterol; 30 g carbohydrates; 315 mg sodium; 1 g fiber

Creamed Tuna and Spaghetti

Yield: 4 servings

You can use whole wheat spaghetti with this, but I think the semolina blends better with the cream sauce.

1/2 cup chicken stock from uncooked or roasted chicken (page 24)
1-1/2 cups chopped onions
1/2 cup sliced carrot
1 cup fresh or frozen green peas
1 teaspoon dried parsley, or 3 tablespoons chopped fresh parsley
2 tablespoons cornstarch
1/4 teaspoon dried red pepper flakes
1 (6-1/2 ounce) can water-packed tuna, drained
1 cup evaporated skim milk
1 teaspoon red hot sauce (not Tabasco)
1/4 teaspoon dried basil
3 cups cooked thin semolina spaghetti
4 tablespoons sapsago cheese

Microwave Directions

Combine the chicken stock, onion, carrot, peas, and parsley in a 2-quart container. Cover and microwave on high 6 minutes. Stir, cover, and cook on high for 4 minutes more, or until the carrot is tender. Sprinkle the cornstarch over the vegetables and mix well. Add the red pepper flakes, tuna, milk, red hot sauce, and basil. Be sure to break the tuna into small pieces. Cover and return the container to the microwave; cook on high 8 minutes. Stir, cover again, and cook on high for 8 more minutes. Remove the container from the microwave and let it sit covered.

Place a 2-quart container with 8 cups of water in the microwave and cook on high for 12 minutes, or until the water bubbles. Add the spaghetti and cook for 7 minutes. Stir and cook for 3 or 4 more minutes, or until the spaghetti is tender. Drain the spaghetti and add it to the tuna mixture. Mix well.

Stove Top Directions

Toss the spaghetti into 2 quarts of boiling water and cook until just tender.

Meanwhile, combine the chicken stock, onion, carrot, peas, and parsley in a medium-size saucepan. Cover, bring to a boil, and boil over high heat for 5 minutes, or until the carrot is tender. Remove the pot from the heat. Sprinkle in the cornstarch and mix well. Add the red pepper flakes, tuna, milk, red hot sauce, and basil. Cook over high heat, stirring constantly, until the sauce has thickened, about 4 minutes.

Drain the spaghetti and put it in a large bowl. Add the sauce to the spaghetti and mix well.

Serve with a tablespoon or less of sapsago cheese over the top. It tastes delicious just plain, too, if you prefer not to use cheese. Each serving will contain 1-1/2 ounces of tuna.

Per serving with cheese: 340 calories; 27 g protein; 2 g fat; tr saturated fat; 26 mg cholesterol; 52 g carbohydrates; 340 mg sodium; 5 g fiber

Tuna-Stuffed Potato

Yield: 4 servings

2 large Irish potatoes
2 tablespoons water
1 medium-size carrot
6 tablespoons low-fat cottage cheese
1 tablespoon skim milk
1 tablespoon chopped onion
1/4 teaspoon turmeric
1/8 teaspoon Tabasco sauce
1 teaspoon dried parsley
1 (6-1/2-ounce) can water-packed tuna, drained
1/8 teaspoon paprika
1 tablespoon sapsago cheese

Microwave Directions

Wash, then prick the potatoes on top with a fork. Bake in a microwave for 16 minutes or until soft. Cool, then cut in half the long way. Carefully scoop out the insides, being careful not to break the skins, and place the contents in a large bowl. Reserve the potato skins in a baking dish.

Pour the water into a 2-cup container. Cut the carrot into chunks and place in the container with the water. Cover. Microwave on high for 4 minutes. Pour the carrots and cooking water into a blender. Add the cottage cheese, milk, onion, turmeric, and Tabasco sauce. Blend on medium speed until the mixture looks very smooth. Pour the mixture into the bowl with the potatoes. With a potato masher, mash the potatoes until creamy and fluffy. Add 1/2 teaspoon of the parsley and mix well. Add the tuna and mix well. Stuff the potato-tuna mixture into the reserved potato skins. Sprinkle the tops of the potatoes first with paprika, then with the remaining 1/2 teaspoon of the parsley, then with the sapsago cheese. You can refrigerate or freeze the potatoes at this point.

Just before serving, microwave the stuffed potatoes on high for 2-1/2 to 3 minutes per potato, depending on how cold the potatoes are.

Per serving: 195 calories; 18 g protein; 1 g fat; tr saturated fat; 24 mg cholesterol; 26 g carbohydrates; 275 mg sodium; 3 g fiber

Tuna Potato Casserole

Yield: 6 servings

4 cups red potatoes, peeled and sliced
1 (6-1/2-ounce) can water-packed tuna
1 cup frozen green peas
3/4 cup raw sliced carrot
1/2 cup chopped onion
2 cups skim milk
3 tablespoons unbleached white flour
1/2 teaspoon dried basil
1 teaspoon dried parsley
1/4 teaspoon dried red pepper flakes
1 tablespoon grated sapsago cheese

Spray an 8-inch square baking dish with nonstick spray. Layer the dish with half the potato slices, all the tuna, peas, carrot, onion, then the remaining potato slices.

Combine the milk and flour in a blender and blend on high until the flour is thoroughly mixed with the milk. Pour the milk mixture over the potatoes and vegetables. Sprinkle the basil, parsley, and red pepper flakes over, then the sapsago cheese on top.

Place in the oven and set the temperature at 300°F. Bake uncovered for 1 hour. Cover with aluminum foil. Slit the foil in several places with a sharp knife tip to release any steam. Increase the temperature to 350°F. Bake for 30 minutes. Pierce the potatoes with a knife. If they are still hard, bake covered for 10 minutes more, or until soft. Turn off the oven and let the casserole sit for 30 minutes in the closed oven. Then serve immediately.

Sprinkle a little wine vinegar or apple cider vinegar over each serving for zing. A little Tabasco sauce with this is good, too. Each serving will contain a little over 1 ounce of tuna.

Per serving: 210 calories; 15 g protein; 1 g fat; tr saturated fat; 17 mg cholesterol; 36 g carbohydrates; 200 mg sodium; 4 g fiber

Codfish Cakes

Yield: 12 cakes

When I was little girl, my mother used to make codfish cakes during Lent. I always thought they were delicious—brown and crisp on the outside and tender and moist on the inside. At that time in New Orleans, codfish, as well as tuna and salmon, only came in cans. Now, I can go to the supermarket and find large refrigerated cases of fillets of so-called fresh codfish, tuna, salmon, swordfish, orange roughy, and many other fish that don't swim anywhere near New Orleans. I doubt if they are really fresh; probably they're freshly un-frozen. The really odd thing is now I can't get codfish in cans. It was strange trying to make codfish cakes with freshly un-frozen codfish, but I did it, and they came out tasting just like Mama's.

3 large Irish potatoes, peeled and quartered
6 ounces fresh codfish fillets, rinsed and cut into
   chunks
2 tablespoons minced dried onions
1 tablespoon dried parsley
2 teaspoons red hot sauce (not Tabasco)
1/2 tablespoon sapsago cheese
1/4 baked banana (page 148)
1/2 teaspoon crumbled or powdered thyme
1 tablespoon apple cider vinegar
1/8 teaspoon cayenne pepper
1 jumbo egg white

In a 2-quart pot, cover the potatoes with water and cook uncovered over high heat for about 20 minutes until tender. Pierce with a sharp knife to test. Drain off the water. Set aside.

Place the fish in a food processor fitted with a cutting blade and process briefly, just until the fish starts to form a ball. Leave a little texture of the fish, don't chop it up until it's soup.

Mash the potatoes. Mix in, one ingredient at a time, the fish, onion, parsley, hot sauce, cheese, banana and its baking juices, thyme, vinegar, cayenne pepper, and egg white. Taste. If the potatoes were huge, you might want to add a little more cayenne pepper, vinegar, and sapsago cheese. Let the mixture sit, out of the refrigerator, for about 20 minutes. Make 12 circular flat patties about 2 inches in diameter and 1/2-inch thick.

Spray a nonstick frying pan with nonstick spray. Preheat it over high heat until a drop of water dropped on it sizzles. Place patties in a circle, not touching, in the pan. Leave the center empty. Brown on one side, then turn the patties over and brown on the other side. Remove to a hot ovenproof plate and put in a 200°F oven to keep warm. Put the next batch of patties in the pan and cook as you did the first batch. If the pan begins to smoke while you are cooking, reduce the heat, then increase it as the pan cools. Try to keep an even high heat.

Serve hot with lemon wedges and some steamed carrots and peas.

You can freeze and reheat these patties. Freeze each one separately wrapped in plastic wrap. Use a conventional oven or microwave to reheat. Each cake will contain 1/2 ounce of fish.

Per codfish cake: 50 calories; 4 g protein; tr fat; tr saturated fat; 6 mg cholesterol; 8 g carbohydrates; 20 mg sodium; 1 g fiber

Crab Cakes

Yield: 6 servings

Zucchini and banana, while adding good taste, also give the right amount of moistness and texture.

4 slices Pritikin or other whole wheat bread
1/2 teaspoon garlic powder
1 teaspoon dried parsley
1/4 teaspoon dried basil
1/4 teaspoon cayenne pepper
1/2 teaspoon crumbled or powdered thyme
1/2 cup finely chopped onions
1 celery rib, finely chopped
1 cup finely chopped zucchini (about 1/2 zucchini)
1/4 baked banana (page 148)
2 jumbo egg whites
Juice of 1 medium-size lemon
1 (6-ounce) can crabmeat, white or claw, rinsed

In a food processor fitted with a cutting blade, combine the bread, garlic powder, parsley, basil, cayenne pepper, and thyme. Process to make seasoned bread crumbs.

Combine the onions, celery, and zucchini in a nonstick frying pan and turn the heat on high. Saute, turning the vegetables over and over, until the zucchini looks limp. Remove the pan from the heat and let it cool. Add the seasoned bread crumbs. Combine the banana and egg whites and beat with a fork. Add the mixture to the vegetables. Add the lemon juice and crabmeat.

Spray a nonstick pan with a nonstick spray because these cakes tend to stick. Form 6 crab cakes about the size of hamburgers and place them on the pan. Place on the middle rack of the oven, turn the setting to 350°F and bake uncovered for 15 minutes. Turn over and bake for 10 to 15 minutes more, until brown. Serve immediately with lemon wedges.

Per serving: 110 calories; 10 g protein; 2 g fat; tr saturated fat; 28 mg cholesterol; 15 g carbohydrates; 250 mg sodium; 2 g fiber

Oven-Fried Soft-Shell Crabs

Yield: 6 servings

Use fresh or frozen soft-shell crabs. They will measure 4 to 6 inches across the top of the shell. Wash them, then clean them. To clean, set them on a board top side up. Lift one side of the shell where it points. Look under and you will see some gray pointed things over the whole side of the crab, growing from where the legs attach. Those are the lungs, or dead men's fingers. Just pull them off. Repeat on the other side of the crab. Now cut off the eyes and mouth. If any part of the crab feels papery, rather than soft, smooth and rubbery, the shell has already started to harden. Pull off the papery part; it will come off as if the crab had been wrapped in cellophane.

1 cup yellow cornmeal
1/4 teaspoon marjoram
1/4 teaspoon ground thyme
1/4 teaspoon cayenne pepper
1/4 teaspoon ground sage
6 cleaned soft-shell crabs

Spray a nonstick pan with nonstick spray.

In a plastic or paper bag, combine the cornmeal, marjoram, thyme, cayenne pepper, and sage. Shake well to mix. Wet the crabs, and one at a time, toss in the bag of seasoned cornmeal and shake to coat. Place the crabs on the pan, not touching each other, top side up.

Place in the oven on the middle rack. Set the temperature at 400°F. Bake for 15 minutes. Turn the crabs over and bake for 5 minutes more. Serve immediately with lemon wedges, Piquante Sauce (page 150), or ketchup if you want to cheat a little.

Per serving: 128 calories; 11 g protein; 1 g fat; tr saturated fat; 43 mg cholesterol; 18 g carbohydrates; 120 mg sodium; 2 g fiber

Crab Souffle

Yield: 4 servings

2 white scalloped bush squash (patty pan)
2 slices whole wheat or Pritikin bread
1 large onion, chopped
1 large green pepper, chopped
1/4 teaspoon garlic powder
1 tablespoon dried parsley
1/4 teaspoon dried red pepper flakes
1/2 teaspoon crumbled or powdered thyme
2 tablespoons dry vermouth
1/4 baked banana (page 148)
1 (6-1/2-ounce) can crab claw meat, rinsed
6 jumbo egg whites at room temperature
1 tablespoon sapsago cheese

Microwave Directions

With a knife, pierce the tops of the squash in several places. Bake uncovered on high for 15 minutes. If they are still hard, cook for another 2 minutes, or more, if needed. Remove the squash from the microwave and let cool.

Stove Top Directions

In a large pot, cover the squash with water and simmer for about 45 minutes. Test with a knife for tenderness and continue cooking until tender. Remove the squash to a large dish to cool.

While the squash is cooling, make bread crumbs by processing the bread in a food processor fitted with a steel blade. Set aside.

Combine the onion and green pepper in a nonstick 5-quart pot. Turn the heat on high and saute by turning the vegetables over and over until the onions look transparent and are a little brown around the edges. Remove the pot from the heat. Cut the tops off the squash and scrape the pulp from the insides, including the seeds. Add the pulp and seeds to the onion and green pepper. Add the garlic powder, parsley, red pepper flakes, thyme, vermouth, banana and its baking juices, and the crabmeat. Mix well. Add the bread crumbs and mix well again.

Beat the egg whites with an electric mixer until they form stiff peaks. Fold the egg whites into the crabmeat and spoon the mixture into a 2-quart souffle dish or an 8-inch square baking dish. Sprinkle with sapsago cheese and place in the oven on the top shelf. Set the temperature at 350°F and bake uncovered for 40 to 45 minutes. When the top is brown, it's done. Serve immediately.

Per serving: 155 calories; 18 g protein; 2 g fat; tr saturated fat; 46 mg cholesterol; 15 g carbohydrates; 350 mg sodium; 3 g fiber

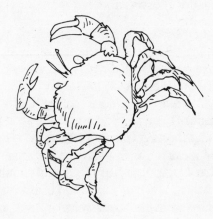

Oysters Mardi Gras

Yield: 4 servings

If you grew up in uptown New Orleans as I did, and you wanted to honor a bride-to-be or a debutante, you gave her a ladies' luncheon at Corinne Dunbar's Restaurant on St. Charles Avenue. In the old Victorian house, with its elegant and quiet dining rooms, there was no menu, but even so, you would be sure to enjoy Corinne Dunbar's most memorable dishes: Oysters Mardi Gras and Banana Fritters. Corinne Dunbar's is just a memory now, like vétivèrt cologne and the days when ladies wore hats and white gloves to lunch and uptown New Orleans was a small city unto itself, hardly conscious of the rest of the world, or of the rest of the city.

2 fresh artichokes
1/2 cup finely chopped onion
1 bay leaf
12 to 18 fresh oysters or 1 (10-ounce) jar of unwashed
   fresh oysters (save the liquid)
Stock from roasted chicken (page 24)
1 tablespoon dry vermouth
1/4 teaspoon Tabasco sauce
1/16 teaspoon garlic powder
1 tablespoon cornstarch
1 teaspoon apple juice concentrate
1 teaspoon dried parsley

Place the artichokes on their sides in a 5-quart pot. There is no need to trim them in any way. Add about 1 inch of water. Cover and cook over medium heat for about 1 hour or until leaves pull out easily and the meat at the bottom of the leaves is soft. Check every now and then to make sure the water has not boiled away. Add more water if necessary. Drain the artichokes and cool them.

Place the onion and bay leaf in a 1-1/2-quart pot. Pour the oyster water into a measuring cup. Then add enough chicken stock until you have 1/2 cup of liquid in all. Pour the liquid into the pot. Bring the liquid to a boil and cook uncovered over high heat until the onion is tender, about 5 minutes. All the liquid will just about disappear, so watch this closely. Remove the pot from the heat.

Deleaf the artichokes, saving the prettiest and strongest leaves. Remove and discard the hairy part of the artichoke bottom. Chop the bottom and add it to the pot.

Place the oysters and any remaining oyster juice in a blender. Pulse the blender on-off, on-off, 5 times. Pour the oysters into the pot. Pour the vermouth into the blender. Swoosh it around to rinse the blender and pour it into the pot. Add the Tabasco sauce, garlic powder, cornstarch, juice concentrate, and parsley to the pot.

Over high heat, bring the mixture to a bubbling boil and let boil for about 1-1/2 minutes, stirring all the time. Pour into 4 custard cups or miniature souffle dishes. Place them on salad plates and surround with the cooked artichoke leaves, points toward the edges of the plates. Serve warm as an hors d'oeuvre. Scoop the oyster mixture up with the artichoke leaves to eat. Each serving will contain about 2-1/2 ounces of oysters.

Per serving: 105 calories; 8 g protein; 2 g fat; 1 g saturated fat; 39 mg cholesterol; 14 g carbohydrates; 140 mg sodium; 5 g fiber

Oysters St. Croix

Yield: 4 servings

On the island of St. Croix, Virgin Islands, Ray and I tried an oyster and pasta dish that was very similar to the oyster and pasta dishes we cook in Louisiana. In fact, Louisiana cooks have been very much influenced by Caribbean cooking. That's because so many people emigrated to Louisiana from the West Indies during various slave rebellions on the Caribbean Islands around the late 1700s.

12 ounces uncooked semolina vermicelli
1 (10-ounce) jar fresh unwashed oysters, about 12
  to 18 oysters plus juice
1 cup finely chopped broccoli florets
1 medium-size onion, finely chopped
1/2 cup sliced mushrooms
1 (12-ounce) can evaporated skim milk
1/4 teaspoon garlic powder
2 tablespoons cornstarch
1/2 teaspoon Tabasco sauce
1/2 teaspoon red hot sauce (not Tabasco)

Boil the vermicelli in plenty of water to cover until just tender. Drain.

While the pasta water is heating, drain the oysters, reserving the juice. Combine the oyster juice, broccoli, onion, and mushrooms in a 2-quart pot. Cover, turn the heat on high, and cook for 5 minutes at a rapid boil. Stir occasionally.

In the meantime, scald the milk and remove any skin that forms. Chop the oysters in a bowl so no juice is lost.

Remove the vegetables from the heat. Sprinkle the garlic powder and cornstarch over the cooked vegetables. Mix. Add the Tabasco and red hot sauce. Mix. Slowly add the milk, mixing it into the cornstarch until smooth. Turn the heat on high and cook, stirring constantly, until the mixture has thickened, 3 to 4 minutes. Add the oysters and any remaining juice and cook on high heat, stirring constantly for about 2 minutes. Serve over the hot cooked vermicelli.

Per serving with pasta: 335 calories; 19 g protein; 3 g fat; 1 g saturated fat; 42 mg cholesterol; 57 g carbohydrates; 190 mg sodium; 3 g fiber

Variation

Oyster Dip. Use Oysters St. Croix without the spaghetti for an oyster dip with Toasted Tortilla Chips (page 20). Serve in a chafing dish that has water in the bottom and a small flame underneath. Yield: 48 tablespoons.

Per tablespoon without chips: 10 calories; 1 g protein; tr fat; tr saturated fat; 4 mg cholesterol; 2 g carbohydrates; 15 mg sodium; tr fiber

Oysters Rockefeller Casserole

Yield: 4 servings

If you order Oysters Rockefeller at Antoine's in New Orleans, where it was invented, you may or may not get it. The menu there is entirely in French and the waiters don't really expect you to be able read it (especially since most of the customers are tourists). Every time I went there (before Ray and I started watching our diets) and ordered something from the menu, the waiter looked at me with his mouth open. Then he cleared his throat and said, "May I suggest the filet mignon. It is very good tonight." When I said no, I'd rather have what I ordered, I was informed that they didn't have whatever it was, that I would have to order that a day ahead (which it does say you have to do on a couple of items, but not on what I ordered). Then when I continued down the menu, I was informed that they didn't have any of those other dishes either, that they were sorry, but there was a big convention in town and they had 70 people in some dining room, and they were so busy with that they didn't have everything on the menu. We always ended up taking whatever the waiter suggested. Once they did have the Oysters Rockefeller. But to be frank, I'd eaten better at Houlahan's, where the oysters were much more succulent.

Anyway, Oysters Rockefeller can be a delectable dish. Normally, it is oysters on the half-shell with a spicy spinach concoction on top, but because you need a lot of butter to keep the oysters moist, I decided to make this as a casserole.

1 (10-ounce) package frozen chopped spinach
8 slices Pritikin or commercial whole wheat bread
1/8 teaspoon cumin
1/8 teaspoon garlic powder
1/4 teaspoon cayenne pepper
1/2 teaspoon dried parsley
1/2 teaspoon dried oregano
1/2 teaspoon dried basil
1 (10-ounce) carton fresh unwashed oysters and juice (12 to 18 oysters)
6 large egg whites
1/4 baked banana (page 148)
Skim milk
2 tablespoons sapsago cheese

Cook the spinach according to package directions and drain. Set aside.

Place the bread in a food processor fitted with a steel blade or blender and process to make crumbs. Add the cumin, garlic powder, cayenne pepper, parsley, oregano and basil; process unitl the herbs are blended into the crumbs.

Drain the oysters, and reserve the juice. Pour the oyster juice into a 2-cup measure. Add the egg whites and banana and its baking juices. Then add enough skim milk to make 1-1/2 cups. Beat together until well mixed.

Gently mix the oysters with the spinach. Then mix in half of the oyster juice mixture.

Spread half the bread crumbs in the bottom of an 8-inch square nonstick baking pan. Spread the oysters and spinach mixture over the crumbs. Spread the remaining crumbs on top. Poke little holes all over the top with a fork. Pour the remaining oyster juice mixture very slowly over the top, poking more holes with the fork and patting the top gently to encourage the liquid to seep through the bread crumbs. Sprinkle with sapsago cheese.

Cover the baking pan very loosely with aluminum foil, not letting it touch the bread crumbs, and slash the foil in several places to release steam. Let the casserole sit in the refrigerator for 2 hours or more.

Place the casserole in the oven, set the temperature at 325°F and bake for 1 hour. Serve immediately. There will be about 2-1/2 ounces of oysters per serving.

Per serving: 280 calories; 21 g protein; 5 g fat; 1 g saturated fat; 39 mg cholesterol; 41 g carbohydrates; 715 mg sodium; 7 g fiber.

Eggplant Jambalaya

Yield: 12 servings

1 large onion, chopped
1 (14-ounce or 16-ounce) can no-salt tomatoes
2 medium-size chopped fresh tomatoes
1/4 cup water
1/2 cup red rosé wine
1/2 cup apple juice concentrate
1 large eggplant, peeled and chopped
1 large carrot, sliced
1 teaspoon dried parsley
1/4 teaspoon cayenne pepper
1 teaspoon crumbled or powdered thyme
1 (14-ounce) box uncooked instant brown rice
   (4-2/3 cups)
1 (6-1/2-ounce) can claw crabmeat, rinsed
1 (4-1/2-ounce) can shrimp, rinsed

Saute the onion over high heat in a 5-quart non-stick soup pot. Remove the pot from the heat. Add the canned tomatoes and juice, and break up the tomatoes with the edge of your spoon.

Add the fresh tomatoes, water, rosé, juice concentrate, eggplant, carrot, parsley, cayenne pepper, and thyme. Cover and bring to a boil. Reduce the heat to medium and cook for 25 to 30 minutes, stirring frequently. Remove the pot from the heat.

Measure the vegetables and liquid. You should have about 6-1/2 cups. If you don't, add enough water to make 6-1/2 cups. Return mixture to the soup pot.

Add the rice, and mix it in well, then gently toss in the crabmeat and shrimp. Cover and bring to a boil. You won't be able to see it's boiling, but you'll hear a popping sound. Reduce the heat to low and simmer for 5 minutes. Remove the pot from the heat and let it stand, covered, for 15 minutes to allow the rice to absorb the liquid. Serve hot. Green peas on the side tastes good.

Per 1-cup serving: 200 calories; 9 g protein; 2 g fat; tr saturated fat; 36 mg cholesterol; 37 g carbohydrates; 85 mg sodium; 4 g fiber

Oven-Fried Shrimp

Yield: 8 servings

These shrimp taste very good with fresh lemon squeezed over, or with some Horseradish Sauce (page 151) or Piquante Sauce (page 150) on the side. By the way, after you peel your shrimp, don't wash them because you will wash much of the flavor away. Cut this recipe in half if you like.

1 cup yellow cornmeal
1/4 teaspoon marjoram
1/4 teaspoon crumbled or powdered thyme
1/4 teaspoon cayenne pepper
1/4 teaspoon ground sage
1 pound fresh peeled shrimp

In a plastic or paper bag combine the cornmeal, marjoram, thyme, cayenne pepper, and sage. Shake well to mix.

Spray a nonstick pan with nonstick spray. Throw a few shrimp at a time into the bag with the seasoned cornmeal and shake to coat. Place the shrimp, not touching, on the pan. Place on the middle rack of the oven at 400°F. Bake for 15 minutes. Serve immediately.

Per serving: 125 calories; 13 g protein; 1 g fat; tr saturated fat; 86 mg cholesterol; 14 g carbohydrates; 85 mg sodium; 1 g fiber

Crawfish Pie

Yield: 12 servings

Bet you never thought you'd see crawfish pie in a diet cookbook. Would you believe I never saw a crawfish until I was 12 years old? My brother brought home some boiled ones, and that's when my love affair with crawfish began. We Créoles were quite unfamiliar with crawfish because they were one of the Cajuns' best-kept secrets.

From deep in Cajun country—Palmetto, Louisiana, to be exact—neatly picked crawfish tails are packaged and sold in 1-pound portions. Though picking crawfish and sharing tales is half the fun of preparing crawfish, I am very grateful to be able to purchase picked crawfish. This recipe calls for washed crawfish. Whit Brown, the Marketing Director at Louisiana Premium Seafoods in Palmetto, told me they package both washed and unwashed crawfish. The washing gets the fat off. He said the ones with the fat have a sign of the package in a red oval that says "Fat On." The washed ones don't have any signs on their packages. The ones with the fat look like they are packaged in a yellow sauce. If you can't get any other kind of crawfish except those with fat, just put the crawfish in a colander and rinse them.

By the way, it takes 8 to 8-1/8 pounds of live or cooked unpeeled crawfish to make 1 pound of peeled crawfish.

Potato Base

6 medium-size Irish potatoes
5 slices Pritikin or commercial whole wheat bread in crumbs
1-1/2 cups frozen or fresh green peas

Filling

1 pound cooked, peeled, washed crawfish tails (2 cups pressed down or about 125 tails)
1 large onion, chopped
1 large green pepper, chopped
5 celery ribs, chopped
2 cups stock from roasted chicken or turkey (page 24)
2 bay leaves
1/4 teaspoon cayenne pepper
1 teaspoon garlic powder
1 teaspoon crumbled or powdered thyme
2 teaspoons dried parsley
2 teaspoons low-sodium soy or tamari sauce
3 tablespoons red rosé wine
4 jumbo egg whites

Topping

7 medium-size Irish potatoes, peeled and quartered
6 tablespoons low-fat cottage cheese
1/4 baked banana (page 148)
5 tablespoons evaporated skim milk
1/4 teaspoon red pepper flakes
1 tablespoon sapsago cheese
Fresh lemon wedges

To make the potato base, boil or bake 6 potatoes in their skins. Let cool. Peel and slice. In a 9-inch by 13-inch baking dish, make a layer of the potato slices.

Process the bread in a food processor or blender to make bread crumbs. Sprinkle the crumbs over the potato slices. Sprinkle the green peas over the bread crumbs.

Pick through the crawfish tails and remove any black veins from the backs.

Combine the onion, green pepper, and celery in a nonstick frying pan and turn the heat on high. Saute the vegetables by tossing them over and over until the onions look a little transparent and brown at the edges. Reduce the heat to medium-low. Add the stock, bay leaves, cayenne pepper, garlic powder, thyme, parsley, soy sauce, and rosé. Stir, reduce the heat to low. Cover and simmer for 15 minutes. Stir occasionally. Remove from the heat and let the mixture cool for 20 minutes. Add the egg whites and stir well. Add the crawfish tails. Pour the crawfish mixture over the potato base.

To make the topping, cover the remaining 7 potatoes in water and boil until very tender, 10 to 15 minutes. Pierce with a knife to test.

In the meantime, process the cottage cheese, banana and its baking juices, and milk in a blender until smooth.

Drain the potatoes and mash. Pour in the cottage cheese-milk mixture and continue to mash until the potatoes are fluffy and creamy. Spread the potatoes over the crawfish mixture in the baking pan. Sprinkle with red pepper flakes and sapsago cheese.

Place the crawfish pie in the oven on the middle rack and turn the heat to 350°F to bake for 40 minutes. Place under the broiler for 5 minutes to brown the top. Let sit outside the oven for 10 minutes, then serve in squares with 1 fresh lemon wedge on each plate. Each serving will contain about 1-1/3 ounces of crawfish.

Per serving: 240 calories; 16 g protein; 2 g fat; tr saturated fat; 34 mg cholesterol; 42 g carbohydrates; 250 mg sodium; 5 g fiber

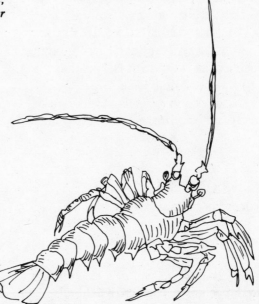

7

Meatless
Main Dishes

If you're not a vegetarian already, meatless meals may seem like a deprivation. But you will be surprised by just how satisfying these meals are.

Cabbage Jambalaya

Yield: 6 servings

Cabbage

2 tablespoons apple juice concentrate
2 medium-size purple turnips, cubed (do not peel)
1-1/2 cups plus 1 tablespoon chicken or turkey stock (page 24)
1 bay leaf
1 (16-ounce) can no-salt tomatoes and juice
1/2 large green cabbage, cut up in small pieces (about 4 cups)
1/4 teaspoon cayenne pepper
1/4 teaspoon crumbled or powdered thyme

Rice Base

2-1/4 cups instant uncooked brown rice
1-1/2 cups chicken stock (page 24)
1/2 cup no-salt tomato paste

Add the juice concentrate to a nonstick 5-quart pot. Heat over high heat until the liquid begins to sizzle. Add the turnips. Let them sit in the liquid to cook for about 2 minutes or until you see the liquid is evaporating. When the liquid begins to evaporate rapidly in the pan, stir the turnips constantly until they are a little bit brown. Continue until all the liquid is gone and the turnips are partially cooked. Add the stock and bring to a boil. Remove the pot from the heat. Add the bay leaf, tomatoes, and cabbage. Chop up the tomatoes with your spoon. Sprinkle on the cayenne pepper and thyme. Cover with a tightly fitting cover. Cook over high heat for 15 minutes, or until the cabbage is tender. Mix all the ingredients together. Serve as is as a vegetable, or make the rice base for jambalaya.

In a 9-inch by 13-inch baking dish, combine the rice, stock, and tomato paste. Add the cooked cabbage mixture including any juice left in the pot. Mix well. Cover with aluminum foil and place on the middle rack of the oven. Set the temperature at 350°F and bake for 20 minutes. Remove the dish from the oven and let it sit covered 10 minutes. Serve immediately. This is nice served with green peas and a salad.

Per serving without rice: 50 calories; 3 g protein; 1 g fat; tr saturated fat; tr cholesterol; 10 g carbohydrates; 40 mg sodium; 2 g fiber

Per serving with rice: 150 calories; 7 g protein; 2 g fat; tr saturated fat; 1 mg cholesterol; 55 mg sodium; 4 g fiber

Variations

Cabbage with Chicken Jambalaya. Add 6 ounces raw or cooked chopped chicken meat to the uncooked rice base and add the cabbage mixture. Cover with aluminum foil and place on the middle rack of the oven. Set the temperature at 350°F and bake for 25 minutes. Remove the dish from the oven and let it sit covered for 10 minutes, then serve. Each serving will contain 1 ounce of chicken.

Per serving: 195 calories; 15 g protein; 3 g fat; 1 g saturated fat; 24 mg cholesterol; 29 g carbohydrates; 80 mg sodium; 4 g fiber

Cabbage with Shrimp Jambalaya. Add 1 pound fresh shrimp (weighed before peeling) or 2 (4-1/2-ounce) cans of shrimp, rinsed, to the uncooked rice base and add the cabbage mixture. Cover with aluminum foil and place on the middle rack of the oven. Set the temperature at 350°F and bake for 20 minutes. Remove the dish from the oven and let it sit covered for 10 minutes, then serve. Each serving will contain 1-1/4 ounces of shrimp.

Per serving: 190 calories; 15 g protein; 2 g fat; tr saturated fat; 83 mg cholesterol; 29 g carbohydrates; 150 mg sodium; 4 g fiber

Southern Casserole

Yield: 8 servings

Grits, if you've never seen it (not them), is something like cornmeal, but different in taste and texture. It is made by grinding and sifting cleaned white corn and removing the corn bran and germ. It looks coarser than cornmeal.

8 jumbo egg whites
4 cups chicken stock (page 24)
1/8 teaspoon cayenne pepper
1/4 teaspoon turmeric
1 cup finely chopped onion
1-1/2 cups uncooked quick (5-minute) grits
7 ounces cooked or raw white meat chicken, chopped
2 cups low-fat cottage cheese
2 teaspoons dried parsley
2 to 4 tomatoes, sliced (enough to cover the top of the casserole)
1 (4-ounce) can peeled green chilies
2 tablespoons sapsago cheese

In a large bowl, beat the egg whites, chicken stock, cayenne pepper, and turmeric with an electric mixer until well blended. Add the onion, grits, chicken, cottage cheese, and parsley. Stir well. Pour into a nonstick 9-inch by 13-inch glass baking dish. Distribute the ingredients evenly in the dish. Slice the tomatoes and distribute them over the top of the casserole, edges touching. Slice the chilies into thin strips and arrange the slices over the top. Sprinkle the sapsago cheese over all.

Place the uncovered casserole on the middle rack of the oven. Set the temperature at 350°F and bake for 1 hour. Remove from the oven and let the casserole sit uncovered for 15 minutes to absorb the juices. Serve hot.

Per serving: 255 calories; 24 g protein; 3 g fat; 1 g saturated fat; 24 mg cholesterol; 31 g carbohydrates; 340 mg sodium; 5 g fiber

Huevos con Papas

Yield: 8 servings

This colorful dish, translated as "Eggs with Potatoes," is nice to serve for a buffet brunch.

1/2 cup chicken stock (page 24)
4 cups sliced Irish potatoes (1/4-inch thick)
1-1/2 cups chopped onions
1/2 medium-size green pepper, chopped
12 jumbo eggs whites
3 tablespoons sapsago cheese
1/4 teaspoon turmeric
1/8 teaspoon dried basil
1/4 teaspoon dried oregano
1/2 teaspoon dried parsley
1/8 teaspoon cayenne pepper
1/2 teaspoon red hot sauce (not Tabasco)
1 (4-ounce) jar pimiento pieces

Pour the chicken stock into a 5-quart soup pot. Add the potatoes, onions, and green pepper. Cover. Bring to a boil, then simmer on very low heat for about 50 minutes until the potatoes are soft. There's no need to stir. Drain off the liquid, and use it for soup later if you like.

Put the egg whites into a 2-quart container and add 2 tablespoons of the sapsago cheese, and all of the turmeric, basil, oregano, parsley, cayenne pepper, and red hot sauce. Beat with an electric mixer until the eggs begin to froth. Add the drained potatoes, onions, and green pepper. Mix well.

Spray a 3-quart baking dish with nonstick spray and pour the egg mixture into it. Chop the pimiento pieces in a bowl (to keep from losing the juice), and pour them and their juice over the top of the egg mixture. Mix them in just slightly. You want them to stay near the top because they look pretty when this is cooked. Bake uncovered on the middle rack at 350°F for 40 minutes, or until the top browns.

Per serving: 105 calories; 8 g protein; tr fat; tr saturated fat; tr cholesterol; 17 g carbohydrates; 130 mg sodium; 2 g fiber

Chilies Relleños

Yield: 2 servings

You could eat this for breakfast, as well as dinner. It tastes especially good with Mexican-Style Red Beans (page 93). Yes, these eggs will come out yellow because of the turmeric.

4 jumbo egg whites
1/16 teaspoon garlic powder
Less than 1/16 teaspoon cumin
1/8 teaspoon turmeric
1/2 teaspoon dried chives
1/8 teaspoon dried red pepper flakes
1/2 cup finely chopped onion
1 (4-ounce) can peeled green whole chilies, rinsed

In a small mixing bowl, combine the egg whites, garlic powder, cumin, and turmeric. Beat with an egg beater until the eggs are close to forming soft peaks. Stir in the chives, red pepper flakes, and onion.

Cut each chili into thirds and arrange evenly spaced in a nonstick frying pan. Pour the egg mixture over. Turn the heat on high and cook until the egg on the bottom begins to set, just a few minutes. Divide the mixture in half with a spatula and turn each section over. Cook for a minute or so more, until the egg looks cooked. Serve immediately.

If you want to cook more servings, either have another frying pan ready, or plan to wash the one you are using before cooking another batch. You can keep the finished servings warm in the oven, covered with aluminum foil. Set the oven temperature very low and slit the foil to allow steam to escape.

Per serving: 75 calories; 9 g protein; tr fat; tr saturated fat; 0 mg cholesterol; 10 g carbohydrates; 115 mg sodium; 2 g fiber

Yellow Squash and Tomatoes over Spaghetti

Yield: 4 servings, with spaghetti

1 (14-1/2-ounce) can no-salt tomatoes, chopped (save the juice)
2 medium-size yellow squash, sliced
1 large onion, sliced in rings
1 tablespoon apple juice concentrate
1/8 teaspoon dried red pepper flakes
1/8 teaspoon dried basil
1/2 teaspoon dried parsley
2 cups cooked whole wheat or semolina spaghetti
2 tablespoons sapsago cheese

Drain the tomatoes, reserving the juice.

Layer first the squash, then the onion, then the tomatoes in a 2-quart pot. Pour in the juice from the tomatoes. Sprinkle the juice concentrate over the top, then the red pepper, then the basil, then the parsley. Don't stir. Cover the pot and turn the heat on high. Cook for 8 to 10 minutes, or until the squash is soft. Watch the pot carefully so the bottom doesn't burn. Shake the pot back and forth a couple of times while cooking.

Cook the spaghetti in plenty of boiling water while the vegetables are cooking. Drain. Stir the cooked vegetables, then serve them and the pan juices over the spaghetti. Sprinkle sapsago cheese over the top.

Per serving, vegetables only (4 servings): 55 calories; 2 g protein; 1 g fat; tr saturated fat; 0 mg cholesterol; 12 g carbohydrates; 20 mg sodium; 3 g fiber

Per serving with spaghetti and cheese (2 servings): 320 calories; 15 g protein; 3 g fat; tr saturated fat; 0 mg cholesterol; 65 g carbohydrates; 140 mg sodium; 8 g fiber

Stewed Okra and Tomatoes over Rice

Yield: 4 servings

This is a very old New Orleans dish, brought by the African slaves who were taken to New Orleans by white masters who were fleeing slave uprisings in the Caribbean Islands in the late 1700s. Of course, okra (*gombo* in one African language) is an African vegetable to start with and is frequently served in the Caribbean. I used to make this dish with ham, but I was very surprised at how nice this tastes without meat.

If you only eat a couple of servings of the okra and tomatoes, you can use the leftover vegetables, without the rice, as a substitute for the 5 cups of okra in Quick and Easy Seafood Gumbo (page 29).

2 cups chopped onions
1 large green pepper, chopped
1 pound fresh okra, sliced
1 (16-ounce) can no-salt tomatoes
1/2 cup water
1/8 teaspoon cayenne pepper
2-3/4 tablespoons apple juice concentrate
Cooked brown or white rice

In a nonstick 5-quart pot, combine the onions and green pepper. Saute over high heat by turning the vegetables over and over until the onions become a little transparent and brown around the edges. Remove the vegetables to a bowl. Immediately add the okra to the pot, and saute until the okra begins to give up its liquid, which forms sticky threads between pieces. Saute just a little more, then pour the tomatoes into the pot. Reduce the heat to low. Break up the tomatoes with a wooden spoon. Return the onions and green pepper to the pot. Add the water, cayenne pepper, and juice concentrate. Stir, cover, and cook over low heat for 1 to 1-1/4 hours, until the okra is tender. Stir often.

To serve, place 2/3 cup of cooked rice on each plate and pour the stewed vegetables over. Corn-on-the-cob tastes good with this.

Per serving, vegetables only: 115 calories; 4 g protein; 1 g fat; tr saturated fat; 0 mg cholesterol; 26 g carbohydrates; 25 mg sodium; 5 g fiber

Per serving with rice: 260 calories; 8 g protein; 2 g fat; tr saturated fat; 0 mg cholesterol; 56 g carbohydrates; 30 mg sodium; 7 g fiber

Variations

Stewed Okra and Tomatoes with Shrimp over Rice. Make the recipe as above. During the last 10 minutes add 1 pound of fresh peeled shrimp (weighed with heads and peel) or 1 (4-1/2-ounce) can of shrimp, rinsed. Each serving will contain a little over 1 ounce of shrimp.

Per serving with rice: 290 calories; 14 g protein; 2 g fat; tr saturated fat; 62 mg cholesterol; 56 g carbohydrates; 105 mg sodium; 8 g fiber

Stewed Okra and Tomatoes with Chicken over Rice. Make the recipe as above, adding 8 ounces of cooked or raw chopped white meat chicken immediately after you add the juice concentrate. Each serving will contain a little over 2 ounces of chicken.

Per serving with rice: 355 calories; 25 g protein; 4 g fat; 1 g saturated fat; 48 mg cholesterol; 56 g carbohydrates; 75 mg sodium; 7 g fiber

Turnip Pie

Yield: 6 servings

5 no-salt puffed rice cakes
1/2 cup unsweetened apple juice (not concentrate)
1 medium-size onion, chopped
3 medium-size turnips, cubed (2 cups)
2 tablespoons apple juice concentrate
1/4 teaspoon cayenne pepper
6 jumbo egg whites
2 tablespoons sapsago cheese

Grind the rice cakes in the food processor until the texture resembles coarse cornmeal. Measure out 2 cups. Pour the crumbs into a 9-inch nonstick pie pan. Pour in the apple juice and mix well with the crumbs. Press and spread the crumbs to form a pie crust.

Place the onion in a nonstick frying pan and saute over high heat.

Add the turnips to the pan, along with 1 tablespoon of the juice concentrate. Saute over high heat, turning the turnips over and over, until they are light brown and all the juice has evaporated.

Place the browned turnips and onions in a food processor fitted with a cutting blade and process until they are very finely chopped.

Combine the onions, turnips, cayenne pepper, egg whites, and the remaining tablespoon of juice concentrate in a large bowl. Mix very well. Pour the mixture into the pie crust.

Place the pie on the middle rack of the oven and set the temperature at 350°F. Bake for 30 minutes. Sprinkle sapsago cheese over the top and bake for 15 minutes more, or until a knife inserted in the center of the pie comes out clean. Cool on a wire rack for 10 minutes before serving. Cut slices with a plastic spatula. Serve as is, or with a few squirts of lemon juice or Tabasco sauce.

Per serving: 115 calories; 6 g protein; tr fat; tr saturated fat; 0 mg cholesterol; 21 g carbohydrates; 125 mg sodium; 2 g fiber

Quick and Easy Pinto Beans

Yield: 7 servings

1 pound dried pinto beans (2-2/3 cups)
9 cups water
1/4 cup dried celery
1/4 cup dried chopped onion
1/4 cup no-salt chili powder
2 teaspoons garlic powder
1/4 cup dried green (sweet bell) pepper
1/4 to 1/2 teaspoon cayenne pepper
3 tablespoons apple juice concentrate
2 teaspoons low-sodium soy or tamari sauce
2 tablespoons fresh lemon juice

Slow Cooker Directions

Rinse the beans and combine with the water in a 5-quart slow cooker. Cover and cook on high for 4-1/2 hours. Add the remaining ingredients, except the lemon juice, and cook for 30 to 40 minutes more. Stir in the lemon juice just before serving.

Stove Top Directions

Rinse the beans and combine with the water in a 5-quart soup pot. Cover and simmer for 3-1/2 hours, stirring often. Add the remaining ingredients, except the lemon juice, and simmer for 30 to 40 minutes more. Stir in the lemon juice just before serving.

Per 1-cup serving: 260 calories; 16 g protein; 2 g fat; tr saturated fat; 0 mg cholesterol; 49 g carbohydrates; 60 mg sodium; 4 g fiber

Variation

Pinto Beans and Pineapple. For a tropical touch and really good flavor, cook the beans as above, but add a 20-ounce can of unsweetened pineapple chunks, well-drained, instead of the lemon juice. Makes 8 servings.

Per 1-cup serving: 270 calories; 14 g protein; 1 g fat; tr saturated fat; 0 mg cholesterol; 54 g carbohydrates; 55 mg sodium; 4 g fiber

Mexican-Style Red Beans

Yield: About 12 servings

On hearing about red beans mixed with cornmeal, my 82-year-old first-cousin-once-removed (that makes her my mother's generation) asked me, "How in the world do you think up such concoctions?" I told her, "It turns out really good and tastes something like a burrito."

Chilies Relleños (page 90) taste delicious on the side and really complete the dish. Cook the beans in a slow cooker; on top of the stove, the pot would require too much watching.

1 pound dry red kidney beans (2-2/3 cups)
9 cups water
1/4 cup no-salt chili powder
1 cup chopped green pepper
2 tablespoons minced dried onion
1 tablespoon dried parsley
2 teaspoons dried celery flakes
1/4 teaspoon dried red pepper flakes
1/2 cup apple juice concentrate
1-1/2 cups frozen corn or 1 (17-ounce) can no-salt
   whole kernel corn, drained
1 cup yellow cornmeal
Chopped raw onions (optional)
Chopped raw jalapeño peppers (optional)
Apple cider vinegar (optional)
Tabasco sauce (optional)

Pour the beans into a slow cooker and add the water. Cover and cook on high for 4-1/2 hours. (Cook covered on low if you are going to be out of the house for more than 4-1/2 hours.) When the beans are soft, add the chili powder, green pepper, onion, parsley, celery flakes, red pepper flakes, and juice concentrate. Cover and continue cooking on high for 1 hour. Add the corn and cornmeal. Stir very well. Cover and cook for 40 minutes on high, stirring twice. Serve (1-cup portions) immediately. At the table, pass the chopped onions, jalapeños, vinegar, and Tabasco sauce.

If you can't serve this immediately, set the temperature of the slow cooker on low and stir occasionally.

Freeze leftovers in 1-cup and 2-cup portions. Reheat covered in the microwave or on top of the stove in a double boiler. Add a little water if the mixture seems too thick.

Per serving without toppings: 220 calories; 11 g protein; 1 g fat; tr saturated fat; 0 mg cholesterol; 44 g carbohydrates; 10 mg sodium; 11 g fiber

Quartée Beans and Rice

Yield: 7 servings

Three months before my daddy died, he started talking about his grandfather, and I ran to get a pencil and paper to record his stories. He said his grandfather's daddy owned a big sugar-cane plantation with quite a few slaves near Baton Rouge before the Civil War.

Now, according to my daddy, his grandfather, John Peyronnin, was mischievous as a boy. He would steal whiskey from his father's plantation store and sell it to the Indians.

Later, John ran away from medical school to join the Confederate Army. During the Battle of Shiloh, he was in the medical corps; he pulled General Albert Sidney Johnston off his horse when he saw the general was injured. He pulled off the general's boot and saw it was full of blood. The general had already lost too much blood, so John was unable to save his life. During the same battle, John was shot in the face and sides. He was sent home to die, but he lived until the age of 95, with the bullet still lodged near his ear.

After the war, John didn't have much money, but he was able to open a grocery store in New Orleans on Poydras Street near Baronne. People kept coming in and asking for a half nickel's worth of beans and a half nickel's worth of rice. Sometimes they would only want a half nickel's worth of one or the other, and they would give John a nickel. How do you give a person 2-1/2 cents change? My clever great-grandfather solved that problem. He minted his own coin with 2-1/2 cents printed on one side, and a "P" for Peyronnin on the other. He called it a quartée. People would come in and ask for a quartée of beans and a quartée of rice. The practice spread all over New Orleans; hence the poem you can find in New Orleans history books:

> *Gimme a quartée red beans,*
> *Quartée rice,*
> *Little piece of salt meat to make it*
> *Taste nice.*
> *Lend me the paper, tell me the time,*
> *When papa passes by he will pay you a dime.*

1/2 pound dried red kidney beans (1-1/3 cups)
1/2 pound dried large lima beans (1-1/3 cup)
1 (14-ounce or 16-ounce) can no-salt tomatoes
7-1/2 cups water
1 cup frozen whole kernel corn
1 onion, chopped
1 carrot, sliced
1 green pepper, sliced in strips
1/4 teaspoon cayenne pepper
7 cups cooked instant brown rice

Slow Cooker Directions

Rinse the beans and pour into a 5-quart slow cooker. Add the tomatoes and water. Break up the tomatoes with a spoon. Cover, and cook on high for 4-1/2 hours. Add the remaining ingredients and cook for 30 to 40 minutes, or until the green pepper is tender.

Stove Top Directions

Rinse the beans and pour into a 5-quart soup pot. Add the tomatoes and water. Break up the tomatoes with a spoon. Cover, and cook on high for about 3 hours. Add the remaining ingredients and cook for 30 to 40 minutes, or until the green pepper is tender.

Serve 1 cup of beans on individual plates over 1 cup of cooked instant brown rice.

Per serving, beans only: 270 calories; 16 g protein; 1 g fat; tr saturated fat; 0 mg cholesterol; 52 g carbohydrates; 25 mg sodium; 20 g fiber

Per serving with beans and rice: 510 calories; 22 g protein; 3 g fat; tr saturated fat; 0 mg cholesterol; 104 g carbohydrates; 35 mg sodium; 24 g fiber

Pinto Beans and Macaroni

Yield: 14 servings

This is good served with Christmas Salad (page 115) on the side. Use medium-size elbow macaroni, the type that's used in boxes of macaroni and cheese.

1 pound dried pinto beans (2-2/3 cups)
9 cups water
1 large carrot, sliced
1-1/2 cups chopped onion
1-1/3 cups chopped green pepper
4 tablespoons no-salt tomato paste
6 tablespoons apple juice concentrate
1-1/2 teaspoons no-salt chili powder
1/4 teaspoon cayenne pepper
2 cups uncooked semolina or whole wheat elbow
  macaroni

Slow Cooker Directions

Rinse the beans and combine them with the water in a 5-quart slow cooker. Cover and cook on high for 4-1/2 hours. Add the remaining ingredients and cook for 30 to 40 minutes more, until the green pepper is tender.

Stove Top Directions

Rinse the beans and combine them with the water in a 5-quart soup pot. Cover and simmer for 3-1/2 hours. Stir often. Add the remaining ingredients and simmer for 30 to 40 minutes more, until the green pepper is tender.

Remove 1 cup of the beans and puree in a blender, or mash with a fork. Return them to the pot to make the beans extra creamy.

Boil 2 quarts of water in a 5-quart pot. Add the macaroni and stir. Cook the semolina elbows for about 10 minutes and the whole wheat elbows for about 15 minutes. Stir frequently. Drain.

To serve, place 1/2 cup of macaroni on each individual serving plate and top with 1/2 cup of the beans. A little chopped onion is good on top, as is Tabasco sauce.

Per serving, not including a topping of onion or Tabasco: 200 calories; 10 g protein; 1 g fat; tr saturated fat; 0 mg cholesterol; 39 g carbohydrates; 10 mg sodium; 3 g fiber

Bean Tostados

Yield: 8 servings

8 frozen or refrigerated corn tortillas
2 cups Bean Dip (page 20)
1 cup Piquante Sauce (page 150)
1/2 cup chopped onions
2 cups shredded lettuce
2 cups low-fat cottage cheese
2 tomatoes, chopped

Place the tortillas on the racks of the oven and set the temperature at 350° F. Bake for 3 to 5 minutes. Watch the tortillas on the bottom rack carefully. They will be done very quickly.

When the tortillas are crisp, remove them from the oven and spread each toasted tortilla with 1/4 cup Bean Dip, then layer with 2 tablespoons Piquante Sauce, 1 tablespoon chopped onions, 1/4 cup shredded lettuce, 1/4 cup low-fat cottage cheese, and finish with chopped tomato on top.

Per serving: 215 calories; 14 g protein; 2 g fat; .5 g saturated fat; 3 mg cholesterol; 37 g carbohydrates; 285 mg sodium; 5 g fiber

Soppin' Good Beans and Eggplant Bread

Yield: 10 servings

To make meatless meals you really have to use your imagination. I'm always amazed, though, how good meatless dishes taste once I set my mind to making them. My husband sops up all the beans and pot liquor with this eggplant bread. He loves it. I do, too.

Red Beans

1 pound dried red or kidney beans (2-2/3 cups)
1 (16-ounce) can no-salt tomatoes
7-1/2 cups water
2 tablespoons no-salt chili powder
1 (4-ounce) can peeled green roasted chilies, drained and chopped
1 large onion, chopped
2 tablespoons apple juice concentrate
1/4 teaspoon cayenne pepper (optional)

Eggplant Bread

1 tablespoon water
1/2 cup plus 1 tablespoon apple juice concentrate
3-1/2 cups cubed, peeled raw eggplant (1 small or 1/2 large)
1/16 teaspoon cayenne pepper
1-1/2 cups yellow cornmeal
2 tablespoons no-salt chili powder
1 tablespoon low-sodium baking powder
1/4 teaspoon red pepper flakes
1/4 teaspoon garlic powder
1 (16-ounce) can no-salt tomatoes
4 jumbo egg whites
1 large onion, chopped
1 large green pepper, chopped
1 cup frozen chuck wagon corn
3/4 cup sliced fresh mushrooms
1/4 baked banana (page 148)
1 (12-ounce) carton low-fat cottage cheese

Paprika
1 large fresh tomato, sliced
2 tablespoons grated sapsago cheese
Extra red pepper flakes
1/2 cup chopped raw onion

Slow Cooker Directions for the Beans

Rinse the beans. Combine with the tomatoes and water in a slow cooker. Cut the tomatoes up right in the cooker. Add the water. Cover and cook on high for 4-1/2 hours. Add the remaining ingredients, except the cayenne pepper, and cook for 30 to 40 minutes, until the onion is tender.

Stove Top Directions for the Beans

Cooking beans on top of the stove is at least a half-day job, so be sure you will not have to leave the house once you start. Rinse the beans. Combine the beans and tomatoes in a 5-quart pot. Cut up the tomatoes right in the pot, then add the water. Cover and simmer for about 3 hours. Stir every so often to keep the beans from burning on the bottom. Add the remaining ingredients, except the cayenne pepper, and simmer for 30 to 40 minutes, until the onion is tender. You shouldn't need any more water, but if the beans start to dry out, add more.

Taste the beans. If the chili powder you are using contains cayenne pepper, you probably won't need any more. Add more if the beans taste at all bland.

When your red beans are just about cooked, preheat the oven to 400°F. Spray a 9-inch by 13-inch baking dish with nonstick spray. Pour 1 tablespoon of water and 1 tablespoon of juice concentrate into a nonstick frying pan. Add the eggplant. Sprinkle the cayenne pepper over the eggplant. Turn the heat to high and let the eggplant sit until it is sizzling quite a bit and getting brown on the bottom, then turn it over. Let it sizzle some more, then start stirring to brown all over, until the eggplant has changed to a darker color and is almost cooked through. Set aside.

In a large bowl, combine the cornmeal, chili powder, baking powder, 1/4 teaspoon red pepper flakes, and garlic powder. Add the tomatoes and juice and cut them up right in the bowl. Mix. Add the egg whites and the remaining 1/2 cup of juice concentrate. Mix. Add the onion, green pepper, chuck wagon corn, mushrooms, banana and its baking juices, and cooked eggplant, mixing after each addition.

Pour the mixture into the baking dish and spread evenly. Spread the cottage cheese over the top, and if some red shows through here and there, don't worry about it. Sprinkle a little paprika over for color. Slice the tomato and decorate the top with the slices. Sprinkle the sapsago cheese over all. Sprinkle a few extra red pepper flakes for still more color and flavor. Cover the dish with aluminum foil and slit it with a knife to release steam.

Place the dish on the middle rack of the oven and bake for 25 minutes, or until the top browns a bit, the tomatoes look cooked, and a toothpick inserted into the center comes out clean. Let the bread sit out of the oven for 10 minutes before serving.

To serve, cut the bread in squares and serve with 1 cup of beans poured around. Sprinkle about 3/4 tablespoon chopped raw onions over. Cooked spinach tastes good with this. A dab of Cabbage Relish (page 152) on the side is also good. Piquante Sauce (page 150) can add extra flavor. I like just the onions on top. My husband adds a squirt of Tabasco sauce or Crystal or Louisiana hot sauces.

This bread can be frozen in pieces for future meals. Freeze the beans separately in cup-size containers.

Per serving, beans only: 175 calories; 11 g protein; 1 g fat; tr saturated fat; 0 mg cholesterol; 33 g carbohydrates; 130 mg sodium; 11 g fiber

Per serving, bread, beans, and extra raw onion: 355 calories; 21 g protein; 2 g fat; tr saturated fat; 2 mg cholesterol; 67 g carbohydrates; 325 mg sodium; 15 g fiber

Kartoffelpuree

Yield: 11 servings

When my husband and I were vacationing in Germany, we would order Sauerkraut and Kartoffelpuree, the Kartoffelpuree being mashed potatoes formed into balls about the size of baseballs. I believe they had been boiled. The mashed potato balls had eggs mixed in them and, I suspect, a little flour. I used egg whites instead of whole eggs, substituted cottage cheese for flour, and baked them in a dish. Talk about delicious!

3 large Irish potatoes
6 tablespoons skim milk
6 tablespoons low-fat cottage cheese
4 jumbo egg whites
1/16 teaspoon cayenne pepper
1 tablespoon sapsago cheese

Preheat the oven to 350°F.

Peel, then boil the potatoes in water for about 15 minutes, covered, or until they feel soft when pierced with a knife. Drain the potatoes and set aside.

In a blender, combine the milk, cottage cheese, and egg whites. Blend on medium speed until very smooth. Add the mixture to the potatoes. Add the cayenne pepper. Mash until smooth and fluffy.

Pile the potatoes into a 1-1/2-quart baking dish. Don't push the potatoes down. Leave them in a mountain shape. You want lots of surface. Sprinkle the sapsago cheese over the potatoes. Bake for 25 minutes. Then put the potatoes under the broiler for about 2 minutes to brown the top; watch carefully. Serve hot, dishing the potatoes out with an ice cream scoop.

Per scoop: 50 calories; 3 g protein; tr fat; tr saturated fat; tr cholesterol; 8 g carbohydrates; 65 mg sodium; 1 g fiber

Potato Latkes

Yield: 8 pancakes

This is a typical Jewish dish, served during Hanukkah and other times as well. Serve with store-bought unsweetened applesauce or with a mock sour cream topping (recipe below). My husband likes to eat these with pinto beans.

Potatoes

2 large Irish potatoes
1 small onion
1/4 cup low-fat cottage cheese
2 jumbo egg whites
1 tablespoon unbleached flour
Cayenne pepper

Mock Sour Cream Topping

1-1/2 cups low-fat cottage cheese
1 small onion
1/2 teaspoon Tabasco sauce
1 tablespoon skim milk

Peel the potatoes, place in a bowl, and cover with cold water.

Combine the onion and cottage cheese in a food processor fitted with a steel cutting blade and process until almost smooth. Pour the cheese mixture into a mixing bowl. Set aside.

Fit the food processor with a grating blade and grate the potatoes. Put the grated potatoes in a colander over a bowl and squeeze them as though you were wringing out clothes. Press out any moisture, reserving the drained liquid. Let them sit a minute. While you wait, add the egg whites and flour to the cottage cheese mixture and beat with an electric mixer for about 2 minutes until the mixture looks very creamy. Squeeze the potatoes one last time and add them to the cheese mixture. The potato liquid should have a starchy sediment by now. Pour off the clear liquid on top and add the sediment to the potatoes and cheese mixture. Toss all together.

Preheat the oven to 200°F.

Preheat a nonstick frying pan over medium heat. Drop large spoonfuls of the potato mixture into the pan. Make the cakes about 2-1/2 inches in diameter and pat them a little on top to flatten them. Sprinkle each cake with cayenne pepper. Cook for about 5 minutes on each side. Turn over carefully. Remove to a nonstick cookie sheet and place in the oven for about 10 minutes more.

To make the topping, place all the ingredients in a blender or food processor and process until the cottage cheese is smooth. This blends more easily on medium speed than high speed in a blender. Yield: 53 tablespoons.

Serve the potato pancakes warm and pass the mock sour cream on the side.

Per serving, latkes only: 45 calories; 2 g protein; tr fat; tr saturated fat; tr cholesterol; 8 g carbohydrates; 45 mg sodium; 1 g fiber

Per tablespoon with mock sour cream: 5 calories; 1 g protein; tr fat; tr saturated fat; tr cholesterol; tr carbohydrates; 25 mg sodium; tr fiber

8

Cooked Vegetables

If you will notice, this is a small chapter. That is because in Louisiana we tend to mix our vegetables with everything else. We sort of fancy them up, or maybe the vegetables fancy up the other foods.

For instance, should I have put Crawfish Pie in the vegetable section as fancied-up peas? That's mighty fancied up for peas. And Cabbage Jambalaya—should that go in the vegetable section? It's a whole meal.

What I actually do is serve a dish such as Crawfish Pie, which has a complicated flavor, with something plain, such as steamed cabbage, on the side. Or I might serve Cabbage Jambalaya, which has lots of flavor, with plain steamed peas or spinach on the side.

You don't want two complexly flavored foods on one plate. They won't complement each other; they will confuse the palate. Moreover, you shouldn't as a rule have two dishes with sauce or gravy on the same plate. It's too messy and too much.

Artichoke Casserole

Yield: 9 servings

1-1/2 cups commercial whole wheat or Pritikin bread crumbs (3 slices of bread)
1/4 cup yellow cornmeal
1 medium-size onion, chopped
1 (14-ounce) can artichoke hearts, rinsed and quartered
1 (8-ounce) can sliced water chestnuts, rinsed
1 cup frozen French-style green beans
1/4 teaspoon dried basil
1/4 + 1/8 teaspoon garlic powder
1/2 teaspoon dried oregano
1/8 teaspoon cumin
1/8 teaspoon cayenne pepper
2 tablespoons sapsago cheese
2 jumbo egg whites

1/2 teaspoon red hot sauce (not Tabasco)
1-1/4 cups strong chicken stock (page 24), cooled
1/2 fresh lemon

Mix the bread crumbs with the cornmeal. Set aside.

In a nonstick frying pan over high heat, saute the onions tossing them over and over until they are transparent and brown around the edges. Remove the pan from the heat. Add the cornmeal and bread crumbs.

Combine the artichoke hearts, water chestnuts, and green beans with the onion and bread crumb mixture, mixing well. Mix in the basil, garlic powder, oregano, cumin, cayenne pepper, and 1 tablespoon of the sapsago cheese.

Add the egg whites and red hot sauce to the cooled chicken stock, beat slightly, then combine very well with the rest of the ingredients. If you don't have a nonstick 8-inch square baking dish, spray an ovenproof glass baking dish with nonstick spray. Turn the casserole mixture into the dish. Cover with aluminum foil and place on the middle rack of the oven. Set the temperature at 300°F and bake for 1 hour. Remove the foil and bake for 15 minutes more.

Squeeze the lemon over the casserole, sprinkle the remaining 1 tablespoon of sapsago cheese over, and serve immediately with lemon wedges on the side.

Per serving: 110 calories; 5 g protein; 1 g fat; tr saturated fat; tr cholesterol; 20 g carbohydrates; 140 mg sodium; 6 g fiber

Fresh Beets

Yield: 2 servings

Water
3 medium-size beets, peeled and sliced

Pour enough water into a medium-size saucepan to cover the beets. Cover and bring to a boil. Immediately add the beets. Cover and cook over high heat for 6 to 7 minutes, or until tender. Watch carefully.

Serve hot as a vegetable, or cold in Beet Salad (page 113). Reserve the cooking liquid for red food color.

Per serving: 25 calories; 1 g protein; tr fat; tr saturated fat; 0 mg cholesterol; 5 g carbohydrates; 35 mg sodium; 1 g fiber

Steamed Broccoli and Cabbage

Yield: 4 servings

2-1/2 cups water
1 medium-size green cabbage
4 broccoli spears
3 tablespoons apple cider vinegar
1/8 to 1/4 teaspoon cayenne pepper

Bring the water to a boil in a covered 5-quart soup pot. Quarter the cabbage from top to bottom and wash well. Peel the broccoli stems and cut into 4 pieces, or as many as seem needed by the size and shape of the broccoli. When the water is boiling, place the cabbage on the bottom of the pot, and arrange the broccoli over it. Sprinkle the vinegar over the vegetables, then the cayenne pepper. Cover and steam over high heat for 7 to 10 minutes, or until the vegetables are tender. Watch carefully. Serve hot.

Per serving: 75 calories; 6 g protein; 1 g fat; tr saturated fat; 0 mg cholesterol; 16 g carbohydrates; 65 mg sodium; 8 g fiber

Cabbage and Green Beans

Yield: 4 servings

Sometimes you just have to mix foods in an unusual way to get variety. This combination turns out surprisingly good.

3 cups water
4 cups chopped green cabbage
1 cup frozen French-style green beans
1/4 cup apple cider vinegar
1/16 teaspoon cayenne pepper

Pour the water into a 5-quart soup pot, cover, and bring to a boil. Add the cabbage and green beans. Pour the vinegar over and sprinkle the cayenne pepper on top. Cover and cook over high heat for 8 to 10 minutes, stirring occasionally, until the cabbage is tender and the liquid is almost evaporated. Serve hot.

Per serving: 30 calories; 1 g protein; tr fat; tr saturated fat; 0 mg cholesterol; 7 g carbohydrates; 15 mg sodium; 3 g fiber

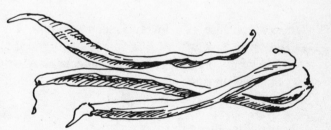

Cabbage and Potatoes

Yield: 4 servings

3 cups degreased corn beef juice from Easy Corned
   Beef (page 41)
4 to 5 medium-size potatoes, peeled and quartered
1/2 head medium-size green cabbage, chopped

Pour the corn beef juice into a 5-quart soup pot.
Add the potatoes, cover, and bring to a boil. Cook over
high heat for 5 minutes. Add the cabbage, cover, and
cook over high heat for 7 minutes. Stir. Cook for 5 or
6 minutes or more, until both the potatoes and cabbage
are tender. Check to make sure the mixture doesn't
burn.

*Per serving (assuming the corn beef juice has the same nutritive
value as unsalted beef stock): 175 calories; 6 g protein; 1 g fat;
tr saturated fat; tr cholesterol; 38 g carbohydrates; NA mg
sodium; 4 g fiber*

Carrots Lyonnaise

Yield: 3 servings

Carrots Lyonnaise is a lovely French creation. I
learned to make it when I was first married and it
became a family favorite. It calls for butter or margarine, but chicken stock makes a very good substitute
and the recipe turns out just as good.

1 large onion, sliced in rings
1 cup plus 3 tablespoons chicken stock (page 24)
3 large carrots
1/16 teaspoon cayenne pepper
1 tablespoon unbleached white flour
2 teaspoons apple juice concentrate

Place the onion rings and 1/2 cup of the chicken
stock in a frying pan. Cover, bring to a boil, and cook
for 8 to 10 minutes over high heat until the onions are
soft.

In the meantime, cut the carrots into thirds, then
cut each section into 4 or 5 long sticks.

Pour 1/2 cup of the chicken stock into a 1-quart
pot, cover, and bring to a boil. Add the carrots, cover,
and cook for about 5 minutes over high heat until the
carrots are tender-crisp.

When the onions are done, sprinkle the cayenne
pepper and flour over them. Stir over medium heat to
blend in the flour. Add the carrots and liquid they were
cooked in plus the remaining 3 tablespoons of chicken
stock and the juice concentrate. Stir until the flour
thickens the liquid and makes a nice sauce for the
carrots and onions. If too thick, add just a little more
chicken stock. Serve immediately.

*Per serving: 70 calories; 3 g protein; 1 g fat; tr saturated fat; tr
cholesterol; 13 g carbohydrates; 30 mg sodium; 3 g fiber*

Cauliflower with Carrot Topping

Yield: 4 servings

If you want a cheesy taste, sprinkle sapsago cheese
over the cauliflower. For fewer servings, use a smaller
pot and half the vegetables.

Water
1 large cauliflower, in florets
1/4 teaspoon dried dill weed (optional)
4 tablespoons finely grated carrot
Sapsago cheese (optional)

Pour about 3/4 inch water into a 5-quart pot, cover,
and bring to a boil. Place the cauliflower pieces in the
boiling water, sprinkle dill weed and the carrot over
the cauliflower. Cover, bring to a boil, and cook for 5
to 8 minutes, until the cauliflower is tender. Serve hot.
Sprinkle a little sapsago cheese over if desired.

*Per serving without cheese: 45 calories; 3 g protein; tr fat; tr
saturated fat; 0 mg cholesterol; 9 g carbohydrates; 25 mg
sodium; 5 g fiber*

Breaded Eggplant

Yield: 6 servings

My mother used to sprinkle sugar over breaded eggplant, but I find sliced bananas cooked under the bread crumb coating make the eggplant moist and sweet on the inside while the bread crumbs are crisp on the outside.

4 slices Pritikin or commercial whole wheat bread
1/8 teaspoon cayenne pepper
1/8 teaspoon garlic powder
1 teaspoon dried parsley
1/4 teaspoon marjoram
1 teaspoon basil
1 large eggplant
2 jumbo egg whites
Skim milk
1 tablespoon whole wheat flour
1-1/2 bananas, sliced

Combine the bread, cayenne pepper, garlic powder, parsley, marjoram, and basil in a food processor and process to make crumbs. Set aside.

Peel and slice the eggplant the long way into 1/8-inch thick slices.

Measure the egg whites and combine with an equal amount of milk; add the flour and mix well. Dip the eggplant slices, one by one, into the egg-milk mixture. Using a fork, pierce the eggplant slices all over while they are in the egg-milk mixture. Remove the eggplant slices and coat with the bread crumbs on one side. Place the slices, coated side down, on a nonstick baking sheet. Coat the banana slices with the egg-milk mixture and arrange them on top of each slice of eggplant. Sprinkle with the remaining bread crumbs. Place on the middle rack of the oven. Set the temperature at 350°F and bake for 30 minutes.

Serve hot as is. If you want to get fancier, serve with heated unsweetened apple sauce. Or if you would rather not have a sweet taste, sprinkle a little red hot sauce over for pizzazz, and/or serve with Horseradish Sauce (page 151).

Per serving: 110 calories; 5 g protein; 1 g fat; tr saturated fat; 0 mg cholesterol; 22 g carbohydrates; 170 mg sodium; 4 g fiber

Green Beans

Yield: 4 servings

Green beans are the hardest vegetable to make flavorful without salt, but I finally hit on this recipe and they come out fine. Be sure to use green beans and not pole beans, which look almost the same, but are tougher and stringier and take longer to cook.

2 cups water
3/4 pound fresh green beans, trimmed
3 celery ribs, coarsely chopped
2 tablespoons dried chopped onions
1/16 teaspoon cayenne pepper

Bring the water to a boil in a covered 5-quart pot. Remove the pot from the heat. Add the beans and celery. Sprinkle the onions and cayenne pepper over the top. Cover and cook over high heat for 4 minutes. Stir. Cover and cook over high heat for 4 to 5 minutes more, or until the vegetables are tender. Serve hot.

Per serving: 15 calories; 1 g protein; tr fat; tr saturated fat; 0 mg cholesterol; 4 g carbohydrates; 30 mg sodium; 1 g fiber

Collards Tchoupitoulas

Yield: 8 servings

Tchoupitoulas was the name of an Indian tribe and is also the name of a street in New Orleans. With all the mispronunciations of street names in New Orleans, believe it or not, this one is pronounced properly by everyone: chop-a-too-las. However, maybe everyone in New Orleans is mispronouncing the word. Still, it is phenomenal that we agree on something. Tchoupitoulas Street runs along the Mississippi River in New Orleans through a neighborhood of people who know the true meaning of collard greens.

1 large onion, chopped
3 cups, more or less, peeled and cubed eggplant
   (1 small or 1/2 large eggplant)
1 medium-size carrot, sliced
2 tablespoons apple juice concentrate
2-1/2 cups plus 1 tablespoon water
1/4 teaspoon cayenne pepper
2 cups water
1 bunch collard greens, chopped (about 2 quarts)
1 large tomato, chopped
Vinegar

Combine the onion, eggplant, carrot, 1 tablespoon of the juice concentrate, and 1 tablespoon of the water in a nonstick 5-quart pot. Sprinkle with 1/8 teaspoon of the cayenne pepper. Turn the heat to high and saute the vegetables by turning them over and over. When the eggplant looks a shade darker, add 2-1/2 cups of water and reduce the heat to low. Cover and let cook while you prepare the greens.

Wash each leaf separately and cut off the stems. Chop the greens and stuff them into the pot. Two quarts of greens is only an approximate figure; use whatever you have. Distribute the chopped tomato over the top. Sprinkle the remaining 1 tablespoon of the juice concentrate over. Sprinkle with remaining 1/8 teaspoon of the cayenne pepper. Cover and cook on high for 15 minutes, or until the greens are just about tender. Watch carefully. Add water if the pot starts to dry out. After the first 15 minutes, stir thoroughly, distributing the eggplant and onions and carrot through the greens. Cover, cook for 5 minutes more over high heat, or a little longer until the greens are tender. Mix again with 2 spoons as if tossing salad.

Serve hot with a sprinkling of wine vinegar or apple cider vinegar. Tabasco sauce is good, too.

Per serving, without vinegar: 40 calories; 1 g protein; tr fat; tr saturated fat; 0 mg cholesterol; 9 g carbohydrates; 15 mg sodium; 3 g fiber

Boiled Potatoes and Cauliflower

Yield: 4 servings

This is an easy way to cook two vegetables at once and save a pot. For variety, add some carrots and/or peas to this, or substitute broccoli for cauliflower, or use both broccoli and cauliflower.

4 medium-size Irish potatoes, peeled and cut in
   halves
Water
1 large cauliflower, in florets

Cover the potatoes with water in a 5-quart pot. Cover and bring to a boil over high heat; cook for 5 minutes. Place the cauliflower over the potatoes. Continue to cook covered for 8 to 10 minutes, or until the potatoes are soft.

Use a slotted spoon to remove the vegetables from the pot. Serve hot.

Per serving: 115 calories; 4 g protein; tr fat; tr saturated fat; 0 mg cholesterol; 26 g carbohydrates; 20 mg sodium; 4 g fiber

Potato Fritters

Yield: 14 fritters

8 medium-size Irish potatoes, peeled
6 tablespoons low-fat cottage cheese
6 tablespoons skim milk
2 tablespoons dried minced onion
1/2 teaspoon dried parsley

Microwave Directions

Place the potatoes in a microwave-proof container. Cover with water. Cook on high for about 25 minutes or longer, until they are soft when pierced with a sharp knife.

Stove Top Directions

Cover the potatoes with water and boil for about 25 minutes, until they are soft when pierced with a sharp knife.

While the potatoes are cooking, combine the cottage cheese and milk in a blender and blend on medium speed until the mixture is free of lumps.

Drain the potatoes and place in a large bowl; add the cottage cheese mixture. Mash the potatoes until they are smooth and fluffy. Add the onion and parsley. Place the potato mixture in the refrigerator for about 2 hours to blend the flavors and to plump the onions.

Make small flat cakes from the potato mixture, about 2-1/2 inches in diameter and 3/4 inch thick. Place 6 or 7 cakes at a time in a nonstick frying pan and cook over high heat to start. When you can see the bottom sides are brown, turn the cakes over and reduce the heat to medium-low. Fry until the second side is brown. Remove to a hot plate and cook the rest of the cakes the same way.

Serve hot. If you like, sprinkle the fritters with a little Crystal hot sauce, Louisiana hot sauce, Tabasco sauce, or lemon juice.

To freeze extra fritters, spray pieces of plastic wrap with a nonstick spray and wrap each fritter individually, spray side against the fritter. Place them in a container and freeze. Reheat frozen fritters in a microwave oven on high or on a nonstick cookie sheet in the oven at 400°F., until the centers are hot.

Per serving: 75 calories; 2 g protein; tr fat; tr saturated fat; tr cholesterol; 16 g carbohydrates; 30 mg sodium; 1 g fiber

Variation

Potato Corn Fritters. Prepare the recipe as above, adding 1/2 cup of frozen whole kernel corn to the potato mixture just before shaping into cakes.

Per serving: 80 calories; 3 g protein; tr fat; tr saturated fat; tr cholesterol; 17 g carbohydrates; 30 mg sodium; 1 g fiber

Summer Vegetable Medley

Yield: 4 servings

1-1/2 cups water
1-1/2 pounds fresh green beans, trimmed
3 celery ribs, coarsely chopped
1 large onion, chopped
1 large tomato, chopped
6 fresh basil leaves, chopped, or 1/4 teaspoon dried basil (optional)

Bring the water to a boil in a covered 5-quart pot. Immediately add the beans, celery, onion, and tomato. Sprinkle the basil over if you like it. Cover and cook over high heat for about 8 minutes, or until the vegetables are tender-crisp. Stir twice while cooking, and watch that the water doesn't boil away. Add a little more water if necessary. Serve hot.

Per serving: 70 calories; 4 g protein; tr fat; tr saturated fat; 0 mg cholesterol; 16 g carbohydrates; 40 mg sodium; 5 g fiber

Sweet Potatoes St. Hilaire

Yield: 5 servings

St. Hilaire is a favorite name in my family—from the hoop-skirt days—it is pronounced "sant eelair." They used to make sweet potatoes that tasted like this dish on Louisiana plantations. A lot of people in Louisiana still do.

It's so nice to know you can get sweet potatoes in a can that don't have sugar or salt added.

2 jumbo egg whites
1-1/4 large over-ripe baked bananas (page 148)
1/4 cup apple juice concentrate
1/16 teaspoon cinnamon
1/16 teaspoon nutmeg
1 (15-1/2-ounce) can sugar-free and salt-free mashed yams or 1-1/2 pounds cooked fresh sweet potatoes
3/4 cup raisins
1 large apple (preferably Granny Smith)

Preheat the oven to 375°F. Spray an 8-inch square baking dish with nonstick spray.

Combine the egg whites, banana, juice concentrate, cinnamon, and nutmeg in a blender. Blend until foamy. Put the sweet potatoes in a bowl and pour the contents of the blender over. Mix. Add the raisins and mix. Peel and core the apple, and slice as you would for apple pie, in nice thick slices. Fold the apple slices into the potato mixture.

Pour the potato mixture into the baking dish. Bake on the middle rack of the oven for 25 minutes. The apple should still be crunchy when done. Serve immediately.

Per serving: 290 calories; 4 g protein; 1 g fat; tr saturated fat; 0 mg cholesterol; 69 g carbohydrates; 45 mg sodium; 7 g fiber

Variation

Sweet Potatoes St. Hilaire with Brandy Topping. Two to three days before making the potatoes, combine 1/4 cup raisins, 1 tablespoon apple juice concentrate, and 1/2 tablespoon brandy in a small container and refrigerate. When the sweet potatoes have baked 20 minutes, pour on the topping and bake for 5 minutes more.

Per serving: 325 calories; 5 g protein; 1 g fat; tr saturated fat; 0 mg cholesterol; 78 g carbohydrates; 50 mg sodium; 7 g fiber

Baby White Squash and Carrots

Yield: 3 servings

Use squash no larger than 2-1/2 inches in diameter. They are very tender—there is no need to peel them.

2 cups water
2 small white scalloped bush squash (patty pan), cut into bite-size pieces
2 medium-size carrots
1/16 teaspoon cayenne pepper
1/4 teaspoon dried basil (optional)

Bring the water to a boil in a covered 1-1/2-quart pot. Immediately add the squash, carrots, and cayenne pepper. Add the basil if you like it. Cook covered at a rapid boil for 5 to 7 minutes or until the vegetables are tender. Save the cooking water for soup.

Per serving: 35 calories; 2 g protein; tr fat; tr saturated fat; 0 mg cholesterol; 8 g carbohydrates; 20 mg sodium; 3 g fiber

Spinach Casserole

Yield: 5 servings

1 (10-ounce) package chopped frozen spinach, defrosted
1/2 cup low-fat cottage cheese
1 cup sliced mushrooms
3 jumbo egg whites
1/4 cup skim milk
1 teaspoon red hot sauce (not Tabasco)
1/4 teaspoon turmeric
2 slices Pritikin or commercial whole wheat bread
1 tablespoon sapsago cheese

In a 1-1/2-quart casserole dish, layer half the spinach, all the cottage cheese, the mushrooms, and then the rest of the spinach.

In a bowl, lightly beat together the egg whites, milk, hot sauce, and turmeric. Pour the egg mixture over the casserole. Push the spinach down wherever it sticks up out of the egg mixture so it is covered. Cover the dish with aluminum foil, pressing it down so it is touching the top of the spinach. Place on the middle rack of the oven and set the temperature at 350°F. Bake for 25 minutes.

While the casserole bakes, break up the bread and combine with the sapsago cheese in a food processor. Process to make bread crumbs.

After 25 minutes, remove the aluminum foil from the casserole and sprinkle the crumb mixture over. Pat it down a little. Continue baking uncovered for 10 minutes. Reduce the temperature to 150°F and let the casserole sit uncovered in the oven for 30 minutes more. Serve hot.

Per serving: 90 calories; 9 g protein; 1 g fat; tr saturated fat; 1 mg cholesterol; 12 g carbohydrates; 290 mg sodium; 3 g fiber

Turnip Greens and Mustard Greens

Yield: 6 servings

The blacks in New Orleans have always mixed turnip greens and mustard greens—the turnip greens for sweetness and the mustards for nipping the tongue. It's a lot of trouble to fix fresh greens, but the texture and taste are so much better than frozen.

1 bunch mustard greens (about 2 quarts chopped)
1 bunch turnip greens (about 2 quarts chopped)
7 cups water
2 tablespoons apple cider or wine vinegar
1/4 teaspoon cayenne pepper

Don't worry about how big the bunches of greens are. This is not an exact science. Wash the greens, leaf by leaf, in a big pan of water. You have to make sure to get rid of all the sand. With kitchen shears, cut off the stems and cut out the big center veins. Then tear the leaves up into small pieces. Pour the water into a roasting pan that is big enough to bake a large turkey. Place over 2 burners, cover, and bring to a boil. Add the greens, sprinkle the vinegar over the leaves, then the cayenne pepper. Cover and cook over high heat for 15 to 20 minutes, or until the vegetables are tender. Stir once while cooking and stir again when the vegetables are cooked. Serve hot. Freeze extra portions.

Per serving: 25 calories; 2 g protein; tr fat; tr saturated fat; 0 mg cholesterol; 5 g carbohydrates; 30 mg sodium; 4 g fiber

Zucchini Squares

Yield: 25 squares

Somewhere between a quiche and a souffle, Zucchini Squares can be prepared ahead and frozen for a party, then reheated.

5 jumbo egg whites
1/4 cup skim milk
1 tablespoon low-sodium baking powder
1/2 cup oat bran
1/2 cup whole wheat flour
1-1/2 cups low-fat cottage cheese
2 tablespoons grated sapsago cheese
1/4 teaspoon cayenne pepper
1/2 teaspoon dried oregano
1 teaspoon dried parsley
1/4 teaspoon dried basil
1/4 teaspoon garlic powder
1 cup cubed zucchini squash
1/3 cup finely chopped onion

Mix all the ingredients in a large bowl, then pour into an 8-inch square nonstick cake pan. Place on the middle rack of the oven. Set the temperature at 400°F. Bake for 35 to 40 minutes, until the top is almost fully brown and a toothpick comes out clean.

Cool in the pan for 10 minutes, then turn out onto a board. Cut into squares with an electric knife or a good serrated knife. Serve at once.

I like to put the squares on a cookie sheet and bake at 400°F for about 10 minutes more to crisp the sides of the squares. These can be reheated, uncovered, one at a time in the microwave for 20 seconds on high. Use more time for more squares. Reheat, uncovered, in the oven on a cookie sheet for about 10 minutes at 300°F.

Per square: 30 calories; 3 g protein; tr fat; tr saturated fat; 1 mg cholesterol; 4 g carbohydrates; 75 mg sodium; 1 g fiber

9

Salads and Dressings

Salads are fun because you don't have to follow the recipes exactly. For example, I don't always specify a variety of lettuce in the recipes because you can use any kind of lettuce you want. Sometimes I don't even know the name of the lettuce I'm using; there are so many kinds, I can't keep track. As far as the calorie count goes, lettuce is so low in calories you don't have to worry if you put a leaf or two more into your salad. The same goes for cucumbers, tomatoes, radishes, cabbage, asparagus, watercress, mushrooms, celery, artichokes, cauliflower, and parsley, to name a few. Do watch the calories with carrots, green peas, and broccoli; they contain more than the first group of vegetables I listed. Celery, broccoli, and artichokes have a bit more sodium than other vegetables.

My husband likes to go in the kitchen after dinner to make himself a snack. To combat that tendency, I usually leave out salad fixings. That way Ray can go wild after he eats his main meal, tearing up lettuce and chopping vegetables in the kitchen.

Chicken Salad

Yield: 4 servings

This chicken salad is as delicious as any you will ever eat.

6 ounces diced cooked white meat chicken (1 to 2 chicken breasts)
1 cup chopped celery
1/2 cup plus 1 teaspoon chopped onion
1/2 cup low-fat cottage cheese
1 teaspoon apple juice concentrate
1/16 teaspoon cayenne pepper
1/16 teaspoon curry powder
1/2 teaspoon red hot sauce (not Tabasco)
Juice of 1/4 large lemon
4 medium-size tomatoes
8 lettuce leaves

In a mixing bowl, combine the chicken, celery, and 1/2 cup of the chopped onion.

In a blender, combine the remaining 1 teaspoon chopped onion, the cottage cheese, juice concentrate, cayenne pepper, curry powder, hot sauce, and lemon juice. Blend until very smooth.

Combine the cottage cheese mixture with the chicken. Refrigerate for at least 20 minutes to mingle the flavors.

Cut across the tomatoes in perpendicular cuts at least 4 times, but do not cut all the way through. Open the tomatoes to look something like a flower. Place the tomatoes on beds of lettuce. Stuff the tomatoes with the chicken salad mixture and serve. There will be 1-1/2 ounces of chicken in each tomato.

Per serving: 145 calories; 17 g protein; 4 g fat; 1 g saturated fat; 39 mg cholesterol; 11 g carbohydrates; 190 mg sodium; 3 g fiber

Chicken Salad Waikiki

Yield: 20 servings

Top

1 (20-ounce) can unsweetened pineapple slices and juice
Reserved juice from 1 (20-ounce) can unsweetened pineapple chunks
2 tablespoons apple juice concentrate
1 envelope unflavored gelatin
6 red seedless grapes

Bottom

16 ounces cooked white meat chicken, diced
1/2 cup chopped onion
1/2 cup chopped celery
1 cup cubed red apple (do not peel)
2 cups canned pineapple juice (not reserved juice from above)
2 tablespoons apple juice concentrate
2 envelopes unflavored gelatin
1-1/2 cups low-fat cottage cheese
1/4 teaspoon cayenne pepper
1 (20-ounce) can unsweetened pineapple chunks (2 cups)
1 banana, sliced
Reserved pineapple rings (for garnish)
More grapes (for garnish)

To make the top layer, drain both cans of pineapple and reserve the juice. You will have 2 cups of juice. Set the pineapple aside. Add the juice concentrate to the 2 cups of pineapple juice. Pour 1/2 cup of the apple-pineapple juice mixture into a 2-cup container and mix in 1 envelope of gelatin to soften it. Heat the remaining juice mixture to the boiling point. Mix the hot juice with the gelatin mixture and stir until all the gelatin is dissolved.

Pour 1-1/4 cups of the gelatin-juice mixture into a 4-quart ring mold or bundt cake pan. Refrigerate for about 40 minutes, until almost solid.

Lay 6 pineapple rings on top of the gelatin, and put a grape inside each pineapple ring hole. Reserve the leftover pineapple rings. Pour the rest of the gelatin mixture over the fruit carefully, so you don't disturb the design. Refrigerate for about 20 minutes, until almost solid. Meanwhile, prepare the bottom of the salad.

To make the bottom of the salad, place the chicken, onion, celery, and apple in a large bowl. Set aside.

Mix the 2 cups canned pineapple juice and the remaining 2 tablespoons of juice concentrate. Pour 1/2 cup of the juice mixture into a 2-cup container; sprinkle 2 envelopes of gelatin over and mix to soften. Heat the rest of the juice to the boiling point. Mix the hot juice with the gelatin mixture until the gelatin dissolves.

Place the cottage cheese, juice-gelatin mixture, and cayenne pepper in a blender. Blend until smooth.

Pour the cottage cheese mixture into the bowl with the chicken. Mix. Add the pineapple chunks and the banana. Let the mixture cool a little, then pour it over the gelled mixture in the ring mold. Refrigerate for at least 4 hours, or overnight.

To unmold, fill a sink with hot water. Hold the mold for just 5 or 6 seconds in the hot water. Put a serving plate on top of the mold and turn it over. If the contents don't fall out, hold the mold in the hot water again, but not for too long. You don't want a melted salad.

For garnish, fill the center with red grapes and pineapple pieces cut from the extra pineapple rings which you will have leftover from the 20-ounce can of unsweetened pineapple rings. Place more red grapes and pineapple chunks around the salad on the plate.

Cut with a serrated knife and serve with a pie server. Be sure to give everyone some grapes.

Per serving without garnish: 120 calories; 11 g protein; 1 g fat; tr saturated fat; 20 mg cholesterol; 17 g carbohydrates; 90 mg sodium; 1 g fiber

Tuna Salad

Yield: 3 servings

The first time I made this, I said to myself, "Why didn't I think of this before?" It turns out just the same as any really good tuna salad and is very simple to make.

1 cup chopped onion
2 celery ribs, chopped medium-coarse
1/2 cup low-fat cottage cheese
1/2 teaspoon apple juice concentrate
1/16 teaspoon cayenne pepper
1/8 teaspoon Tabasco sauce
1/8 teaspoon curry powder (optional)
1 (6-1/2-ounce) can water-packed tuna, drained
1 teaspoon dried parsley or 3 tablespoons chopped
   fresh parsley
3 fresh tomatoes
3/16 teaspoon paprika
12 lettuce leaves
3 lemon wedges

Combine the onions and celery in a bowl and set aside.

Combine the cottage cheese, juice concentrate, cayenne pepper, Tabasco sauce, and curry powder in a blender. Purée until very smooth. Add the cottage cheese mixture to the onion and celery. Add the tuna and parsley and mix well.

To serve, cut 3 tomatoes crisscross almost all the way through 4 times and open the tomatoes to form "stars"; there is no need to dig out the seeds. Arrange the lettuce leaves on 3 salad plates and place a tomato on each plate. Stuff the tuna salad into the tomatoes; sprinkle a little paprika on top. Serve with lemon wedges on the side. Squirt the lemon over the salad, if desired.

Per serving: 160 calories; 24 g protein; 1 g fat; tr saturated fat; 33 mg cholesterol; 14 g carbohydrates; 390 mg sodium; 4 g fiber

Tuna Apple Salad

Yield: 4 servings

1/4 cup finely chopped white onion
1 large Red Delicious apple, cubed (do not peel)
1 banana, sliced
1/2 lemon
1 (6-1/2-ounce) can water-packed tuna, drained
1/2 cup coarsely chopped celery (include no leaves)
8 iceberg lettuce leaves
Apple Dressing (page 120)

Combine the onion, apple, and banana in a medium-size salad bowl. Squeeze the lemon juice over and toss to mix in evenly. Add the tuna and celery and toss everything together.

Arrange beds of lettuce in 4 individual salad bowls and spoon 1 cup of salad on each. Pass the Apple Dressing at the table.

Per salad without dressing: 115 calories; 13 g protein; 1 g fat; tr saturated fat; 23 mg cholesterol; 15 g carbohydrates; 165 mg sodium; 2 g fiber

Sort of Caesar Salad

Yield: 4 servings

8 to 12 Romaine lettuce leaves
2 medium-size tomatoes, sliced
1/2 medium-size onion, sliced in very thin rings
2 slices Pritikin or commercial whole wheat bread
Garlic Green Pepper Dressing (page 117)

Place the lettuce on 4 salad plates, arrange the tomato slices over the lettuce. Place the onion rings over the tomatoes. Trim the crusts off the bread and cut into small squares for untoasted croutons. Sprinkle the croutons over the salads. Pass the Garlic Green Pepper Dressing at the table.

Per salad without dressing: 60 calories; 3 g protein; 1 g fat; tr saturated fat; 0 mg cholesterol; 12 g carbohydrates; 120 mg sodium; 3 g fiber

Fresh Beet Salad

Yield: 2 servings

Canned no-salt beets could be used for this, but the fresh ones are really special.

2 cups torn iceberg lettuce
3 fresh cooked beets (page 101), sliced
1 small white onion, sliced paper thin
Dill Dressing (page 118)

Arrange the lettuce on 2 salad plates. Layer the beets over the lettuce. Top with the onion, then pass the Dill Dressing at the table.

Per serving without dressing: 35 calories; 2 g protein; tr fat; tr saturated fat; 0 mg cholesterol; 8 g carbohydrates; 40 mg sodium; 2 g fiber

Antipasto Salad

Yield: 4 servings

My husband says this salad could be served at Antoine's.

1 (14-1/2-ounce) can cut asparagus, drained and rinsed
2 (4-ounce) jars pimiento pieces and juice
1/2 medium-size onion, sliced in paper-thin rings
1 celery rib, chopped
1/2 large carrot, finely chopped in a food processor
1 cauliflower floret about an inch in diameter, finely chopped in a food processor
3/4 cup Antipasto Dressing (page 119)
12 lettuce leaves
1 cup low-fat cottage cheese
2 tomatoes

Place the asparagus in a 1-1/2-quart bowl. Pour the pimiento juice into the bowl. Cut the pimientos up just a little and add them along with the onion, celery, carrot, and cauliflower. Pour the dressing over and mix well. Marinate the salad for an hour or longer in the refrigerator.

To serve, arrange the lettuce on salad plates. Place 1/4 cup of low-fat cottage cheese on each plate to one side. Put some tomato wedges on the other side. Over the tomatoes, spoon the marinated vegetables. Spoon a little more dressing over the lettuce, if you desire.

Per serving with dressing: 120 calories; 12 g protein; 1 g fat; 1 g saturated fat; 3 mg cholesterol; 18 g carbohydrates; 265 mg sodium; 6 g fiber

Créole Cole Slaw

Yield: About 10 servings

1-1/4 cups shredded cabbage
1 cup grated carrot (1 large carrot)
1/4 cup finely chopped onion
1/2 medium-size green pepper, sliced in thin strips
1/2 large cucumber, peeled and sliced
1/4 cup raisins
6 tablespoons Creamy Créole Dressing (page 119)

Combine the cabbage, carrot, onion, green pepper, cucumber, and raisins in a large salad bowl. Add the dressing and toss to mix thoroughly. Marinate for 2 hours in the refrigerator. Serve well chilled.

Per 1/2-cup serving: 35 calories; 2 g protein; tr fat; tr saturated fat; .5 mg cholesterol; 7 g carbohydrates; 50 mg sodium; 1 g fiber

Hominy Salad

Yield: 4 servings

Hominy (grits *before* it is ground) is really large corn kernels, but it has a much different texture from canned corn. The texture is something like chickpeas.

8 lettuce leaves (Boston lettuce, preferably)
2 medium-size tomatoes, sliced
2 celery ribs, chopped coarsely
1 (15-1/2-ounce) can white hominy (1-1/2 cups), rinsed
1 medium-size white onion, sliced in thin rings
3/4 cup Kiwi Dressing (page 120)

In 4 individual salad bowls, layer first the lettuce, then the sliced tomatoes, then the celery, then 3/8 cup of hominy in each bowl. Top with the onion rings. Pass the Kiwi Dressing at the table.

Per salad without dressing: 162 calories; 4 g protein; 1 g fat; tr saturated fat; 0 mg cholesterol; 35 g carbohydrates; 35 mg sodium; 2 g fiber

Hot German Potato Salad

Yield: 8 servings

A friend of mine from Wisconsin, whose parents came directly from Germany, introduced me to Hot German Potato Salad. In Wisconsin they add hot bacon grease to the vinegar, but I think the Hot and Sour Dressing, without oils or grease, is excellent, in keeping with how this salad is supposed to taste. The salad can be used as a main meal and tastes really terrific with steamed cabbage on the side. Pour a little of the dressing over the hot cabbage.

1-1/2 cups Hot and Sour Dressing (page 119)
1 medium-size onion, sliced in thin rings
2 celery ribs, coarsely chopped
1 (4-ounce) jar pimiento pieces and juice
10 ounces lean ground top round beef or flank steak
2 cups water
1 quart cubed good-size Irish potatoes (4 to 5 potatoes), peeled and diced (1-inch pieces)

Pour the dressing into a bowl. Add the onion, celery, and liquid from the pimientos. Cut up the pimientos in another small bowl and add them. Set aside to marinate.

Brown the ground beef in a nonstick frying pan. Remove the beef to paper towels to drain. Pat the meat with more paper towels. Wipe any grease out of the pan.

Pour the water into the frying pan. Add the potatoes. Cover and cook over high heat for about 20 minutes, until just tender. Drain the potatoes, saving the cooking water to make soup. Add the dressing, onions, celery, meat, and pimientos to the pan, and mix well. Let marinate for about an hour, mixing every now and then.

Serve at room temperature. The leftovers taste good served cold.

Per serving: 165 calories; 12 g protein; 3 g fat; 1 g saturated fat; 29 mg cholesterol; 24 g carbohydrates; 40 mg sodium; 2 g fiber

Eggplant Salad

Yield: 8 servings

3 cups peeled and cubed eggplant (1 very small eggplant)
1 (16-ounce) can peeled no-salt tomatoes
1/2 teaspoon red hot sauce (not Tabasco)
1/4 teaspoon dried basil
1/2 large onion, sliced in rings
1 large carrot, thinly sliced
1 large green pepper, sliced in strips
2 celery ribs, coarsely chopped
1 (15-1/2-ounce) can whole no-salt green beans, drained
1-1/2 teaspoons dried parsley or 3 tablespoons finely chopped fresh parsley
1-1/2 cups Simple Garlic Dressing (page 117)
4 fresh sliced tomatoes (optional)
32 lettuce leaves (optional)

Put the eggplant in a 5-quart soup pot; add the canned tomatoes and juice. Break the tomatoes up with the edge of a spoon. Add the red hot sauce and basil. Cover, bring to a boil, and cook over medium heat for about 10 minutes, or until the eggplant is just tender, but will hold its shape. Uncover and remove from the heat to cool.

Meanwhile, combine the onion, carrots, green pepper, celery, green beans, and parsley in a salad bowl. Add the eggplant mixture. Pour the dressing over and mix. Let the salad marinate in the refrigerator for at least an hour.

Serve over fresh tomato slices and lettuce if desired. If you are serving this at a buffet dinner, serve it directly out of a salad bowl, without the lettuce and tomato.

Per serving with lettuce and tomato slices: 80 calories; 3 g protein; 1 g fat; tr saturated fat; 0 mg cholesterol; 18 g carbohydrates; 35 mg sodium; 5 g fiber

Christmas Salad

Yield: 6 servings

This salad is pretty for the holidays, and it can be made as much as 4 hours ahead. It's a layered salad with a topping of Creamy Dill Dressing, decorated on top with pimientos and green peppers. To make this for a large crowd or for a bring-a-dish affair, just double the ingredients and use a 9-inch by 13-inch casserole dish.

1/4 head iceberg lettuce, shredded and chopped
1 medium-size tomato, chopped
1/2 medium-size onion, sliced in rings
2/3 cup frozen green peas
2/3 cup frozen whole kernel corn, cooked and cooled
1-1/3 cups Creamy Dill Dressing (page 118)
1 green pepper, sliced
1 (4-ounce) jar pimientos, chopped or sliced

On the bottom of an 8-inch square baking dish or some similar container, layer the lettuce first. Sprinkle the tomatoes over, then the onion rings. Next sprinkle the peas over, and then the corn. Pour the dressing over the salad and spread it evenly. Place the green pepper slices decoratively on top. Place the pimientos, as many as you like, decoratively on top, between, and/or on top of the green pepper slices. Refrigerate.

Serve when you are ready. Do not leave this salad in the refrigerator overnight, though, because the dressing will liquefy and sink into the rest of the salad.

Per serving: 80 calories; 7 g protein; 1 g fat; tr saturated fat; 2 mg cholesterol; 13 g carbohydrates; 180 mg sodium; 3 g fiber

Salade la Mer

Yield: 6 servings

Many people say sheepshead, a large fish caught all up and down the Atlantic coast, tastes like crabmeat in a salad. It does, sort of, and is very good for making salad, so I called this Salade la Mer, or loosely translated, seafood salad. You start with a whole poached sheepshead (be sure to leave the head on). You could try this with any fish that has flaky white meat.

2-1/2-pound Poached Sheepshead (page 74)
1 small onion, finely chopped
1 celery rib, chopped
2 cooked celery ribs from the poaching liquid, chopped
1/4 cup cooked onion from the poaching liquid, finely chopped
1/2 cup Creamy Onion Dressing (page 118)
1/4 teaspoon Tabasco sauce
12 lettuce leaves, torn
3 tomatoes, sliced

After the sheepshead has marinated and cooled in the poaching liquid, remove it to a platter. Pick the meat off the fish and place it in a salad bowl. As you pick the meat, feel it carefully to remove all the bones and possible scales. Pick the white meat out of the head, too. It has the most flavor. Discard the bones and head when finished. You should have about 14 ounces of meat. Add both the uncooked and cooked onions and celery. Combine the Creamy Onion Dressing with the Tabasco and then combine it with the fish mixture. Refrigerate for at least 3 hours, preferably overnight.

Serve the Salade la Mer on top of a bed of lettuce and sliced tomatoes on 6 individual salad plates.

Per serving: 100 calories; 17 g protein; 1 g fat; tr saturated fat; 35 mg cholesterol; 6 g carbohydrates; 160 mg sodium; 2 g fiber

Tomato Aspic

Yield: 2-1/2 cups

2 (16-ounce) cans no-salt tomato sauce
1 celery rib, cut in large pieces
1 teaspoon crumbled thyme
1 bay leaf
1 teaspoon onion powder
1/4 teaspoon garlic powder
1/2 teaspoon dried basil
1 teaspoon red hot sauce (not Tabasco)
1 teaspoon dried parsley
1/16 teaspoon dried red pepper flakes
2-1/2 tablespoons apple juice concentrate
Juice of two lemons
2 envelopes unflavored gelatin

Microwave Directions

Combine the tomato sauce, celery, thyme, bay leaf, onion powder, garlic powder, basil, red hot sauce, parsley, red pepper flakes, and juice concentrate in a 2-quart microwave bowl. Cover and cook at 50% power for 35 minutes, stirring twice.

Stove Top Directions

Combine the tomato sauce, celery, thyme, bay leaf, onion powder, garlic powder, basil, red hot sauce, parsley, red pepper flakes, and juice concentrate in a 2-quart saucepan. Cover and cook over low heat for 30 minutes, stirring frequently. Remove from the heat.

Remove the celery and bay leaf. Add the lemon juice, then sprinkle the gelatin over the top and work it in with a spoon until well dissolved. Pour into a 1-quart mold and chill until firm, 3 to 4 hours. Serve alongside meat or fish.

Per tablespoon: 15 calories; 1 g protein; tr fat; tr saturated fat; 0 mg cholesterol; 3 g carbohydrates; 10 mg sodium; 1 g fiber

Simple Garlic Dressing

Yield: 1-1/2 cups

1 cup apple cider vinegar
1/4 cup water
1/4 cup apple juice concentrate
1/8 teaspoon cayenne pepper
1/4 teaspoon garlic powder

Combine all the ingredients in a pint jar and shake. Use immediately. Leftovers will keep well for several days in the refrigerator.

Per tablespoon: 6 calories; tr protein; tr fat; tr saturated fat; 0 mg cholesterol; 2 g carbohydrates; tr sodium; tr fiber

Garlic Green Pepper Dressing

Yield: 1-3/4 cups

I like to use the frozen chopped green peppers in this because they are soft when they defrost, which is right for the consistency of this dressing.

1 garlic clove
2 tablespoons low-fat cottage cheese
1 cup apple cider vinegar
1/4 cup water
1/4 cup apple juice concentrate
1/4 cup frozen chopped green pepper
1/8 teaspoon cayenne pepper
2 jumbo egg whites

Combine the garlic, cottage cheese, vinegar, water, juice concentrate, green pepper, and cayenne pepper in a blender and process briefly on a slow speed. Do not chop up too much. You want to see pieces of green pepper.

Put the eggs into rapidly boiling water for 3 minutes. Remove and cool. Crack the eggs and carefully remove the yellows. Scrape the whites into the blender with the rest of the dressing. Blend on a low speed for 1 second—I just touch the blender button and stop it immediately. You want to see pieces of egg white. Pour over the salad immediately. Leftovers will keep in the refrigerator for about 4 days.

Per tablespoon: 8 calories; tr protein; tr fat; tr saturated fat; tr cholesterol; 2 g carbohydrates; 10 mg sodium; tr fiber

Mustard Seed Dressing

Yield: 2 cups (32 tablespoons)

1 cup apple cider vinegar
1/4 cup water
1/4 cup apple juice concentrate
1/4 cup low-fat cottage cheese
1/8 teaspoon cayenne pepper
3 teaspoons mustard seeds

Combine the vinegar, water, juice concentrate, cottage cheese, cayenne pepper, and 2 teaspoons of the mustard seeds in a blender. Blend on high until the mixture looks smooth. Pour into a pint jar and add the remaining 1 teaspoon mustard seeds. Shake well before using. Pour over the salad immediately. Leftovers should keep well in the refrigerator for several days.

Per tablespoon: 10 calories; tr protein; tr fat; tr saturated fat; tr cholesterol; 2 g carbohydrates; 10 mg sodium; tr fiber

Dill Dressing

Yield: 1 cup

1/2 cup apple cider vinegar
1/2 cup water
1/2 teaspoon dried dill weed
1/2 teaspoon garlic powder
1/16 teaspoon cayenne pepper
1/2 tablespoon dried onion flakes
2 tablespoons apple juice concentrate

Combine all the ingredients in a salad dressing bottle, shake, and let sit in the refrigerator for at least 1 hour. Shake well before serving. Leftovers keep well in the refrigerator for several days.

Per tablespoon: 5 calories; tr protein; tr fat; tr saturated fat; 0 mg cholesterol; 2 g carbohydrates; 1 mg sodium; tr fiber

Creamy Dill Dressing

Yield: 1-1/3 cups

2 tablespoons skim milk
1 cup low-fat cottage cheese
2 tablespoons apple juice concentrate
2 tablespoons finely chopped onion
1/16 teaspoon cayenne pepper
1/4 teaspoon dillweed

Combine all the ingredients in a blender or food processor and blend on medium speed until smooth. Use immediately. Leftovers will keep for about a day in the refrigerator.

Per tablespoon: 12 calories; 1 g protein; tr fat; tr saturated fat; .5 mg cholesterol; 1 g carbohydrates; 45 mg sodium; tr fiber

Creamy Onion Dressing

Yield: About 1/2 cup

1/2 cup low-fat cottage cheese
1 teaspoon finely chopped onion
1 teaspoon apple juice concentrate

Combine all the ingredients in a blender or food processor and blend or process until smooth. Use immediately.

Per tablespoon: 12 calories; 2 g protein; tr fat; tr saturated fat; tr cholesterol; 1 g carbohydrates; 60 mg sodium; tr fiber

Chive Dressing

Yield: About 1 cup

1/2 cup apple cider vinegar
1/2 cup water
2 tablespoons apple juice concentrate
1/4 teaspoon garlic powder
1/16 teaspoon cayenne pepper
1 tablespoon dried chives

Combine all the ingredients in a salad dressing bottle. Shake well, let the dressing sit for several hours in the refrigerator, then serve over salad. Shake before each serving. Leftovers will keep well in the refrigerator for several days.

Per tablespoon: 5 calories; tr protein; tr fat; tr saturated fat; 0 mg cholesterol; 1 g carbohydrates; tr sodium; tr fiber

Creamy Créole Dressing

Yield: 3/4 cup

1/2 cup low-fat cottage cheese
4 teaspoons apple juice concentrate
1 teaspoon red hot sauce (not Tabasco)
2 tablespoons apple cider vinegar
1/4 teaspoon garlic powder
1/16 teaspoon cayenne pepper

Combine all the ingredients in a blender and process until very smooth. Use immediately, or within an hour or so. This dressing doesn't keep its texture well. You can store it for a maximum of 2 days in the refrigerator.

Per tablespoon: 11 calories; 1 g protein; tr fat; tr saturated fat; tr cholesterol; 1 g carbohydrates; 40 mg sodium; tr fiber

Hot and Sour Dressing

Yield: 1-1/2 cups

1 cup apple cider vinegar
1/4 cup water
1/4 cup apple juice concentrate
2 teaspoons red hot sauce (not Tabasco)

Combine all the ingredients in a pint jar. Use immediately. Leftovers will keep well in the refrigerator for several days.

Per tablespoon: 6 calories; tr protein; tr fat; tr saturated fat; 0 mg cholesterol; 2 g carbohydrates; tr sodium; tr fiber

Antipasto Dressing

Yield: 1-1/3 cups

1/2 cup apple cider vinegar
2 tablespoons apple juice concentrate
3/4 cup water
1/16 teaspoon cayenne pepper
1/2 teaspoon garlic powder
1/8 teaspoon dried basil
1/4 teaspoon dried oregano
1/16 teaspoon cumin
1/2 teaspoon onion powder
1/2 teaspoon coriander seeds

Combine all the ingredients in a blender and set on high, or liquefy. Blend until the coriander seeds are pulverized. Use immediately. Leftover dressing will keep well for several days in the refrigerator.

Per tablespoon: 4 calories; tr protein; tr fat; tr saturated fat; 0 mg cholesterol; 1 g carbohydrates; tr sodium; tr fiber

Kiwi Dressing

Yield: 3/4 cup

This dressing is delicious on fruit salad and over any type of tomato salad. I like to pour this over banana slices, too.

1 tablespoon cornstarch
1/4 cup water
1/4 cup apple juice concentrate
1/4 cup apple cider vinegar
1 kiwi

In a small saucepan, mix the cornstarch, water, juice concentrate, and vinegar until there are no more lumps in the cornstarch. Turn the heat on high and stir constantly until the mixture has thickened and looks almost transparent. Let the mixture bubble and cook, stirring all the time, for about 25 seconds more to make sure the cornstarch is fully cooked. Remove from the stove and leave the pan at room temperature for about 10 minutes.

In the meantime, cut the kiwi in half and scoop the pulp out into a blender. Pour the cornstarch mixture into the blender with the kiwi and blend until smooth.

Use immediately. Leftovers don't keep well.

Per tablespoon: 16 calories; tr protein; tr fat; tr saturated fat; 0 mg cholesterol; 4 g carbohydrates; tr sodium; tr fiber

Apple Dressing

Yield: 1 cup

1 tablespoon cornstarch
1/4 cup water
1/4 cup apple juice concentrate
1/4 cup apple cider vinegar
1/2 large Red Delicious apple, peeled and quartered
Lemon juice
1/16 teaspoon dry mustard
1/16 teaspoon curry powder
1/16 teaspoon celery seeds
1/8 teaspoon cayenne pepper or to taste

Combine the cornstarch, water, juice concentrate, and vinegar in a saucepan, mixing until the cornstarch is dissolved. Cook over high heat, stirring constantly. Nothing will happen for a while, but then you will start to see what looks like lumps forming. Continue to stir. The mixture will begin to thicken up and become almost transparent. Keep stirring until the mixture bubbles; cook for about a minute more, stirring all the time. Remove the mixture from the heat and cool for about 10 minutes.

Peel and cut up the apple; then rub the pieces with lemon juice. Combine the apple pieces in a blender with the mustard, curry powder, celery seeds, and cayenne pepper. Add the cornstarch mixture. Blend on medium speed until the mixture is liquefied.

Serve immediately over Tuna Apple Salad (page 112) or any fruit salad. Leftovers do not keep well.

Per tablespoon: 15 calories; tr protein; tr fat; tr saturated fat; 0 mg cholesterol; 4 g carbohydrates; tr sodium; tr fiber

10

Cooking with Grains

How about a slice of Banana Bread (page 124) spread with Cherry Preserves (page 154) for breakfast? Now, who would have thought that, on a salt-free, sugar-free, fat-free diet, you could have goodies like that? And they actually taste delicious!

I know. Sometimes you buy items in health food stores and you think they are going to be sweet and they aren't, which is surprising because the bakers probably had the advantage of adding honey or molasses. They even use oils or fats of some kind, and nuts.

You don't need honey or molasses or fat to make banana bread taste good. It's wonderful with just the sweetness and moistness of bananas and apple juice concentrate.

You will be amazed at how inventive you can be when making muffins by adding different fruits. What's nice is that you can make big batches of muffins, pancakes, and breads, and freeze them so you don't have to be up early every morning, scrambling around in the kitchen when you should be getting ready for work or school, or whatever else you may have to do.

Banana Bran Muffins

Yield: 12 muffins

2-1/2 cups oat bran
1 teaspoon baking soda
2 teaspoons low-sodium baking powder
1-1/4 cups plus 2 tablespoons apple juice concentrate
2 jumbo egg whites, slightly beaten
2 medium-size to large very ripe bananas

Preheat the oven to 400°F. Spray full-size nonstick muffin pans with nonstick spray.

Combine the oat bran, baking soda, and baking powder in a large mixing bowl. Add the juice concentrate and egg whites. Mix thoroughly. Slice the bananas into 1/4-inch slices and add them. Spoon the mixture into the muffin cups, making sure each muffin will have some banana slices. Bake on the middle rack of the oven for 15 to 20 minutes, until golden brown and not too dark around the edges. Remove the muffins from the oven and let them cool in the pans for 10 minutes. Remove the muffins to a wire rack to cool completely, if desired, or eat piping hot.

Freeze extras in a plastic bag.

Per muffin: 100 calories; 4 g protein; 2 g fat; tr saturated fat; 0 mg cholesterol; 30 g carbohydrates; 85 mg sodium; 4 g fiber

Variation

Banana Bran Blueberry Muffins. Prepare exactly as Banana Bran Muffins, but add 1 cup of unsweetened frozen or fresh blueberries when you add the banana slices. Yummy!

Per muffin: 110 calories; 4 g protein; 2 g fat; tr saturated fat; 0 mg cholesterol; 33 g carbohydrates; 90 mg sodium; 4 g fiber

Pineapple-Blueberry Bran Muffins

Yield: 12 muffins

The first time I made these, I gave four to my friend Margie. She was going to her exercise class to meet our mutual friend Gerry. Margie was supposed to have two and give Gerry two. I asked Gerry later how she liked them. Gerry knew nothing about them. Margie fessed up. Gerry wasn't at exercise class that day, so guess what happened to the muffins.

2-1/2 cups oat bran
1 tablespoon low-sodium baking powder
4 jumbo egg whites, beaten lightly
1 cup pineapple juice concentrate
1 (20-ounce) can crushed unsweetened pineapple, drained
1/2 cup frozen or fresh blueberries

Preheat the oven to 425°F. Spray full-size muffin pans with nonstick spray, even if they are nonstick pans.

Mix together the oat bran and baking powder. Add the egg whites and pineapple juice concentrate. Add the pineapple and blueberries and mix well. Spoon the mixture into the cups. Bake on the middle rack of the oven for about 20 minutes, until brown bumps appear on top. If you wait until the muffins are totally brown on top, they will be burned on the bottom. Cool in the pan for about 10 minutes before turning out on a wire rack to cool completely.

Freeze in a plastic bag if you like. They are good reheated in a microwave oven.

Per muffin: 110 calories; 5 g protein; 1 g fat; tr saturated fat; 0 mg cholesterol; 32 g carbohydrates; 20 mg sodium; 4 g fiber

Bran-Cherry Muffins

Yield: 36 miniature muffins

Sometimes you get a break and can use a commercially prepared product. These moist and delicious oat bran muffins contain black cherry all-fruit preserves that you can buy in most health food stores and many groceries. Polaner is the brand I used to create this recipe.

2-1/2 cups oat bran
1 tablespoon low-sodium baking powder
4 jumbo egg whites, slightly beaten
1 (10-ounce) jar or 1 cup black cherry all-fruit preserves
6 tablespoons apple juice concentrate

Preheat the oven to 425°F. Spray 3 nonstick miniature muffin tins (12 cups each) with nonstick spray.

Mix together the oat bran and baking powder. Add the eggs, preserves, and juice concentrate. Mix well. Fill each muffin cup almost to the top. Place the tins on the middle rack of the oven. Bake for 10 to 12 minutes. When you see the muffins getting brown around the edges, remove them from the oven. Cool the muffins in the pan for about 10 minutes before turning them out onto wire racks to cool completely.

Refrigerate or freeze in a plastic bag or covered container.

Per muffin: 18 calories; 2 g protein; tr fat; tr saturated fat; 0 mg cholesterol; 6 g carbohydrates; 10 mg sodium; 1 g fiber

Pumpkin Muffins

Yield: 18 muffins

These are great for breakfast along with herb tea and skim milk. And surprise!—the centers are soft, like pumpkin pie. Just think how nice these would be on the Thanksgiving dinner table, too.

I like to use Granny Smith apples best because they give the muffins a special apple pie taste. But I've made them with Delicious apples when I couldn't find Granny Smiths, and they still came out wonderful.

1/4 cup oat bran
1-1/2 cups whole wheat flour
1/8 teaspoon cinnamon
1/8 teaspoon allspice
1/8 teaspoon mace
1 tablespoon low-sodium baking powder
2 jumbo egg whites, lightly beaten
2 cups unsweetened canned pumpkin or
  1 (16-ounce) can
1 large baked banana (page 148)
Approximately 1 cup apple juice concentrate
1 Granny Smith apple, peeled and sliced in chunks
1/2 cup raisins

Spray 18 full-size muffin cups with nonstick spray.

In a large bowl, combine the oat bran, flour, cinnamon, allspice, mace, and baking powder. Mix in the egg whites and pumpkin.

Beat the baked banana and its baking juices with a fork; pour it into a 2-cup measure. Add enough juice concentrate to come up to the 1-1/2-cup line. Add the mixture to the bowl. Add the apples and raisins. Mix well. Spoon the mixture into the muffin cups, filling each 3/4 full. Place the tins on the middle rack of the oven and bake for 35 minutes at 400°F, or until the muffins are just starting to get dark bumps on top. Since they are soft, cool them in the pans.

Per muffin: 100 calories; 3 g protein; tr fat; tr saturated fat; 0 mg cholesterol; 23 g carbohydrates; 10 mg sodium; 3 g fiber

Banana Bread

Yield: 16 slices

This is so nice and sweet it can be served as a dessert along with herb tea.

2 cups whole wheat flour
2 teaspoons low-sodium baking powder
1 teaspoon baking soda
1/2 large baked banana (page 148)
Approximately 3/4 cup apple juice concentrate
2 to 3 medium-size very ripe bananas, mashed
  (1 cup)
4 jumbo egg whites, beaten until almost foamy

Preheat the oven to 350°F. Spray a 9-1/4-inch by 5-1/4-inch by 3-inch bread pan with nonstick spray, even if it is a nonstick pan.

Sift the flour into a large bowl, and add the whole wheat kernels you will see left behind in the sifter. Add the baking powder and baking soda. Mix well.

Pour the baked banana and its baking juices into a 1-cup measure. Add enough apple juice concentrate to come up to the 1-cup line. Mix the baked banana and juice concentrate. Pour the mixture into the bowl with the flour. Add the mashed bananas and the egg whites. Blend the ingredients with a spoon until they are wet, then beat with an electric mixer for about 2 minutes until the mixture is smooth. Pour the batter into the pan and place on the middle rack of the oven. Bake for 1 hour, or until a toothpick inserted into the center comes out clean. Cool in the pan for 10 minutes, loosen around the edges with a rubber spatula, then turn onto a wire rack to cool completely. For best results, slice with an electric knife or a bread knife.

Per 1-slice serving: 95 calories; 3 g protein; tr fat; tr saturated fat; 0 mg cholesterol; 21 g carbohydrates; 70 mg sodium; 3 g fiber

Cranberry Bread

Yield: 16 slices

My friend and neighbor, Peggy Stanford, gave me her grandmother's recipe for cranberry bread, which I adapted to follow the no-salt, no-sugar, no-fat guidelines. After I tasted this bread, I had to agree that she certainly knows her cranberries. It really is a taste sensation. You wouldn't believe cranberries could taste this good.

1-1/2 cups coarsely chopped fresh or frozen cranberries
1 cup oat bran
1 cup whole wheat flour
1-1/2 teaspoons low-sodium baking powder
1/2 teaspoon baking soda
2 jumbo egg whites, lightly beaten
1/3 cup orange juice concentrate
3/4 cup apple juice concentrate
1 teaspoon finely chopped grapefruit zest

Spray a 9-1/4-inch by 5-1/4-inch by 3-inch non-stick bread pan with nonstick spray.

In the food processor, chop the cranberries very coarsely, leaving some whole. Set aside.

Combine the oat bran, flour, baking powder, and baking soda. Add the eggs, the 2 concentrates, and grapefruit zest, and mix well. Add the cranberries. Pack the mixture into the bread pan. Shake the pan from side to side to even out the batter. Place the pan in the oven and set the temperature at 350°F. Bake for 1 hour.

Remove the pan to a wire rack for 10 minutes. Turn out onto a wire rack to cool.

Per 1-slice serving without grapefruit zest: 70 calories; 3 g protein; 1 g fat; tr saturated fat; 0 mg cholesterol; 18 g carbohydrates; 40 mg sodium; 2 g fiber. Nutritive value of grapefruit zest not available.

Granny's Raisin Bread

Yield: 16 slices

The Granny Smith apples in this give it an apple pie taste.

1-1/2 cups unbleached white flour
1/4 cup oat bran
1 tablespoon low-sodium baking powder
1/4 teaspoon cinnamon
2 jumbo egg whites
1-1/4 cups apple juice concentrate
1 Granny Smith apple, peeled and sliced
1 cup raisins

Preheat the oven to 325°F. Spray a 9-1/4-inch by 5-1/4-inch by 3-inch bread pan with nonstick spray.

In a large mixing bowl, combine the flour, oat bran, baking powder, and cinnamon. Mix in the egg whites, juice concentrate, and apple slices. Add the raisins last and mix well. Pour the batter into the pan and place on the middle rack of the oven. Bake for 1 hour and 20 minutes. Cool in the pan for about 10 minutes. Then loosen around the edges with a spatula and turn out onto a wire rack to cool. Cut with an electric knife or a bread knife.

Per 1-slice serving: 120 calories; 2 g protein; tr fat; tr saturated fat; 0 mg cholesterol; 29 g carbohydrates; 15 mg sodium; 1 g fiber

Muriel's Soft-Centered Spoon Bread

Yield: 5 servings

My cousin Muriel told me about this wonderful tasting bread and gave me her recipe. The bread is almost like a pudding in the center, and a bit crispy on the outside. It tastes very good just by itself, along with some herb tea, or even better, with all-fruit orange, cherry, or grape preserve. Another way to eat it is to put the bread in a bowl with some sliced banana and/or strawberries, then pour a little hot skim milk over. It is also wonderful for sopping up the gravy alongside hot roast beef. Corn tortilla meal (sometimes called masa harina) is a finely ground cornmeal. Don't try regular ground cornmeal, it won't work.

1/2 cup corn tortilla meal
1/4 cup whole wheat flour
1 teaspoon low-sodium baking powder
2 jumbo egg whites
1/4 baked banana (page 148)
3 tablespoons apple juice concentrate
1 cup skim milk

Spray an 8-inch square nonstick baking pan with nonstick spray. Combine the tortilla meal, flour, and baking powder. Set aside.

Beat the egg whites with an electric mixer until they are very frothy. In another small container, beat the banana and its baking liquid together with the juice concentrate. Pour the eggs and the juice mixture into the tortilla meal mixture. Add 1/2 cup of the milk. Beat on high speed with an electric mixer for 2-1/2 minutes until the batter is very smooth. Pour the batter into the pan and shake it back and forth a little to even it out. Place on the middle rack of the oven. In order not to disturb the surface of the batter, reach in and slowly pour the remaining 1/2 cup of milk evenly over the top. Set the oven temperature at 375°F and bake for 25 to 30 minutes, until you see the paper thin edges curling up and getting medium brown.

Per serving: 110 calories; 5 g protein; tr fat; tr saturated fat; 1 mg cholesterol; 21 g carbohydrates; 50 mg sodium; 2 g fiber

Corn Bread

Yield: 16 servings

This is delicious along with cooked beans, or with any dish containing gravy. It's also very good spread with all-fruit preserves or with Blueberry Preserves (page 154).

2 cups yellow cornmeal
1 tablespoon low-sodium baking powder
1/2 very large baked banana (page 148)
Approximately 1/4 cup apple juice concentrate
4 jumbo egg whites, lightly beaten
1 cup water

Preheat the oven to 400°F. Spray a nonstick 8-inch square baking pan or an 8-inch square baking dish with nonstick spray.

Combine the cornmeal and baking powder in a mixing bowl. Pour the baked banana and its baking juices into a 1-cup measure. Add enough apple juice concentrate to make 2 cups. Add the egg whites, water, banana, and juice concentrate to the cornmeal mixture. Mix very well. Pour into the baking pan or dish. Shake the pan from side to side a few times to even out the batter. Place the pan on the top shelf of the oven and bake for 30 to 35 minutes, or until the top is golden brown and a toothpick inserted into the center comes out clean. There is no need to cool. Serve directly from the pan in 2-inch squares.

Per 1-square serving: 80 calories; 2 g protein; tr fat; tr saturated fat; 0 mg cholesterol; 16 g carbohydrates; 15 mg sodium; 1 g fiber

Doctor Vanselow's Rye Bread

Yield: 32 servings

When I was a judge for the New Orleans Dietetic Association's 3rd Annual Culinary Heart's Cookoff in New Orleans, Dr. Neal Vanselow, Chancellor of Tulane University Medical School, was also a judge. I sat next to him and his wife, Mary. Dr. Vanselow said he loved to bake yeast breads, rye being one of his favorites. He said the secret to achieving a good-textured rye bread is to use medium-ground rye flour. If you use stone-ground, the bread will be too heavy. Mary was kind enough to send me her husband's recipe. I adapted it slightly by changing honey to apple juice concentrate, but basically, this is Dr. Vanselow's rye bread.

Where do you find medium-ground rye flour? Mary said she buys it in New Orleans at a bakery called Your Daily Bread on St. Charles between Broadway and Carrollton, and that's where I bought mine. They sold me a pound out of their own big barrel.

Of course, I know if you live in California, that information doesn't help much. Look for it at health food stores first, and if you can't find medium-ground, start calling the bakeries that specialize in bread and they might have it and sell you a little.

2 (12-ounce) bottles of alcoholic or nonalcoholic beer
1/4 cup apple juice concentrate
2 envelopes or 2 tablespoons dry baker's yeast
3-1/8 to 3-1/4 cups unbleached bromated bread flour
1 tablespoon caraway seeds
2 cups medium-ground rye flour

Bring the beer to a boil, reduce the heat, and simmer for 5 minutes. Pour 2 cups of the beer into a large mixing bowl and discard the rest. Add the apple juice concentrate. Cool the mixture until it is just warm, not hot, to the touch. Sprinkle the yeast over the mixture and mix it in until it is dissolved. Put the bowl in a warm place for about 5 minutes or until the mixture looks foamy.

Using a wire whisk or fork, beat in 2 cups of the bread flour until smooth. Add the caraway seeds and mix well. Add the rye flour and mix thoroughly. Gradually work in the remaining flour, adding only enough to form a sticky but workable dough.

When the dough forms a ball, knead briefly in the bowl. Turn the dough out on a lightly floured surface and knead for about 3 minutes, dusting with bread flour when it gets sticky. It's ready when you poke the dough with your finger and the dough bounces back.

Return the dough to the mixing bowl. Spray a piece of plastic wrap with nonstick spray and place it loosely, spray side down, over the dough. Let the dough stand in a warm place until it has doubled in volume, about 1 hour.

Turn the dough out on a lightly floured surface and knead lightly for about 1 minute.

Divide the dough in half and form into 2 long, narrow loaves. Spray either nonstick French bread pans or nonstick baking sheets with nonstick spray. Place the loaves in the French bread pans or diagonally on the baking sheets. Spray plastic wrap with nonstick spray and place the pieces of wrap loosely, spray side down, over the loaves. Place the loaves in a warm place for about 45 minutes until they are doubled in volume. Preheat the oven to 375°F.

Place the pans on the middle and top racks of the oven and bake for 25 to 35 minutes. The loaves are done when they are lightly brown on both top and bottom, and they sound hollow when tapped. Cool on wire racks. Cut with an electric knife or a bread knife.

Per 1-slice serving: 85 calories; 2 g protein; tr fat; tr saturated fat; 0 mg cholesterol; 17 g carbohydrates; 5 mg sodium; 2 g fiber

Onion Rolls

Yield: 17 rolls

These rolls taste very good if you have some roast beef or chicken gravy to dunk them in. I also eat these just as is, as a spicy snack along with hot herb tea.

1/4 cup apple juice concentrate
1-1/4 cups warm water
1 package or 1 tablespoon dry baker's yeast
3-1/2 cups unbleached bromated bread flour
1/2 cup oat bran
1 teaspoon red hot sauce (not Tabasco)
1/4 cup dried minced onions
1/4 teaspoon dried red pepper flakes

Combine the juice concentrate and water. Add the yeast and stir until it dissolves. Put in a warm place for 5 to 10 minutes, or until the top looks foamy.

Combine the flour and oat bran in a food processor fitted with a plastic dough blade. Add the hot sauce to the yeast mixture, then pour that mixture, all at once, into the food processor, and process until the dough is formed. If the mixture seems dry and won't form a ball, add up to 1/4 cup water, a little at a time, until the mixture is moist and forms a ball.

Flour a large board very lightly if the dough is sticky and turn the dough onto it. Flatten the dough out and sprinkle on about 1/3 of the onion and red pepper flakes. Fold the dough, working the onions and red pepper flakes into it. Flatten the dough again, and add more onions and red pepper flakes. Repeat a few times until all the onions and red pepper flakes are folded in and well blended.

If you don't have a food processor, mix the dough in a bowl. If the dough does not pick up all the flour and oat bran, add up to 1/4 cup warm water. Flour a wooden board only if the dough is very sticky and knead the dough until it is elastic and smooth. When the dough is pretty smooth, start adding in the onions and red pepper flakes and work them in. Kneading should take about 10 minutes. The dough should bounce back when you poke it with your finger.

Dust the inside of a zippered plastic bag with flour and place the dough inside. Squeeze out all the air and zip tightly. Set the dough in a warm place to rise until double in bulk, about 1-1/2 hours.

Open the bag and place it on the counter. Beat on it until the dough is all punched down and flat. Break off pieces of the dough about the size of golf balls and roll between your palms to form balls. Place them about 2 inches apart on a large nonstick cookie sheet or regular cookie sheet that has been sprayed with nonstick spray. Set the cookie sheet, uncovered, in a warm spot for about 20 minutes, until the rolls have doubled in size. Preheat the oven to 450°F.

Bake for 15 minutes. Check after 10 minutes. When the rolls look brown, they are done. Cool on the cookie sheet.

You can freeze extras in plastic bags. Defrost at room temperature, or pop in the microwave oven on high for about 20 seconds, or place in a preheated 450°F oven for 4 to 5 minutes.

Per roll: 110 calories; 3 g protein; tr fat; tr saturated fat; 0 mg cholesterol; 24 g carbohydrates; tr sodium; 1 g fiber

Rice and Bran Pancakes

Yield: 16 pancakes

Rice bran as well as oat bran is good for getting bulk into your system, and for reducing cholesterol. I combined the two in these pancakes. I used instant brown rice which, of course, still has the bran on it. For a topping you can use Blueberry Preserves or Cherry Preserves (page 154).

1 cup instant brown rice
1/2 cup oat bran
1 tablespoon low-sodium baking powder
1/2 cup unbleached white flour
2-1/2 cups skim milk
2 jumbo egg whites, lightly beaten
2 bananas, sliced

Put the rice in a food processor fitted with a steel blade. Turn it on and process it while you get the other ingredients ready.

Combine the oat bran and baking powder in a large mixing bowl. Sift in the flour. When the rice is finely ground and has the texture of a gritty flour, add it to the bowl.

Beat in the milk with a wire whisk, preferably an electric one. Blend in the egg whites with the wire whisk.

When the mixture is smooth, let it sit for 10 minutes to allow the rice to absorb some liquid. Beat the mixture again for a moment. Mix in the banana slices.

Spray a nonstick frying pan with nonstick spray and heat over high heat. Pour 3 pancakes into the pan. I use a 1/2-cup metal measuring cup with a handle and fill it about half full for each pancake. It goes quick that way and I can stir the batter between pourings. I make small pancakes with this recipe because big ones are too hard to flip.

The first 3 pancakes probably won't turn out too well. For a reason I can't figure, the first pancakes usually just prime the pan. But, on the other hand, they might be just fine.

Now that you have the pancakes in the pan, watch to see bubbles form on the top. When there are a whole bunch of bubbles, it's time to flip the pancakes with a spatula. It's harder to tell when the other side is done. Peeping under might break them. Be careful not to burn them. When they are done, quickly get them out onto a warm plate.

Continue making batches of 3 in the pan until the batter is gone. (There is no need to spray the pans again.) If, in the middle of making the pancakes, they seem to be browning too fast, reduce the heat to medium.

To freeze leftovers, place plastic wrap between the pancakes so you can remove them one by one. You can reheat the pancakes in the microwave for about 1 minute. Or heat on an ovenproof dinner plate in a preheated oven at 350°F for 5 to 6 minutes or on a piece of aluminum foil in a toaster oven for 3 to 4 minutes.

Per pancake: 70 calories; 3 g protein; tr fat; tr saturated fat; 1 mg cholesterol; 15 g carbohydrates; 30 mg sodium; 1 g fiber

Microwave Oatmeal

Yield: 1 serving

Rolled oats and 1-minute oats work equally well in this recipe. You can get rolled oats at the grocery store. Quaker labels theirs as "Old Fashioned Quaker Oats."

1/3 cup rolled oats or 1-minute oats
1/8 teaspoon cinnamon
1/4 large baked banana (page 148)
2 tablespoons apple juice concentrate
Water
1/4 cup skim milk
Raisins (optional)

In a cereal bowl, combine the oatmeal and cinnamon. Beat the banana in its baking juices with a fork until it is liquefied. Pour the juice concentrate into the measuring cup with the banana and its baking juices, then add enough water to make 2/3 cup. Stir the water-fruit-juice mixture into the oatmeal. Microwave on high uncovered for 2 minutes. Stir. Microwave on high for 1 minute. Stir. Cover and let sit 2 minutes.

In the meantime, heat the milk on high in the microwave for 40 seconds. Pour the milk into the oatmeal and mix. For extra sweetness, stir in a few raisins. Serve hot.

Per serving without raisins: 200 calories; 6 g protein; 2 g fat: tr saturated fat; 1 mg cholesterol; 40 g carbohydates; 40 mg sodium; 3 g fiber

11

Desserts

Your life isn't over. Believe it or not, you can make absolutely wonderful desserts without sugar or butter or margarine or chocolate.

The first time I was told this, I didn't believe it—until I tasted my first apple pie made without sugar and without shortening. And it was delicious.

So many fruits are so wonderfully sweet that it is easy to make scrumptious desserts without sugar. In a couple of recipes, I use a little fructose, which is a sugar made from fruit, not sugar cane. Many nutritionists say fructose is acceptable to use in small amounts on no-sugar diets. But, for the most part, I have stuck to using whole fruits or fruit juices, since they are better for you than fructose.

I think I had a real breakthrough when I was successful in making a sponge cake. It's for real!

The nutritional breakdowns at the end of each recipe do not include vanilla or other extracts because that information is unavailable. The nutritive contribution of those ingredients is negligible.

Sponge Cake

Yield: 10 servings

I never dreamed I could make a sponge cake without sugar, oil, or whole eggs—but I did it. This is the kind of cake you can buy as small sponge cake cups to fill with strawberries and top with whipped cream. My version is light, sweet, and just delicious. Use a nonstick flan pan to make this. A flan pan is fluted around the edges and has a depression in the center. Be sure the pan measures 10-1/2 inches at the widest point and will hold 4 cups of batter. And be sure the indentation will hold 2 cups of fruit filling.

1 cup unbleached white flour
1 teaspoon low-sodium baking powder
4 jumbo egg whites
1 cup apple juice concentrate
1/2 teaspoon lemon extract

Preheat the oven to 325°F. Spray a nonstick flan pan with nonstick spray.

In one bowl, sift the flour. Mix in the baking powder.

In another deep mixing bowl, beat the egg whites with an electric mixer on high speed until they form stiff peaks.

In still another large mixing bowl, combine the juice concentrate and the lemon extract. Gradually beat the flour into the juice-extract mixture. Carefully fold the eggs into the batter, gently mixing until all streaks disappear. Pour the batter into the pan.

Place the pan on the middle rack of the oven and bake for about 30 minutes, or until the cake is golden brown and a toothpick inserted in the center comes out clean. Remove the cake to a cake rack and let it cool in the pan for 10 minutes. Turn the cake out of the pan and let it continue cooling on the cake rack.

Per serving: 95 calories; 3 g protein; tr fat; tr saturated fat; 0 mg cholesterol; 21 g carbohydrates; 30 mg sodium; tr fiber

Peaches and Cream Cake

Yield: 10 servings

With a sponge cake base and whipped topping top, peaches make this cake a taste dream.

1 Sponge Cake (page 132)
Whipped Topping (page 155)
2 (16-ounce) cans sliced yellow cling peaches packed in unsweetened pear juice

Prepare the sponge cake base according to the recipe directions and cool. Begin preparing the whipped topping.

Place the cooled sponge cake on a plate and pour about 1/4 inch of the juice from the peaches into the cavity. Prick the cake with a toothpick so it will absorb the juice. Pour some more juice on the plate around the sides of the cake and on the high sides of the cake. Prick carefully the sides of the cake. As the juice is absorbed into the sides of the cake, pour more juice. Try to get as much juice into the cake as possible. Fill the cavity of the cake with as many peach slices as will fit.

Whip the topping and spread on top. Use the remaining peaches to decorate the top, using as many as you can.

Chill the cake for about an hour before serving. You can also pour more juice around the sides of the cake while you wait. The juicier, the better.

Per serving: 170 calories; 7 g protein; tr fat; tr saturated fat; 1 mg cholesterol; 36 g carbohydrates; 75 mg sodium; 2 g fiber

Blueberry Magic

Yield: 8 servings

1 Sponge Cake (page 132)
Whipped Topping (page 155)
1-1/2 cups unsweetened pineapple juice
1/2 cup apple juice concentrate
1-1/2 cups Blueberry Preserves (page 154)
Fresh blueberries

Prepare the sponge cake according to the recipe directions and cool. Begin preparing the whipped topping.

Prick the cooled sponge cake all over with a fork.

Mix together the pineapple juice and juice concentrate and pour over the cake to moisten it. Fill the cavity in the cake with Blueberry Preserves. Whip the topping and spread it on top of the cake. Decorate with fresh blueberries and serve.

Per serving: 320 calories; 12 g protein; 1 g fat; tr saturated fat; 3 g cholesterol; 67 g carbohydrates; 150 mg sodium; 2 g fiber

Hawaiian Moonlight

Yield: 10 servings

1 Sponge Cake (page 132)
Whipped Topping (page 155)
1 (20-ounce) can unsweetened crushed pineapple
1 (20-ounce) can unsweetened sliced pineapple
About 3-1/2 cups canned unsweetened pineapple juice
2 tablespoons apple juice concentrate
2 bananas, sliced
1 envelope unflavored gelatin

Prepare the sponge cake base according to the recipe directions and cool. Begin preparing the whipped topping.

Drain the crushed pineapple and the sliced pineapple and reserve the juice. Pour the juice concentrate into a 2-cup measure and add enough of the reserved pineapple juice to make 2 cups.

Pierce the cooled sponge cake all over with a fork and place the crushed pineapple in the cavity of the cake. Arrange 1 banana over the pineapple, allowing the slices to touch each other.

Pour 1/2 cup of reserved pineapple juice into another container and add 1 envelope of unflavored gelatin to soften it. Heat the remaining reserved pineapple juice to the boiling point and add it to the gelatin mixture. Mix well. Pour the gelatin mixture over the bananas and the cake, letting it seep in, as much as the cake can absorb. Make sure you pour some juice on all the banana slices to coat them, and on the sides of the cake. Place the cake in the refrigerator to gel. Also place the remaining juice-gelatin mixture in the refrigerator.

After about an hour, whip the Whipped Topping and spread it on top of the cake. (You don't want to whip it sooner because it won't spread as well.)

Take 1 slice of pineapple and dip it into the juice-gelatin mixture, which should be syrupy by now. Place a pineapple slice on the middle of the cake. Cut another slice of pineapple in equal pieces, dip them one by one into the gelatin mixture, and arrange the pieces geometrically around the pineapple ring in the center. Dip the remaining banana slices one by one into the juice-gelatin mixture. Put the first slice inside the pineapple ring and place the others between the cut pieces of pineapple.

Return the cake to the refrigerator for at least 2 hours to gel. If you aren't going to serve the cake within the next day or so, after the cake has gelled for 2 hours, spray some plastic wrap with nonstick spray and cover the cake with it, spray side down.

What do you do with the leftover pineapple juice-gelatin mixture? Well that's what we people in Louisiana call langiappe—pronounced lan-yap, and it means a little something extra for free. Add more banana slices and leftover pineapple to the rest of the juice-gelatin mixture, refrigerate, and you have pineapple gelatin.

Per serving: 275 calories; 8 g protein; 1 g fat; tr saturated fat; 1 mg cholesterol; 62 g carbohydrates; 75 mg sodium; 3 g fiber

Variation

Carob Fruity Chiffon Cake. Make the cake exactly as above, but substitute Carob Banana Mint Pudding (page 139), omitting the bananas and pineapple in the pudding, for the whipped topping. The resulting pudding makes a wonderful creamy chocolate-like top.

Per serving: 280 calories; 8 g protein; 1 g fat; tr saturated fat; 1 mg cholesterol; 64 g carbohydrates; 75 mg sodium; 3 g fiber

Shirley's Carrot Cake

Yield: 128 squares

This is delicious, moist, and as good as, or better than a standard carrot cake. For an extra treat, spread the top with Polaner All Fruit, which is an unsweetened fruit preserve. I like the orange kind, which is just like orange marmalade (14 calories per teaspoon). You can buy it at the grocery or write M. Polaner, Inc., Roseland, NJ 07068. Or make some homemade Blueberry Preserves (page 154).

Shirley is my friend and a wonderful cook. I revised her delicious recipe for carrot cake to make this dietetic version.

2 cups whole wheat flour
1 teaspoon low-sodium baking powder
2 teaspoons baking soda
1 teaspoon cinnamon
8 jumbo egg whites
1-1/2 cups apple juice concentrate
1 teaspoon vanilla extract
1 cup raisins
2 cups finely grated carrots

Preheat the oven to 350°F. Spray two 8-inch square nonstick cake pans with nonstick spray.

Sift the flour into a large mixing bowl. Mix in the baking powder, baking soda, and cinnamon.

Beat the egg whites in another bowl until just very frothy. Add to the flour with the juice concentrate and vanilla extract. Stir with a spoon until all the ingredients are wet. Beat with an electric mixer for 3 minutes. With a spoon, mix in the raisins and carrots. Pour the batter into the pans.

Bake on the middle rack of the oven for 40 to 50 minutes. The cakes are done when a toothpick inserted into the centers comes out clean.

Let the cakes cool in the pans for 20 minutes. Loosen the cakes with a nonstick frying pan spatula, sliding the spatula underneath if necessary. Turn the cakes over onto a clean cloth which is resting on a solid surface. They might just fall out, but if they don't, bang the pan down on the cloth. Try the cloth first because it's hard to bang a cake down on a wire rack. Move the cake to a wire rack to finish cooling. On a chopping board, cut the cooled cake into 1-inch squares with a serrated or electric knife.

Freeze extras in a plastic bag for a long-lasting supply of healthy, sweet snacks. Defrost by placing individual squares in a microwave oven on high for 30 seconds, or let the cake defrost at room temperature.

Per serving: 18 calories; .5 g protein; tr fat; tr saturated fat; 0 mg cholesterol; 4 g carbohydrates; 20 mg sodium; tr fiber

Floating Pineapple Upside-Down Cake

Yield: 25 squares

I never meant for this cake to float, but it just did. I was trying to add a gelatin-fruit juice mixture to the baked cake to add moisture, and lo and behold, the cake floated. Some surprises are absolutely delightful. Be sure to use only canned fruit and juices because fresh pineapple and juice won't gel.

4 sliced pineapple rings canned in own juice
1/2 cup raisins
1-1/3 cups crushed unsweetened pineapple or 1
  (20-ounce) can, drained and juice reserved
1 cup whole wheat flour
1-1/2 teaspoons low-sodium baking powder
1 cup apple juice concentrate
2 jumbo egg whites
1/2 teaspoon vanilla extract
Apple juice concentrate
1 envelope unflavored gelatin

Preheat the oven to 350°F. Arrange the 4 pineapple rings in an 8-inch square nonstick cake pan. Sprinkle the raisins over. Spread the drained crushed pineapple over the raisins. Set aside.

Sift the flour into a large bowl and mix in the baking powder. Add the 1 cup of apple juice concentrate, the egg whites, and vanilla. Beat with an electric mixer for 2 minutes until smooth. Pour the batter over the fruit in the cake pan.

Place on the middle rack of the oven. Bake for 30 to 40 minutes, or until a toothpick inserted into the center comes out clean. Let cool on a wire rack in the pan for 10 minutes

Poke holes all over the cake with a toothpick and loosen the sides with a spatula.

Into a measuring cup, pour the reserved pineapple juice and enough additional apple juice concentrate to equal 2 cups liquid. Pour 1/4 cup of the liquid into another container and add the gelatin. Mix together and let sit to soften the gelatin. Bring the rest of the fruit juice to a boil. Add the hot juice to the gelatin mixture and completely dissolve the gelatin. Pour the gelatin-fruit juice mixture over the cake in the pan. Wait for about 5 minutes. The cake will float up. If it doesn't, poke more holes in the cake and loosen the sides of the cake again with the spatula. I guarantee, the cake will float and you will get a good laugh. It's a funny sight to see.

Chill the cake for about 4 hours, then fill a sink with hot water and place the cake pan in the water for just a second or two. Place a cake plate over the pan and turn the cake over. The cake will fall out onto the plate with the gelatin side up. If it doesn't, repeat the hot water operation, but don't leave the pan in the hot water for too long. You don't want to have runny gelatin.

To garnish, decorate with fresh strawberries. Or slice 1/4-inch thick slivers out of a watermelon and cut out stars or flowers with decorative cutters you can buy at gourmet supply stores. One way or another you will need a little red on this cake. If you want to cheat, use Maraschino cherries. But don't eat them! Take them off as if they were birthday candles.

Per serving: 105 calories; 2 g protein; tr fat; tr saturated fat; 0 mg cholesterol; 25 g carbohydrates; 15 mg sodium; 1 g fiber. Nutritive values may vary slightly depending on how much apple juice concentrate is added.

Bread Pudding

Yield: 12 servings

After the Civil War, many people in New Orleans were left poverty-stricken, so they had to be inventive to save money. Bread pudding, made from stale French bread, became popular at that time. It is a lovely dessert enjoyed in the best French restaurants and by old New Orleans Créole families. This bread pudding is as good as or better than any I've ever tasted. Use fresh bread, though, because stale whole wheat bread doesn't soften up enough. You want this to come out tender, shaky, and shivery. This not only makes a great dessert, you can eat it for breakfast, too. Serve as is, or with Blueberry Preserves or Cherry Preserves (page 154) over it.

4 cups cubed fresh Pritikin or commercial whole wheat bread (about 7 slices)
2 cups skim milk
1/2 cup brandy
8 jumbo egg whites
1 teaspoon vanilla extract
2 baked bananas (page 148)
1 ripe medium-size banana
Zest of 1/2 medium-size orange, cut in pieces
1/16 teaspoon nutmeg
1/16 teaspoon cinnamon
1 cup raisins

Place the bread in a 9-inch by 13-inch baking dish. Set aside.

Combine the milk, brandy, egg whites, vanilla extract, baked bananas and its baking juices, uncooked banana, orange zest, nutmeg, and cinnamon in a blender. Mix with a spoon first to get the spices wet. Blend on slow speed for a few seconds, then switch to high and blend for about 3 minutes, until you can't see the orange zest any more.

Toss the raisins into the bread cubes with your fingertips. Pour the milk mixture over, and push down any bread that doesn't sink. Place the dish in the refrigerator for 1 hour to soak.

Push the bread down again gently, but don't stir. Spray a piece of aluminum foil with nonstick spray and place it spray side down touching the top of the liquid and bread, then crimp the rest of the foil around the edges of the dish. Place in the oven and set the temperature at 350°F. Bake for 45 minutes. Remove the foil carefully and bake for 15 minutes more. Cover the pudding again and let it sit out of the oven for 20 minutes before serving.

When spooning it out, serve it bottom side up. The pudding will taste divine and will keep in the refrigerator for 4 days. You can warm covered portions in the microwave on high for 1-1/2 minutes, or wrap portions with foil and place in a 300°F oven for about 10 minutes to rewarm. Freeze extra portions.

Per serving: 160 calories; 6 g protein; 1 g fat; tr saturated fat; 1 mg cholesterol; 31 g carbohydrates; 190 mg sodium; 3 g fiber

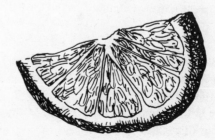

Puffed Rice Pudding

Yield: 12 servings

Louisianans never eat rice pudding. Rice in Louisiana is for pouring gravy over or cooking jambalaya, not for eating with milk and sugar. But hold on, people from Louisiana. I wouldn't make you eat your steamed or boiled rice with milk and sugar. Notice the title of this pudding; you will use puffed rice. That makes all the difference. I use puffed rice cereal or rice cakes made from puffed rice for this, and it comes out very similar to bread pudding, but lighter in texture. I guarantee you will like it—it will have no resemblance to any rice pudding you might have tasted by force or accident (more likely by force).

Incidentally, if the rice cakes you find include oat bran and perhaps some other grains, that's all right.

Serve as is, or with Blueberry Preserves or Cherry Preserves (page 154).

4 cups puffed rice cereal or 5 to 6 no-salt rice cakes,
   crumbled to measure 4 cups
2 cups skim milk
1/2 cup brandy
8 jumbo or extra large egg whites
1 teaspoon vanilla extract
2 baked bananas (page 148)
1 ripe medium-size banana
1/16 teaspoon nutmeg
1/8 teaspoon allspice
1/16 teaspoon ground cloves
1 cup raisins

Put the puffed rice in a 9-inch by 13-inch baking dish. Set aside.

Combine the milk, brandy, egg whites, vanilla extract, baked banana and its baking juices, uncooked banana, nutmeg, allspice, and cloves in a blender. Mix with a spoon first to get the spices wet. Blend on slow speed for a few seconds, then switch to high and blend for about 3 minutes.

Toss the raisins into the puffed rice with your fingertips. Pour the milk mixture over, and push down any puffed rice that doesn't sink. Place the dish in the refrigerator for 1 hour to soak.

Push the puffed rice down again gently, but don't stir. Let soak in the refrigerator for another hour.

Push the puffed rice down into the liquid again. Spray a piece of aluminum foil with nonstick spray and place it, spray side down, touching the top of the wet mixture. Then crimp the rest of the foil around the edges of the dish. Place in the oven and set the temperature at 350°F. Bake for 45 minutes. Remove the foil carefully and bake for 15 minutes more. Let the pudding sit, covered with foil, out of the oven for 20 minutes before serving.

When spooning it out, serve it bottom side up. The pudding will taste divine and will keep for 4 days in the refrigerator. You can warm covered portions in the microwave on high for 1-1/2 minutes, or wrap portions with foil and place in a 300°F oven for about 10 minutes to rewarm. Freeze extra portions.

Per serving: 135 calories; 5 g protein; tr fat; tr saturated fat; 1 mg cholesterol; 28 g carbohydrates; 60 mg sodium; 1 g fiber

Carob Banana Mint Pudding

Yield: 3 servings

This is delicious, just like chocolate pudding. Carob tastes like chocolate except it has none of the caffeine, sugar, fat, emulsifiers, artificial flavor, or other additives that chocolate often has; look at a label on a chocolate bar sometime. And carob is naturally sweet (but do check the label to see if any sugar is added). You can find carob powder at a health food store.

1 (12-ounce) can evaporated skim milk
1 envelope unflavored gelatin
1/2 baked banana (page 148)
2 tablespoons carob powder
1/16 teaspoon peppermint extract
1 sliced banana
1/2 cup unsweetened canned pineapple chunks, drained

Pour about 1/3 cup of the milk into a cup and sprinkle the gelatin over it to soften. Stir well.

Meanwhile, scald the rest of the milk in a microwave on high for 2-1/2 to 3 minutes or on top of the stove. Remove any skin that forms on top of the milk.

Add the gelatin mixture to the scalded milk. Stir well. Let it cool a little, then pour into a blender. Add the baked banana and its baking juices, the carob powder, and the peppermint extract. Blend on high speed until very smooth. Pour into a mixing bowl and cover with plastic wrap. Let the wrap touch the top of the pudding to keep the gelatin from forming a hard skin on top. Refrigerate for 3 to 4 hours until gelled.

When it has gelled, beat with an electric mixer. Start slowly, building up to the fastest speed. Beat until the mixture is fluffy and creamy. Fold in the banana slices and pineapple.

Per serving: 170 calories; 11 g protein; 1 g fat; tr saturated fat; 4 mg cholesterol; 33 g carbohydrates; 135 mg sodium; 3 g fiber

Banana Custard

Yield: 7 servings

Banana custard makes a delicious low-calorie snack.

3/4 cups skim milk
2 baked bananas (page 148)
8 teaspoons water
6 jumbo egg whites
1/2 teaspoon vanilla extract

Pour the milk, baked bananas and its baking juices, and water into a blender. Blend on high until smooth. Pour into a mixing bowl and add the egg whites and vanilla. Beat with a rotary mixer for about 1 minute. Pour the mixture into 7 (4-ounce) custard cups.

Into a wide roasting pan, pour 1/2 inch of water. Set the filled cups in the water and place the pan on the center rack of the oven. Set the temperature at 300°F. Bake uncovered for 50 to 60 minutes, or until a knife comes out clean. Sprinkle a little nutmeg on top if you like.

To reheat 1 serving in a microwave, cover the cup with plastic wrap, and heat for 1-1/2 minutes on high (or less if your microwave is very fast). Or cover with foil and sit the dish in water in an oven and reheat at 300°F for 15 to 20 minutes. I like to eat this ice cold.

Per serving: 55 calories; 4 g protein; tr fat; tr saturated fat; tr cholesterol; 9 g carbohydrates; 60 mg sodium; 1 fiber

Gelled Grape Dessert

Yield: 2 servings

Use beet juice for red food coloring as well as taste in this recipe.

1 envelope unflavored gelatin
1/4 cup water
1/4 cup beet juice from fresh cooked beets (page 101) or from canned no-salt beets
1/2 cup apple juice concentrate
40 red seedless grapes

Microwave Directions

Soften the gelatin in the water. Set aside.

Combine the beet juice and juice concentrate in a 2-cup container. Cook uncovered on high for 1-1/2 minutes, or until it comes to a boil. Add the water with the gelatin and stir until the gelatin is completely dissolved.

Stove Top Directions

Soften the gelatin in the water. Set aside.

Combine the beet juice and apple juice concentrate in a small saucepan. Place over high heat until the liquid comes to a boil. Remove from the heat and add the water with the gelatin. Stir until the gelatin is completely dissolved.

Let the mixture cool, then pour into 2 wine glasses. Add 20 grapes to each glass. Chill in the refrigerator for 2 hours before serving.

Per serving without beet juice: 200 calories; 4 g protein; 1 g fat; tr saturated fat; 0 mg cholesterol; 47 g carbohydrates; 25 mg sodium; 2 g fiber. Nutritive information on beet juice is unavailable.

Déjà Vu

Yield: 8 servings

Do you ever dream you're in the tropics? Squeeze a little fresh lime juice over Déjà Vu and you'll swear you're on a beach in Jamaica. Add chunks of fruit if you like.

2 very ripe nectarines (do not peel)
1-1/4 large ripe bananas
1 envelope non-flavored gelatin
1 cup apple juice concentrate

Cut up the nectarines and banana and place in a blender. Add the gelatin, and, using a spoon, mix it with the fruit to soften it. Set aside in the blender. Heat the apple juice in a microwave or on top of the stove until it comes to a boil. Pour the juice concentrate over the fruit. Cover the blender and blend at a high speed for about 1-1/2 minutes, or until you don't see any signs of fruit peel. Pour into a 1-1/2 quart bowl or into individual pudding or custard dishes. Refrigerate for 3 to 4 hours until set. Enjoy as is or squeeze lime juice over.

Per serving without lime juice: 95 calories; 1 g protein; tr fat; tr saturated fat; 0 mg cholesterol; 23 g carbohydrates; 10 mg sodium; 1 g fiber

Variation

Déjà Vu with Fruit. After you have poured the Déjà Vu into a 1-1/2 quart bowl, add 20 seedless grapes and 2 chopped nectarines, no need to peel. Refrigerate for 3 to 4 hours until set.

Per serving: 120 calories; 2 g protein; 1 g fat; tr saturated fat; 0 mg cholesterol; 29 g carbohydrates; 10 mg sodium; 2 g fiber

Upside-Down Nectarine Cream Pie

Yield: 10 servings

This is a gorgeous dessert, really fancy. It's almost the same as Nectarine Cream Pie (page 142), except you reverse the assembling directions and add a little apple gelatin and banana. Use a 10-inch nonstick flan pan that will hold 4 cups of liquid. A flan pan is a round one fluted around the edges with an indentation to put a filling in. I found mine at the grocery store. Be sure the pan measures 10-1/2 inches at the widest point.

Whipped Topping (page 155)
1 recipe for Déjà Vu (page 140)
40 seedless green grapes
2 nectarines, sliced (do not peel)
1-1/2 cups Grape-Nuts® cereal
1-1/4 cups apple juice concentrate
1 banana, sliced
1/2 envelope unflavored gelatin

Spray the flan pan with nonstick spray.

Spread the Whipped Topping in the pan. Chill until set, about 2 hours.

Prepare the Déjà Vu. Layer the ungelled Déjà Vu over the whipped topping, leaving about 1/4 inch of pan still above the Déjà Vu. (If there is a little Déjà Vu left over, put it in a custard cup and chill it for an extra snack.) Place 20 grapes here and there in the Déjà Vu. Also place slices of 1 nectarine around in the Déjà Vu. Chill for about 3 hours.

In a bowl, mix the Grape-Nuts with 1/4 cup juice concentrate then sprinkle and spread over the Déjà Vu. Chill the pie for 3 hours.

If your flan pan has a little hole in the side, stop it up with some aluminum foil. Fill the sink with a little hot water and set the flan pan in the water for just a few seconds. Place a serving plate on top of the pan and turn the pie over. It should fall out onto the plate. If it doesn't, leave the pan in the hot water for a few more seconds. Unmold the pie on top of the plate. Refrigerate while you prepare the fruit topping.

Put the remaining grapes in a bowl. Add the remaining nectarine slices and the banana slices. Pour 1/4 cup of the remaining juice concentrate into a cup. Add the gelatin to soften it. Bring to a boil the remaining 3/4 cup of the juice concentrate. Pour the hot juice into the gelatin mixture. Mix until the gelatin is dissolved. Let cool. Pour the juice mixture over the fruit in the bowl and mix well. Distribute the fruit around the center of the pie. Pour the juice-gelatin mixture over the fruit and fill the cavity. Pour leftover juice around the sides of the pie, and let it drizzle under it. If it won't go underneath the pie, don't worry about it, just pour it over the leftover Déjà Vu in the custard cup (if you haven't already eaten it), and chill the pie again for 3 to 4 hours. Serve. Sit back and listen to the compliments.

Per serving: 240 calories; 4 g protein; 1 g fat; tr saturated fat; tr cholesterol; 56 g carbohydrates; 125 mg sodium; 4 g fiber

Nectarine Cream Pie

Yield: 10 servings

Even my kids' friends like this one and request it when they come over. It's really marvelous.

Whipped Topping (page 155)
1 recipe for Déjà Vu (page 140)
1/4 cup apple juice concentrate
1-1/2 cups Grape-Nuts cereal
40 seedless green grapes
4 chopped nectarines (do not peel)

Prepare the Whipped Topping, but do not whip. Prepare the Déjà Vu, but do not refrigerate.

Make the crust by mixing the juice concentrate and the Grape-Nuts in a 9-inch pie dish. Spread it around evenly.

Fold half of the grapes and half of the nectarines into the Déjà Vu. Spread the mixture over the crust.

Whip the topping and spread over the pie. Arrange the remaining grapes and nectarines over the top. Refrigerate for 3 to 4 hours until set.

Per serving: 225 calories; 7 g protein; 1 g fat; tr saturated fat; 1 mg cholesterol; 50 g carbohydrates; 150 mg sodium; 4 g fiber

Pears in Cherry Sauce

Yield: 4 servings

Talk about easy to make! And it's great when you're having company.

1 (16-ounce) can Bartlett pears packed in pear juice
1 cup Cherry Preserves (page 154)

Chill the pears in the unopened can. Drain off the juice. Place 2 halves in each dessert dish. Ladle 1/4 cup of Cherry Preserves over each serving of pears and serve.

Per serving: 125 calories; 1 g protein; tr fat; tr saturated fat; 0 mg cholesterol; 32 g carbohydrates; 15 mg sodium; 3 g fiber

Variation

Pears in Blueberry Sauce. Ladle Blueberry Preserves (page 154) over the pears instead of the cherry.

Per serving: 135 calories; 1 g protein; tr fat; tr saturated fat; 0 mg cholesterol; 34 g carbohydrates; 15 mg sodium; 3 g fiber

Raisin Chewies

Yield: 36 candies

Finding the raisins inside these marshmallow-like candies is a real surprise.

2 jumbo egg whites
1 tablespoon fructose
1 teaspoon vanilla extract
1/2 cup raisins

Preheat the oven to 350°F. Spray a nonstick cookie sheet with nonstick spray.

Beat the egg whites until they are stiff and form peaks. Beat in the fructose and vanilla extract thoroughly. Fold in the raisins.

With a teaspoon, spoon the mixture out in bite-size clumps onto the pan, not touching each other. Place in the oven and leave the oven on for 1 minute—no more. Turn the oven off and leave the door closed. Let the candies sit until the oven is totally cool, about 3 hours. The chewies will be ready to eat.

You can refrigerate these or freeze them in a plastic bag and they won't stick together.

Variation

Rum Raisin Chewies. Make as you would Raisin Chewies, but add 1 teaspoon rum extract along with the vanilla.

Per each Raisin Chewie or Raisin Rum Chewie: 10 calories; tr protein; tr fat; tr saturated fat; 0 mg cholesterol; 2 g carbohydrates; 5 mg sodium; tr fiber. Nutritive value for rum unavailable.

Brandy Bon-Bites

Yield: 32 treats

Back in the early 1900s, my mother's uncle Monier, a doctor, was the only one in the family who knew how to cook. When the family moved off Esplanade Avenue in New Orleans to Des Allemands out in the country, they would have starved to death if Uncle Monier hadn't known how to fry oysters, which he did until my mother's Tante Marie, his wife, found a cook. My mother said when her family would visit him in the country, he would always have bon-bites prepared for her. She said a bon-bite was a good bite or something good in the mouth—half French, half English. Brandy Bon-Bites certainly live up to that description.

3/4 cup brandy
2 cups Grape-Nuts cereal
1-1/2 teaspoons carob powder
4 tablespoons fructose
1/2 cup raisins
1 jumbo egg white
1/2 baked banana (page 148)
1/4 teaspoon orange extract
1/4 teaspoon lemon extract
Apple juice concentrate (optional)

In a small saucepan, heat the brandy over high heat until warm. Turn the heat off. Leave the pot on the stove and be sure nothing is around, above, or on the sides that will catch on fire. With a long match, standing well away from the pot, and getting children out of the way, light the fumes coming up from the pan. The alcohol will flame up and the flames will leap a foot or more into the air over the pan. Let the alcohol in the brandy burn itself out. Don't leave the room while the pot is flaming.

Process the Grape-Nuts in a food processor fitted with a chopping blade until they are fine crumbs. Combine the crumbs in a bowl with the carob powder and 1 tablespoon of the fructose. Mix. Add the raisins.

Mix. Combine the egg white, brandy, banana and its baking juices, orange extract, and lemon extract. Add to the crumbs and mix very well. If the mixture isn't wet enough to hold together, add a tablespoon or so of juice concentrate.

Form bite-size balls and roll them in the remaining 3 tablespoons fructose. Store in a tightly covered container in the refrigerator. They will keep for a week.

Per bon-bite without juice concentrate: 55 calories; 1 g protein; tr fat; tr saturated fat; 0 mg cholesterol; 45 mg sodium; 1 g fiber

Paris-Style Peach Ice Cream

Yield: 4 servings

When Ray and I came down from the Eiffel Tower the first time we visited Paris (and before we discovered no-salt, no-sugar, no-fat eating), we found an ice cream man with a rolling cart full of pastel green, pink, peach, and orange fruit-flavored ice creams. His peach ice cream was very refreshing on a hot day because it had tiny crystals of ice in it. Afterward, I discovered most French ice cream is like that, somewhere between American ice cream and sherbet.

The secret to making a similar ice cream is to get everything measured ahead, except the ice cubes. I use ice cubes that measure 2 inches by 1 inch.

10 ice cubes
6 frozen peach slices
1 very ripe banana
1-1/2 tablespoons low-fat cottage cheese
1/4 cup apple juice concentrate
1 tablespoon fructose (optional)

Place the ice cubes in a food processor and process until pulverized. Add the peaches, banana, cottage cheese, and juice concentrate. Process until the ingredients are ground very fine. Taste. If the ice cream is not sweet enough for you, add the fructose and process for a second or two more. Serve immediately.

Per serving with fructose: 100 calories; 1 g protein; tr fat; tr saturated fat; tr cholesterol; 24 g carbohydrates; 30 mg sodium; 1 g fiber

Tropical Ice

Yield: 4 servings

Tropical Ice is very refreshing, with the tangy-sweet taste of kiwi fruit.

2 kiwi fruits, ice cold
1/2 fresh pear (do not peel) or 1/2 canned pear in unsweetened juice, ice cold
2 ice cubes
1/4 cup frozen apple juice concentrate
1-1/2 tablespoons low-fat cottage cheese
1/2 large banana, sliced
Extra kiwi slices for garnish (optional)

Cut the kiwis in half and scoop the contents out into a small bowl. Cut the pear half into 2 or 3 pieces and add it to the bowl.

Place the ice cubes in a food processor and process until finely chopped. Add the kiwis, pear, juice concentrate, and cottage cheese. Process until the mixture is smooth and fluffy, not for too long. You want the texture to be almost as stiff as ice cream, but slushier. Pour into 4 wine glasses. Add sliced bananas to each glass, top with a slice of kiwi, if desired. Eat immediately. Don't try to save leftovers in the freezer. It tends to get bitter.

Per 1/2-cup serving without optional kiwi slices: 80 calories; 1 g protein; tr fat; tr saturated fat; tr cholesterol; 29 g carbohydrates; 30 mg sodium; 2 g fiber

Pear Slushy

Yield: 2 servings

Fruit slushies are very refreshing in hot weather. Enjoy them with almost any kind of fruit. Here are a few ways to make them, beginning with pears.

1 Bartlett pear (do not peel)
10 ice cubes
1 cup sparkling sodium-free bottled water
3 tablespoons apple juice concentrate
1/16 teaspoon peppermint extract (optional)

Core and chop the pear. Combine with the rest of the ingredients in a blender. If you use the peppermint extract, just pour it out of the spoon and don't dunk the spoon in the mixture or the slushy will be too minty. Blend on high speed until the pear is no longer visible. Pour over more ice to drink immediately; or freeze for an hour or so, stir, and serve.

Per 1-cup serving: 95 calories; tr protein; tr fat; tr saturated fat; 0 mg cholesterol; 23 g carbohydrates; 10 mg sodium; 2 g fiber

Nectarine Slushy

Yield: 2 servings

1 nectarine, sliced (do not peel)
10 ice cubes
1 cup water
3 tablespoons apple juice concentrate
1/8 teaspoon vanilla extract

Place all the ingredients in a blender and blend on high until the ice disappears. Add more apple juice concentrate if you want it sweeter.

Freeze for an hour or serve immediately over more ice.

Per 1-cup serving: 75 calories; 1 g protein; tr fat; tr saturated fat; 0 mg cholesterol; 19 g carbohydrates; 10 mg sodium; 1 g fiber

Kiwi Slushy

Yield: 2 servings

2 kiwis
10 ice cubes
5 tablespoons apple juice concentrate
1 cup water

Halve the kiwis. Scoop out the pulp and place in a blender. Add the ice cubes, juice concentrate, and water. Blend on high until the ice is finely chopped.

Pour over ice cubes; or freeze for about an hour, stir, and serve.

Per 1-cup serving: 120 calories; 1 g protein; tr fat; tr saturated fat; 0 mg cholesterol; 29 g carbohydrates; 15 mg sodium; 3 g fiber

Lemonade Slushy

Yield: 2 servings

Juice of 1 medium-size lemon
1 cup water
6 tablespoons apple juice concentrate
10 ice cubes

Combine the lemon juice, water, and apple juice concentrate in a blender with the ice cubes. Blend on high until the ice is pulverized. Taste. Add more apple juice concentrate if it's not sweet enough and blend again.

Serve over more ice cube, or freeze for an hour or so until the mixture is almost like a snowball in texture. Stir and serve.

Per 1-cup serving: 90 calories; tr protein; tr fat; tr saturated fat; 0 mg cholesterol; 23 g carbohydrates; 15 mg sodium; tr fiber

Pineapple-Banana Pops

Yield: 8 pops

You can buy the molds for making frozen fruit pops in your grocery. The kind I found has 8 sections with plastic tops with sticks attached. It holds a total of 2 cups of liquid.

1 cup pineapple juice
1 large banana
1/4 teaspoon vanilla extract

     Pour the pineapple juice into a blender. Add the banana in chunks. If the liquid does not rise to the 2-cup mark, add more pineapple juice. Add the vanilla and blend until smooth. Pour into the pop molds almost to the tops and place the plastic tops on. Freeze for about 5 hours. Unmold by running cool water over the mold. Pull the pops out gently. Note: If these pops are not sweet enough, substitute a little apple juice concentrate for some of the pineapple juice.

Per pop: 30 calories; tr protein; tr fat; tr saturated fat; tr cholesterol; 8 g carbohydrates; tr sodium; tr fiber. Nutritive values will vary slightly if you use apple juice concentrate.

12
Basics

I usually buy the commercial no-sugar-added all-fruit preserves, but sometimes I can't find them. I was thrilled after experimenting with apple pectin powder to come up with absolutely delicious all-fruit preserves. They add so much to a sugar-free diet. The apple pectin powder is loaded with fiber, too, and you can't even tell it's there.

Gravies are important, too, and the Chicken or Turkey Gravy Base from Stock (page 149) has helped me enormously. The recipe provides plenty of deliciously seasoned and thickened stock to flavor gravies, and in a pinch I can use it for gravy all by itself.

The Piquante Sauce (page 150) has almost changed my life—it is so handy and delicious.

I think you will find the recipes in this chapter will make eating the salt-free, sugar-free, fat-free way a lot easier.

Baked Banana

Yield: 1/2 banana

I used to use banana flakes to sweeten many dishes, but now they are almost impossible to find, so I had to rethink my sweetening method.

It turns out that 1/4 baked banana plus a teaspoon of water equals 2 to 3 tablespoons of banana flakes, or 1/2 baked banana plus 1 teaspoon of water equals 1/4 cup banana flakes, or 1 whole baked banana plus 2 teaspoons of water equals 1/2 cup banana flakes. This information will be useful to people who have my first cookbook.

A baked banana becomes very soft, so I beat it with a fork in its baking juices and pour it into whatever I'm making.

1/2 very ripe banana
1 teaspoon water

Microwave Directions

Place the banana in a container with high sides. Add the water. Cover and bake on high for 1 minute 30 seconds to 1 minute 50 seconds, until the banana looks collapsed.

Oven Directions

Place the banana in a small baking dish. Add 1 teaspoon of water and cover. Set the temperature at 400°F and bake for 20 minutes.

Per 1/2 banana: 50 calories; 1 g protein; tr fat; tr saturated fat; 0 mg cholesterol; 13 g carbohydrates; tr sodium; 1 g fiber

Chicken or Turkey Gravy Base from Stock

Yield: About 5 cups

This recipe makes good gravy. However, it is better combined with the strong, pure drippings from a roasted chicken or turkey. If you use this gravy without the drippings, try a little mint jelly alongside it to jazz it up.

Peels of 2 large onions, or 3 or 4 small to medium-size onions
5 cups strong chicken stock or turkey stock from a roasted bird (page 24)
10 tablespoons whole wheat flour
5 tablespoons onion flakes
1 tablespoon celery flakes
2 tablespoons dried parsley
1-1/2 teaspoons dried sage
1-1/2 teaspoons crumbled or powdered thyme
1/4 teaspoon marjoram
1-1/2 teaspoons garlic powder
1/2 teaspoon cayenne pepper
1/3 cup red rosé wine
5 tablespoons apple juice concentrate
2-1/2 cups sliced mushrooms
2 teaspoons red hot sauce (not Tabasco)

Wash the onion peels if they look dirty. Dry the peels well. Place them on a piece of aluminum foil on the bottom rack of the oven. Bake the peels at 500°F for about 10 minutes. When the peels have become very brown, almost black, remove them from the oven.

Microwave Directions

Crumble the peels into a 2-cup container and cover with water. Microwave on high for 3 minutes. Strain the liquid off into another container. Throw away the peels.

Stove Top Directions

Crumble the peels into the smallest saucepan you have. Add water to cover the peels. Boil covered for 3 minutes. Strain the liquid off into another container. Throw away the peels.

While the onion peels are browning, pour 3 cups of the stock into a large pot. Pour the remaining 2 cups stock and the flour into a blender. Mix the flour in with a spoon to wet it, then blend on high until the flour and stock are thoroughly mixed. Pour the stock-flour mixture into the pot with the rest of the stock. Add the onion flakes, celery flakes, parsley, sage, thyme, marjoram, garlic powder, cayenne pepper, rosé, juice concentrate, mushrooms, and hot sauce. Turn the heat on high and cook, stirring constantly. When the mixture starts to bubble, stir, and cook for 1 minute. Reduce the heat to low. Add the reserved liquid from the onion peels. Cover and simmer for 45 minutes, stirring occasionally.

Freeze in cup-size or larger containers to mix with degreased drippings of roasted chicken or turkey. This will make plenty of gravy for one turkey breast at holiday time.

Per tablespoon: 10 calories; 1 g protein; tr fat; tr saturated fat; tr cholesterol; 2 g carbohydrates; tr sodium; tr fiber

Piquante Sauce

Yield: 5 cups

This medium-hot salsa can be served as a dip at a party with Toasted Tortilla Chips (page 20). It disappears faster than most bottled salsas. It's really good—easy to make, too. I usually quadruple this recipe and make it in a big roasting pan on top of the stove. Then I freeze small amounts for my husband to snack on.

1 medium-size onion
1 fresh jalapeño pepper
1 (4-ounce) can roasted, peeled, mild green chili peppers, rinsed and chopped by hand
2 (15-ounce) cans no-salt tomato sauce
1/2 tablespoon no-salt chili powder
2/3 cup apple cider vinegar
2 tablespoons apple juice concentrate
1/8 teaspoon garlic powder
1/3 cup water

Mince the onion and jalapeño in a food processor.
In a 2-quart pot combine the onion, jalapeño, roasted green chili peppers, tomato sauce, chili powder, vinegar, juice concentrate, and garlic powder. Rinse the food processor with the water and add the water to the pot. Bring to a boil, cover, and simmer for 10 minutes. Remove the cover and simmer for 35 to 40 minutes, stirring occasionally.
Cool and serve with Toasted Tortilla Chips or use as a sauce to spice up any dish you can think of.

Per tablespoon: 5 calories; tr protein; tr fat; tr saturated fat; 0 mg cholesterol; 1 g carbohydrates; 20 mg sodium; tr fiber

Cran-Apple Sauce

Yield: 7 cups

Use this instead of cranberry sauce.

1/2 cup beet juice (page 101)
1 cup unsweetened grape juice concentrate
3 envelopes unflavored gelatin
1 (12-ounce) bag or 4 cups fresh or frozen cranberries
1/4 cup raisins
3 cups chopped peeled apple
1 cup chopped celery

Microwave Directions

Combine the beet juice and juice concentrate in a microwave container. Sprinkle the gelatin on top. Set aside to soften.
Pick through the cranberries and remove any stems and bad berries. Combine the raisins and cranberries with the fruit juices and gelatin. Cover and microwave for 15 minutes at 70% or medium power. Stir. Let cool on the counter.

Stove Top Directions

Combine the beet juice and juice concentrate in a 2-quart saucepan. Sprinkle the gelatin on top. Set aside to soften.
Pick through the cranberries and remove any stems and bad berries. Combine the raisins and cranberries with the fruit juices and gelatin. Bring to a boil. Cover and cook for 5 minutes, then simmer for 10 minutes. Stir often. Let cool on top of the stove.

When the mixture has completely cooled, add the apples and celery. (The vegetables will cook if you add them while the mixture is hot.) Pour the mixture into a 7-cup mold and refrigerate for about 4 hours until gelled.

Per tablespoon without the beet juice: 10 calories; tr protein; tr fat; tr saturated fat; 0 mg cholesterol; 2 g carbohydrates; tr sodium; tr fiber. Nutritive values of beet juice not available.

Creamy Horseradish

Yield: 1/2 cup

This is particularly good served alongside Easy Corned Beef (page 41). Horseradish root, of course, may not come in exactly 2-1/4 ounce pieces, so if the roots you find in the produce section of the grocery store are a little heavier or lighter, add more or less water, vinegar, or juice concentrate.

The roots themselves look rather formidable—dried up, unattractive things they are. You may buy them and stare at them in your refrigerator and never get up the courage to peel them. I did that 3 times. I finally got the guts to peel the third set, and found they are not much harder to peel than a potato.

2-1/4 ounces fresh horseradish root
2 tablespoons apple cider vinegar
1/4 cup water
2 teaspoons apple juice concentrate

Wash and peel the root, then wash it again. Cut in small pieces and place in a blender or a food processor. Add the vinegar, water, and juice concentrate. Process until creamy. You may have to open the food processor or blender and push the contents down off the sides a few times and process again. When you push the contents down, stand back—don't lean over the container. The fumes will not only clear your sinuses, they might put them out of commission. This is powerful stuff.

Store in an airtight jar and keep the jar covered as much as possible to retain the flavor. You can freeze this in small amounts to make Horseradish Sauce or to eat straight.

Per tablespoon: 10 calories; tr protein; tr fat; tr saturated fat; 0 mg cholesterol; 2 g carbohydrates; 10 mg sodium; tr fiber

Horseradish Sauce

Yield: 1/2 cup

My husband thinks this is mild. However, he eats jalapeño peppers plain and doesn't drink water afterward, so take it from there. If you also think this is mild, increase the amount of Creamy Horseradish.

You can serve this with Easy Corned Beef (page 41) or with cold chicken. It makes a super dip for raw vegetables.

1/2 cup low-fat cottage cheese
2 tablespoons Creamy Horseradish
1/8 teaspoon dried dill weed (optional)

Combine the cottage cheese and Creamy Horseradish in a blender. Blend until very smooth. Dip out a tiny bit to taste. Now dip out a little more and sprinkle a little dill weed on it. Roll it around in your mouth to see if you like the dill. If you do, add the dill and blend again. I like the dill, but it's a very personal spice. It's good to try it sparingly at first.

Per tablespoon: 15 calories; 2 g protein; tr fat; tr saturated fat; 1 mg cholesterol; 1 g carbohydrates; 60 mg sodium; tr fiber

Barbara's Cabbage Relish

Yield: 2-1/2 cups

Barbara Wellman, who used to live down the bayou from me, is the sister of Geoffery Beene, the famous dress designer. What fun it was to look through her closet and see all the clothes that Geoffery designed just for her. Though Geoffery is famous all over the world and lives in New York, he and Barbara are from Shreveport, Louisiana. You see, we do have some sophisticated people in Louisisana, after all. Barbara is extremely proud of her brother, and can you blame her? And Geoffery is extremely proud of Barbara. He even wrote a letter to me and told me so when I wrote an article about him and Barbara in our hometown newspaper.

Barbara, a wonderful cook, gave me a recipe for cabbage relish that I was able to make without sugar or salt. This version is good when you want something like a pickle, something sweet and sour. My husband likes it over a baked potato, or with Bean Dip (page 20) and Toasted Tortilla Chips (page 20), or with Easy Corned Beef (page 41), and on top of Hamburger (page 45).

1/4 medium-size green cabbage, shredded
   (about 2 cups raw)
1/4 cup chopped green pepper
1/2 cup chopped onion
9 cups water
1-1/2 teaspoons celery seed
1-1/2 teaspoons mustard seed
1-1/2 teaspoons dried red pepper flakes
1/2 cup plus 1 tablespoon apple cider vinegar
6 tablespoons apple juice concentrate

Combine the cabbage, green pepper, and onion in a pot or heatproof bowl. On top of the stove, in another pot, bring to a rapid boil 8 cups of the water. Pour the boiling water over the vegetables and cover. Let sit for 1 hour. Drain. Set aside.

To make a pickling juice, combine the celery seed, mustard seed, red pepper flakes, vinegar, juice concentrate, and the remaining 1 cup of water in a pot or a microwave container. Cover and bring to a boil on top of the stove or in the microwave and boil for 2 minutes. Pour the pickling juice over the drained cabbage mixture. Cover and let sit for 1 hour. Refrigerate. It will keep for 7 or 8 days if refrigerated.

You can cut this recipe in half; just be careful you don't boil all your pickling juice away. Use a lower heat to keep evaporation to a minimum.

Per tablespoon: 5 calories; tr protein; tr fat; tr saturated fat; 0 mg cholesterol; 2 g carbohydrates; tr sodium; tr fiber

Pineapple Preserves

Yield: 2 cups

Apple pectin powder can be found at most health food stores. It's a little expensive, but a 4-ounce jar will make tons of preserves.

1 (20-ounce) can crushed unsweetened pineapple
1/4 cup water
1/2 cup plus 5 tablespoons pineapple juice
  concentrate
1 tablespoon pectin powder

Drain the pineapple in a colander for about 20 minutes and press on it with a spoon to squeeze any remaining juice out. Save the juice to drink later.

Combine the water and pineapple juice concentrate in a blender. Add the pectin and mix it in slightly with a spoon to wet it. Turn the blender on high for about 2 minutes. Pour the mixture into a small saucepan. Turn the heat on high and stir constantly. When the mixture begins to foam and steam, boil it for 3 minutes, stirring all the time and lifting the pot off the heat slightly to keep the pot from boiling over and to keep the bottom of the pan from scorching. Remove the pan from the heat and add the pineapple. Return the pan to high heat and stir constantly for 1-1/2 minutes, lifting the pan almost the whole time.

Pour the mixture into a container and cover it. After it has cooled for about 2 hours, refrigerate it.

Per tablespoon without pectin: 25 calories; tr protein; tr fat; tr saturated fat; 0 mg cholesterol; 6 g carbohydrates; tr sodium; tr fiber. Nutritive values for pectin are negligible.

Mint Jelly

Yield: 3/4 cup

This is lovely to eat with Slow Cooker Lamb (page 53) or roasted chicken. Apple pectin powder can be obtained at a health food store. Apple pectin comes in tablets, too, but you need the powder.

1/4 cup water
1/2 cup plus 5 tablespoons apple juice concentrate
1 tablespoon orange juice concentrate
2 tablespoons apple pectin powder
1 tablespoon dried mint leaves

Combine the water and juice concentrates in a blender. Add the pectin and mix it in slightly to wet it. Turn the blender on high for about 2 minutes. Pour the mixture into a small saucepan and add the mint leaves. Turn the heat on high and cook, stirring constantly. When the mixture begins to foam and steam, boil it for 3 minutes, stirring all the time and lifting the pot off the heat slightly to keep the pot from boiling over.

Pour into a container and cover. After it has cooled for about 2 hours, refrigerate it. Serve as is, or heat the jelly to soften it and make it more like a sauce.

Per tablespoon without pectin or mint: 35 calories; tr protein; tr fat; tr saturated fat; 0 mg cholesterol; 8 g carbohydrates; 5 mg sodium; tr fiber. Nutritive values of pectin and mint are negligible.

Variation

Orange Jelly. Cook exactly as you would the Mint Jelly, but omit the mint leaves. This is good served heated over chicken.

Per tablespoon without pectin: 35 calories; tr protein; tr fat; tr saturated fat; 0 mg cholesterol; 8 g carbohydrates; 5 mg sodium; tr fiber. Nutritive values of pectin are negligible.

Blueberry Preserves

Yield: 1-1/2 cups

This is so good on the various muffins and on Corn Bread (page 126). It is also great on the Whole Wheat Pancakes (page 47) in my *No Apologies Cookbook*.

1/4 cup water
1/2 cup apple juice concentrate
5 tablespoons grape juice concentrate
1 tablespoon apple pectin powder
1 cup fresh or frozen blueberries

Combine the water and juice concentrates in a blender. Add the pectin and mix it in slightly with a spoon to wet it. Turn the blender on high for about 2 minutes. Pour the mixture into a small saucepan. Turn the heat on high and cook, stirring constantly. When the mixture begins to foam and steam, boil it for 3 minutes, stirring all the time and lifting the pot off the heat slightly to keep the pot from boiling over. Remove the pan from the heat and add the blueberries. Return the pan to high heat and cook, stirring constantly, for 1 minute, lifting the pan if it starts to boil over.

Pour the preserves into a container and cover. After it has cooled for about 2 hours, refrigerate.

Per tablespoon without pectin: 25 calories; tr protein; tr fat; tr saturated fat; 0 mg cholesterol; 5 g carbohydrates; tr sodium; tr fiber. Nutritive values of pectin are negligible.

Cherry Preserves

Yield: 2 cups

If you like cherries, you will love this scrumptious jelly.

1 (16-ounce) can pitted tart unsweetened red cherries
1/4 cup water
1/2 cup grape juice concentrate
5 tablespoons apple juice concentrate
1 tablespoon apple pectin powder

Drain the cherries and discard the liquid in which they were canned. Set aside.

Combine the water and juice concentrates in a blender. Add the pectin and mix it in slightly with a spoon to wet it. Turn the blender on high for about 2 minutes. Pour the mixture into a small saucepan. Turn the heat on high and cook, stirring constantly. When the mixture begins to foam and steam, boil it for 3 minutes, stirring all the time and lifting the pot off the heat as needed to keep the pot at a steady rolling boil without boiling over. Remove the pan from the heat and add the cherries. Return the pan to high heat and cook, stirring constantly, for 1-1/2 minutes, lifting the pan to keep at a steady rolling boil and to keep the preserves from boiling over.

Pour the preserves into a container and cover. After it has cooled for about 2 hours, refrigerate it.

Per tablespoon without pectin: 20 calories; tr protein; tr fat; tr saturated fat; 0 mg cholesterol; 4 g carbohydrates; tr sodium; tr fiber. Nutritive values of pectin are negligible.

Whipped Topping

Yield: 10 servings

This makes enough topping to cover one cake.

1 (12-ounce) can evaporated skim milk
1 envelope unflavored gelatin
1/2 baked banana (page 148)
1/2 teaspoon lemon extract

Pour about 1/3 cup of the milk into a cup and sprinkle the gelatin over it to soften. Stir well.

Meanwhile, scald the remaining milk in a microwave on high for 2-1/2 to 3 minutes, or on top of the stove. Remove any skin that forms on top of the milk.

Add the milk mixed with the gelatin to the scalded milk. Stir well. Let it cool a little and then pour the mixture into a blender. Add the banana and baking liquid and lemon extract. Blend on high speed until very smooth. Pour into a mixing bowl and cover with plastic wrap. Let the wrap touch the top of the milk to keep the gelatin from forming a hard skin. Refrigerate for 3 to 4 hours until gelled.

When it has gelled, beat with an electric mixer. Start slowly, building up to the fastest speed. Beat until the mixture is fluffy and creamy.

Per serving: 35 calories; 3 g protein; tr fat; tr saturated fat; 1 mg cholesterol; 5 g carbohydrates; 40 mg sodium; tr fiber

Homemade Crab Boil

Yield: 1 bag

What is crab boil and what do you do with it? This brings to mind a story. When Ray and I were in St. Croix, Virgin Islands, right before Hurricane Hugo, we stayed at a small hotel that had a dress code: you had to wear something. At the open-air, thatched roof bar where we were having some fruit punch, the bartender introduced us to a newspaper reporter from Ohio who had won a Pulitzer prize. I told the man I had once been a newpaper reporter for a newspaper in Slidell, Louisiana. The man said, "I didn't know they had newspapers in Louisiana." I was astonished at the man's ignorance. I said, "Of course we have newspapers in Lousiana! What else would we eat our boiled crabs and crawfish on?"

In Louisiana, we don't eat our boiled crabs, crawfish, and shrimp on plates! No! We eat them in mountains, piled on newspapers. And we boil them out in the yard in big kettles with crab boil. The spices for the crab boil come in perforated boilable plastic bags. You just toss as many bags as you need into the boiling water with the seafood, and add garlic, onions, lemons, and sometimes chili powder. You could try using crab boil with lobster. Dale Porter, who works for Zatarain's, right outside of New Orleans, says they sell their crab boil all over the United States. Look in a gourmet store if you can't find it at your grocery. Zatarain's also makes crab boil for McCormick and it is exactly the same thing. You can ask your grocer to contact Zatarain, Inc., 81 1st Street, Gretna, LA, 70114, and ask for crawfish, shrimp, and crab boil.

However, rather than calling and writing letters, it's not that much trouble to make your own crab boil. How do I know how much of each spice goes into this? Believe it or not, I took a bag of crab boil apart and separated out all the seeds, berries, and spices, then measured them. It took me all morning.

6 tablespoons mustard seeds
5 tablespoons coriander seeds
2 bay leaves
4 allspice berries
4 whole cloves
1/4 teaspoon dried red pepper flakes

Mix all the ingredients in a bowl. Now make a bag to put the spices in. Cut three 1-foot squares of cheese cloth. (You can get cheesecloth in the automotive section of the grocery store.) Cut another strip of cheesecloth for tying the bag closed. Lay the pieces of cloth on top of each other. Pour the spices on top of the cheesecloth. Pull the ends of the cloth up around the spices and tie with the strip of cheesecloth. Submerge the bag of spices in the water next to whatever you may be cooking. After everything is cooked, just throw the whole bag away.

Nutritive values of spices are negligible.

Index